Fish's Daughter

The Memoirs of a Naval Captain's Daughter

By

Judy Corry

for John

Contents

Chapter 1

Yorkshire Childhood

I was born exactly a year after the Second World War began. My father was at sea in the Royal Navy, and I didn't meet him until I was a year old. My mother was afraid that I would cry, but my father said I just stared at him and was really quite friendly. One of my earliest memories is seeing him in uniform: a dark suit, with shiny bands round the edge of the sleeve, and a peaked cap with a shiny badge.

I don't remember ever calling my father Daddy; to me as to everyone else he was just 'Fish'. He'd acquired the nickname when he was at the Royal Naval College at Dartmouth, where he went when he was thirteen.

"What's your name?" a fellow cadet asked him.

"Dalglish," said my father.

"Dalglish, Dogfish," was the reply, and the name stuck.

He was very tall, six foot three inches, and well-built with dark hair and a deep, husky voice. I wasn't a bit scared of him, although he could be quite loud when angry. I was much more scared of my mother, who didn't shout. He was very affectionate and always gave me a big bear hug. He smoked a pipe and it clicked against his teeth, especially if he was concentrating, and he was surrounded by the comforting smell of musty tobacco. He drank beer and would dip his finger in it and give it to me to suck. I'm told that the bitter taste made me shudder but I wasn't averse to opening my mouth for more.

Everyone said I looked just like him, and I think I did. I had the same straight dark hair, and my eyes disappeared when I laughed, as his did. On Speech Day at my senior school, I walked up the steps onto the stage. The presiding admiral smiled as he gave me my O-Level Certificate.

"You must be Fish's daughter," he said.

"Yes, I am," I replied.

As I walked down the steps at the far side I could see my father in the back row, grinning from ear to ear. He could guess just what had been said.

My mother, Eve, was quite tall too, and pretty, with blonde hair and big blue eyes. Although shy, private, and very self-contained, she was also lively and vivacious. She particularly enjoyed the company of men, for whom she 'sparkled'. My parents adored each other and I think it is fair to say that Fish was more important to my mother than were her children. I particularly loved Fish, I suppose because I saw him much less than my mother, and he was easier to please.

Home was with my mother's parents in a vicarage in a hilltop village in North Yorkshire, not far from the coast, although we lived in other places for short periods, when my father wasn't at sea. My grandfather, 'Grandpop', as we knew him, was the vicar. He was tall, bespectacled and white-haired, and, like my father, he smoked a pipe. He was a kindly man, much revered in the village. Before breakfast he always said prayers, with us kneeling on footstools. He said grace before meals too: "Benedictus, Benedicite" or "For what we are about to receive, may the Lord make us truly thankful." He was fond of saying "there's no such thing as a small half" and "neither a borrower not a lender be." He used to wink at me as I sat in my high chair, and one day apparently I winked back.

Grandpop used to swim in the river down in the valley from April to October. He taught the village boys to swim and he tried to teach me too, with a scarf round my waist to hold me up. I hated the feeling of squidgy mud between my toes and only learnt to swim in the sea, when I was older.

My grandmother was little and round, always smiling and laughing, always kind and loving. She never got cross. She was a great mimic, and when she had been out, she regaled us with accounts of the people she'd talked to, in a broad Yorkshire accent. She and my grandfather used to go out on their bicycles every afternoon, visiting people in the parish, whether they were churchgoers or not.

When I was four, I was given a bundle to hold, wrapped in a shawl. It was my brother David, who, like me, was born at the vicarage. Initially, I didn't like him much, especially as my mother seemed to like him much better than she did me. I continued to feel jealous at times, mainly because he got away with things, but I loved him really. He was a chubby, placid baby, and didn't walk until he was eighteen months old.

"Aren't you a ducky thing," said my grandmother to David, sitting in the playpen.

"Ducky," he replied, and that is what everyone called her after that.

David grew into a friendly, mischievous small boy, slightly knock-kneed, with thick brown hair, brown eyes, and large dimples when he smiled, which was often. We rarely saw other children and spent most of the time together, usually outside. We climbed trees – lots of them · went on long scooter rides down the country lanes, played at funerals, burying the small dead animals we sometimes came across. Only at meal times did we go home.

When Fish was at home, he played cricket with us. We were taken to the beach too, which we loved. In the winter there was always lots of snow and we played on a sledge in the fields below the house.

Ducky and Grandpop had two servants. Hilda came to the vicarage when she was sixteen and had already been in service for two years. She was the youngest of a large family who lived nearby. It was her grandmother that Hilda knew as her 'Mam' and who brought her up, although it was May, the oldest girl, who had given birth to her. Joan was her cousin. Hilda had black hair, was very thin, and smoked a lot. She talked a lot too; she talked about her boyfriend Alf and she used funny expressions such as 'I'se brussen', 'I'se like two o'clock half struck today' and 'she's as daft as a brush'. We loved being with them and spent a lot of time in the kitchen. We picked up their broad accents too, but of course we had to talk 'properly' when we were with our family.

The vicarage some few hundred yards from the church was a large, imposing stone house overlooking the valley and the moors beyond. The drive leading down to the house had woods on either side and a large garden sloped away to the left. Inside the front door was a lobby with a red-tiled floor, and a cloakroom. Through another door was a spacious hall and staircase. Leading off it was a drawing room, Grandpop's study, and a dining room. At the end was a large kitchen with a big, black range for cooking and a separate larder and pantry. The smell of fresh bread always reminds me of those days. In spite of wartime rationing we had good, plain food, the menu pretty much the same each week. We always ate what we were given and were never allowed to leave anything. We had rice pudding, sometimes with a dollop of jam, semolina (plain, pink, or chocolate-coloured), cornflower mould, jelly, or junket. For tea we had bread and jam, then caraway seed cake.

Upstairs were five bedrooms, a bathroom, and lavatory, and up another staircase were two attic bedrooms where Hilda and Joan slept. The house was heated downstairs by coal fires, but in upstairs rooms they were only lit if someone was ill. We were used to seeing our breath in the air and it taught us to get dressed very quickly. I can still remember the pungent smell of the paraffin lamps which were lit as it got dark, and how my grandmother pumped a tiny knob up and down until the wick glowed behind the glass chimney. There were candles too, in silver candlesticks, and a small Kelly lamp which stood at the corner of the landing at night. Sometimes David blew it out and Joan got into trouble because it was thought that she'd forgotten to light it. Once he lit the carefully laid fire in the dining room too. The matches were put out of his reach after that. There was no electricity in the village until 1952.

The garden outside was extensive, sloping away from the house. A tennis court had a steep rockery at one end; a hedge divided it from the kitchen garden. Grandpop grew potatoes, carrots, onions, parsnips, swede, peas, broad beans, cabbage, and cauliflowers. We had fruit too: gooseberries, red, black, and whitecurrants, strawberries, rhubarb, and raspberries. Ducky used to make jam and marmalade, putting a dollop on a saucer and tipping it to see if it wrinkled and was ready to set. The rich, fruity smell was lovely.

Sometime in 1946, Fish was posted to Japan, and we were due to follow him but at the last minute he went instead to Hong Kong, and it wasn't until February 1948, when I was seven and David three, that we went with our mother to join him.

This entailed a six week voyage in a troop ship, SS Strathnaver. The food must have been strange after the plain food of wartime, although we had never been hungry. I remember the first time I ate watermelon, and the fascinating sight of the black seeds floating in the lavatory a while later. I remember too the hot wind on my face, and looking through the porthole at the palm trees lining the Suez Canal. We stopped in Bombay, as it was called then, and we looked down at dozens of small boats and dark-skinned men trying to sell things to the passengers. I think we children spent our days in a playroom on board; my mother enjoyed the social life and was popular amongst the many young army officers.

As it wasn't long after the war had ended, accommodation was in short supply, so we lived in the huge Peninsular Hotel in Kowloon. We had a large room with a bathroom, a walk in clothes cupboard, a lobby, and had meals in the hotel dining room. My parents were out at parties every night, or so it seemed. My brother always went to sleep, but I didn't. I used to read books or comics in the clothes cupboard. Sometimes I walked around the corridors, but when my parents found out, they were cross with me. They tied the two doors together so I couldn't get out. I still hate closed doors.

During the day we were with a Chinese *amah* called Ah Soh. She was very young with a round, smiling face, slanting black eyes, and straight black hair in a plait which hung below her waist. David used to wind her plait round her neck; she giggled as he did it and never seemed to mind. She always wore a *cheongsam* tunic, which was fastened diagonally with tiny buttons, up to a high neck, and baggy black trousers. She spoke 'Pidgin English' to us. I went to the Gun Club School in Kowloon and I expect Ah Soh took me, but I remember nothing about it except the day I wet myself, and the feeling of shame as everyone stared at me. I recently found a copy of Alice in Wonderland; inscribed in it, in beautiful copperplate writing, it says: 'Presented to Judy Dalglish for Very Good Progress' so I must have done all right.

On Sundays we often went to beautiful sandy beaches by boat, with a picnic, and Fish taught me to swim in the warm, shallow sea. We went by ferry to Hong Kong Island and ate delicious green peppermint ice cream at a cafe called the Dairy Farm; a great treat. I remember the tall buildings, lots of clothes shops, hanging signs with strange writing, and most of all the teeming crowds of people in the streets. I had never seen so many people before, chattering at the tops of their voices in their strange-sounding language.

There were long, rattling, clanging trams, and masses of rickshaws, little open carts with two seats and a roof over them. They had long handles and were pulled by a 'coolie', their bare feet making a slapping thud as they jogged along. They wore large, shallow, cone-shaped waxed paper hats, and had brown, wizened faces. Local umbrellas had the same waxed paper over a slatted wooden frame; rain falling on them made a distinctive sharp tapping sound.

Hong Kong was an exciting place, but often I didn't like being there. I didn't want to enjoy it, and was sulky and cross. I think I must have missed the vicarage, and especially Ducky and Grandpop, as I wasn't usually a naughty child.

On one occasion I was taken to a children's party on board my father's ship. One of the sailors made a gramophone record of me reading a poem aloud – I cringed when I heard it! I thought it sounded absolutely awful and I still don't like the sound of my voice.

Another bad memory is the Royal Naval Hospital where I was sent when I got chicken pox. My mother and David got it too, a fortnight later. She stayed in the hotel, but David joined me in hospital and I had to stay there throughout. One night, a male nurse called Mr Smith woke me up, got me to take my nightie off, and took photographs of me. Another night I woke up to find him touching my bare body, and making me touch his. It seemed as if it happened every night, but I don't suppose it did. I just remember hating it and knowing it was wrong, but I didn't know how to stop him.

When we did get out of hospital, my father's ship had just returned from China following the incident in the Yangtse River, which was later made into a film. In the excitement of all this, our hospital stay was forgotten and I never had the courage to tell my mother. Anyway, I don't think I knew how to. But it did stay with me, particularly in adolescence. I hated taking my clothes off in front of people and felt that Mr Smith had done something to my body so it wasn't like everybody else's.

The weather was usually very hot and sunny, but one day there was a typhoon. All the ships in the harbour went out to sea. It was very dark. The howling wind rattled the windows, and water poured through them, with my mother trying in vain to mop it up. I was very frightened.

It was lovely when we all returned to England by sea and were back in our familiar life at the vicarage. For the next four years, David and I went to a small private school in a village in the valley, some two miles away. We walked there together, taking two fig rolls in a tobacco tin to have for break. It was harder coming home, as it was uphill most of the way. I used to tell David stories to keep him going, as his legs were so much shorter than mine.

The school was run by Miss Seller, who had taught my mother and her two sisters. She had ginger hair worn in plaits coiled round her ears. She must have done her hair like this since she was a young woman; it was always the same, the colour eventually fading to white. She had eight pupils of varying ages, and we were only there for the morning. Miss Seller taught us a lot in that short time, and gave me in particular a lifelong love of learning. "Fancy," she would say when we told her our news or showed her anything… "Fancy," and a happy little laugh.

We were taken regularly to have our teeth examined. I always hated these visits. My heart used to sink as we climbed up a long flight of stone steps to the surgery and waited for our turn to be seen. Mr Green had a large head with straight, black hair, a huge jowly red face, and a hearty laugh. Once I simply refused to open my mouth.

"Come on, Judy, it won't take a minute," said Mr Green.

"Open your mouth, Judy," snapped my mother.

But I just sat there, scowling, lips tightly closed. I was eventually taken home again, and my mother hardly spoke to me for days afterwards.

The year following my ninth birthday I remember feeling concerned about Grandpop. I began helping him up from his footstool after prayers and often brought him bunches of wild flowers which I'd picked on the way home from school. He always came to say goodnight to us when we were in bed, and one evening he'd blown us an extra lot of kisses. A while later I heard Ducky talking on the telephone.

"My husband has just passed away…"

That means dead, I thought. *He can't be.*

But Grandpop was dead. He'd had a heart attack whilst having dinner, the day after his seventieth birthday. Some men from the village carried him on a chair, past our room, to the spare room. No one noticed me watching, and David was fast asleep. Our parents had gone to London for a wedding.

The next day was Sunday.

Ducky came into our room and said, "I've got something very sad to tell you. Grandpop died last night."

I didn't tell her that I already knew. She took us to church as usual, and the service was taken by someone else. Once we'd arrived home, the house was soon filled with solemn, red-eyed people dressed in black, talking in hushed voices. We weren't allowed to go to the funeral, but were sent to Dr and Mrs Lyne for the day. Their children, Susan and Nicky, were the same ages as us. They lived in a large terraced house in Whitby, perched above the street, with steps up to the front door, garden on each side. I didn't want to be there and I hated every minute.

Ducky had to leave the vicarage, of course, as a new vicar would be appointed in due course, but the church authorities gave her plenty of time. Luckily, her brother Clifford and sister Mamie came to her rescue. They lived about half a mile away at the family home, Park Hall, which had some disused stables next door. They had them converted into an unusual house on several levels, and two years later we all moved into it. It was called Park Lodge. Hilda came with us, but Joan went to a job in Leeds. My parents helped Ducky to make a garden in the surrounding grounds, as they were all keen gardeners. We children had the run of both gardens, which had a high stone wall between them and lots of lovely trees and shrubs.

We already knew Park Hall as we often went there for tea with Aunt Mamie, who was little and round, always full of fun. She never minded what we did, such as putting gooseberries in our cups of tea.

Two days before we all moved, Mamie was found unconscious in the churchyard, having had a massive stroke. This was so sad, as Ducky and Mamie had been looking forward to living next door to each other. Mamie never got over it; for a few months David and I would take her out in a wheelchair, but after that she became bedridden, and she died two years later. Uncle Clifford taught music at Aysgarth, a boys' prep school near York. He was a wonderful pianist and played the organ too, but I remember him less well.

Since Hong Kong, Fish had been in shore jobs, but was about to go to sea again, this time in command of a ship, HMS Aisne, a frigate. At the same time came the highly secret information that he was being considered for a post as commander of the new royal yacht. He had a few months in his new ship, during which time his new appointment was confirmed, and in April 1953 he duly went to Glasgow, not long before the royal yacht was to be launched by the Queen. My mother was very excited, as she was asked to 'stand in' for the Queen during rehearsals.

Fish's job had no immediate impact on our lives, as he still came home to Park Lodge for holidays. We did go to London for the coronation though, which was a great adventure. We stayed with friends of my parents at the naval college at Greenwich and were taken by boat to Westminster, very early in the morning. It was still only just getting light when we arrived in the mall, where we had seats.

The crowd started singing, "What shall we do with the drunken sailor" when they saw Fish in uniform! I remember the soldiers lining the streets, many, many carriages going by, and the very, very large Queen of Tonga happily waving at us despite the teeming rain.

Soon after this it was the end of the summer term, and we left Miss Seller. I was almost thirteen and David almost nine. Our mother was going to join Fish in Glasgow and we were being sent to boarding schools. The only thing I knew about them was that my mother had hated hers, and Fish wasn't all that keen about his either.

I had to take an entrance exam. For this, I needed Latin, Algebra, and Geometry, so I had extra lessons with Miss Hatfield who lived near Miss Seller. I duly passed the exam, as did David for his school. During the holidays, our mother was busy sewing name tapes on to loads of new clothes, which were packed in two large trunks and sent off in advance, and all too soon the dreaded day arrived. I felt partly excited, partly apprehensive, wondering what it would be like. I knew it would be a different world; quite how different was soon to become apparent.

Chapter 2
Schooldays

On the bright, sunny September day we left Yorkshire, the thing I remember most clearly is getting dressed in my brand new school uniform. First I put on a woolly vest, two pairs of knickers, and a suspender belt which held up long, black lisle stockings. I wore a dark navy skirt and jacket, a white shirt, and a thing called a 'tippet'; a bit of folded black ribbon pinned just under my shirt collar. On my head was a straw hat with a black ribbon round it. I had never worn such uncomfortable clothes; they felt horribly hot and itchy.

We went by train from Sleights. Fish was on his way south from Glasgow, so my mother handed us over to him at York, and he took us the rest of the way, including crossing London from Kings Cross to Waterloo, where we got on our respective school trains. I was going to The Royal Naval School, for naval officers' daughters, at Haslemere in Surrey. David went to St Peter's Court, Broadstairs, in Kent, a boy's preparatory school which had been founded many years previously by a great great uncle.

That first evening was all confusion. I was surrounded by masses of girls who all seemed to know each other, milling about and chatting at the tops of their voices. One of the first things to happen was assembly, in the main hall. I heard my first roll-call read out,

anxiously listening for "Dalglish", to which I had to say "Present".
This was followed by the hymn, "Oh God our help in ages past, our
hope for years to come". I couldn't sing for the lump in my throat.
I think supper was after this, but maybe it was before. I can only
remember having a tummy ache.

I was sleeping in a different house to the main part of the school,
maybe ten minutes walk away, my first experience of walking two
by two in a 'crocodile'. My dormitory had eight beds with girls of
mixed ages, so I had to strip wash at a basin on a marble table with
several younger pairs of eyes watching me, before I could get into my
narrow, lumpy bed. I lay under the rough sheets and blankets and
quietly cried into my pillow until I fell asleep.

Next morning I was woken by a loud bell. Someone showed me
how to strip my bed; to fold the sheets and blankets and lay them
neatly at the end of it. Another bell went and we had to kneel on the
hard wooden floor by our beds to say our prayers. Five minutes later,
a third bell; time to make beds again, with hospital corners. This
was inspected by the head of the dormitory, an intimidating senior
girl, and then we walked in a crocodile up to the main school for
breakfast, followed by assembly.

My year was divided into two classes and I started in the B
stream. A few weeks later, I was told that the headmistress wanted
to see me after lunch. I was petrified, wondering what I had
done wrong. I asked for a small helping of stew because I felt so
miserable, but was given a huge one, and could hardly swallow
it for incipient tears. I have hated butter beans ever since. Miss
Oakley-Hill (known as O.H.) just wanted to tell me that I was
being moved into the A stream. Lessons were no problem for me as
Miss Seller had given me such a good grounding. It was everything
else that was difficult.

I usually woke up before the rising bell and needed to go to the
lavatory nearby. One day, the dormitory head said to me "Judy,

don't use the lavatory before the rising bell. I don't want to be woken up early." The next day I lay rigid in bed, too scared to get up, doing my best to 'hold on' until I couldn't bear it, and let go. Luckily, it was my turn to have a bath so I quickly scuttled off. When I got back my bed had been stripped and the mattress propped against the radiator. Nobody said anything about it, but oh the shame and embarrassment.

Another thing to be endured was GAMES. I had never played any formal games, just cricket on the beach or in the garden with my father, so I had no idea what to do. I was tall, awkward, shy, inhibited, and the worst of it was that games were so IMPORTANT. If you were no good at games you were regarded as pretty hopeless. I eventually got the hang of netball, but lacrosse – definitely not. Most of the time I was sent down to the 'bottom pitch' in a field further away, a few minutes walking through a wood, with all the other non-players. The only good thing about the dreaded 'monthlies' was that you could ask to be excused games for a couple of days.

Worst of all was tennis in the summer term. We had to play on Saturday afternoons, organising ourselves. No-one ever chose me and I was left till last. Everyone was 'tried' for the house tennis team, regardless of ability or lack of it. The hard court was overlooked by a rocky escarpment, where all the seniors stood watching. I was paired with Sophia-Ann Davis, younger than me, and very short-sighted. I don't think the ball went over the net once and I wished the ground would swallow me up.

Another big problem for me was free time, as I had not mixed with so many girls before. Most of my form had started school two years earlier, so friendships were already formed. Gradually I became friendly with three other girls who had started at the same time as me. Jill was tall, lanky, and rather dreamy; Sue had olive skin and big, dark eyes. She and Jill already knew each other. The other Sue was small, blonde, and bossy, and went on to become a doctor.

Also in 'Rodney' was Angela, who should have been in my year but had missed a few months due to illness and was now in the year below me. Somehow we discovered that our grandmothers both lived in North Yorkshire. Her mother and my parents became good friends (her father had died during the war), and we used to meet on the beach at Sandsend during the summer holidays. Her younger sister, Penny, the same age as my brother David, duly followed Angela to school; I remember feeling very sorry for her, she was so homesick.

My parents were still in Scotland for the first long half-term weekend. I and a few other girls whose families lived further away were invited to spend a day with the Dolmetsch family, of recorder fame. Their twin daughters, a bit younger than me, were day girls. They were very kind but I can only recall a persistent lump in my throat all day and a lingering sense of shame that I didn't send them a thank you letter afterwards. Soon after this, my mother inherited a house near Farnham, in Surrey, only half an hour's drive away from Haslemere, so I could go home for half-terms and the two visiting days.

At meal times we sat on long tables, each with our own table napkin and ring. Sometimes a member of staff or a prefect would come and one would have to 'bunk off' and find another place to sit. I've already mentioned my dislike of butter beans; stews were fairly horrible too, the meat always had gristle and fat on it. What I dreaded most and which caused much amusement was my aversion to watery, reconstituted dried egg on fried bread. Ugh. We had to eat everything on our plates, however much we hated it, and could never ask for someone to pass the salt; we had to ask our neighbour "would you like some salt?" and hope they'd take the hint. Some food was all right though, a universal favourite being 'sick-up' whipped evaporated milk on fruit salad. I liked fried bread and marmite too.

What I did enjoy about school was academic work. I did quite well, except for French, and was usually near the top of the class in exams. My favourite subject was History, taught by Miss Hussey, the deputy head who was known as 'Boot'. An imposing, broad, intimidating figure always clad in a tailored suit worn with academic gown, she had iron grey cropped hair, a moustache, and a deep, low voice. Those sitting near the front were liable to be showered with spray as Boot talked about "Schleswig-Holstein". I liked her, she made history come alive.

A few of the staff were young and we gave them a hard time. Mr Plant taught Physics and used to blush whenever blonde Miss Dickinson (Chemistry) came into the classroom, all us girls giggling. Most staff seemed ancient and many of them were sarcastic and unkind, especially the house matrons.

We were taken out on various trips, which were fun. We went to the Royal Mint, which was very interesting, and a glass factory where we watched glass being blown. I've never forgotten that. One very hot day we went to Wimbledon to see the tennis, and another, to the theatre for 'Midsummer Night's Dream' which we did for O-Level. We went to the occasional concert as well. On Saturday evening we sometimes had a film, some girls having a crush on Cary Grant and David Niven.

On Sundays we went to church in Haslemere for communion, before breakfast of course. I can still recall the smell of wet leaves as we walked down the long, wooded avenue, and having to put my head between my knees as I felt faint in the service, having had to kneel for so long.

I can't say that I ever much liked school and it wasn't the happiest time of my life. I was there for three and a half years, but never really 'fitted in'. I always preferred listening to talking; "Tak' all in any say now't" as they say in Yorkshire. I felt as if I'd left my real self at the front door and was just watching life go on around me. I always dreaded going back, and for years the smell of bacon and eggs reminded me of those Sunday nights when I could hardly swallow for misery as the time to leave home approached. I think when it came to it I was sad to leave, only because of facing the unknown and not being at all sure that I wanted to be a 'grown-up'. I did know that I was lucky to have had a good basic education and the seven O-levels I gained stood me in good stead when I applied to go to teacher training seventeen years later.

Chapter 3

Eastbourne

I completed my education at the Eastbourne School of Domestic Economy, starting after Easter not long before I was seventeen. My mother had been there twenty-five years before, in 1932. The same principal was still there – Miss Randle, known as 'Rannie'. She was tiny, very thin, with frizzy curly hair and a lined, humorous face. She used to come round the classrooms every day to see what we were doing, and to show people round.

"Never slim, darlings," she said, more than once. "It's bad for the future generation."

Mummy's father had thought it was a good idea for her to be taught to cook and housekeep. He realised after the First World War that society was changing and there wouldn't always be servants. Actually, my family did still have one, as Mrs Cowburn, who lived in the wing at Park Hall, cooked for us when we were there.

The first night at Eastbourne I met a slim blonde girl, with short curly hair and big blue eyes, coming downstairs into the common room, looking rather red-eyed.

"Are you feeling homesick?" I asked her.

"Yes," she said. "It's my first time away from home."

"It's horrible," I said. "I was away at school. I'm Judy, by the way."

"I'm Pauline," she said. "I just went to day school, and I really miss my family."

Like me, she had a younger brother, and her father was very special to her; she had two boy cousins who lived with them as well. We were happy to find that our rooms were adjacent, in the main building. We soon got to know each other and got on very well; we had a similar sense of humour. Pauline was bubbly and outgoing, and was very capable and practical, and I was quiet, shy, and lacked confidence. I'd never had a close friend like Pauline before, so it made college such fun after the naval school. Just sharing a room with one person and not being in a dormitory, being able to wear our own clothes, going out and about in free time, and, not least, not having compulsory games.

Pauline and I were amongst the youngest girls in the college. Although there was a boys' college nearby we never sought boys out – or they us, for that matter. We were perfectly happy walking along the seafront or sitting on the beach, looking at shops, or seeing an occasional play at the local repertory theatre. We spent a lot of time in our rooms, chatting about make-up and clothes, what we'd been doing in class, and what our teachers were like.

The first term I shared with Lois Lowry, a South African girl who was prickly and critical. I was quite upset when she told me I should use deodorant, not having come across it before. I felt very embarrassed and bought some as soon as I could. She also told me I put my make-up on very badly; equally embarrassing but probably quite right.

It was a relief that the following term Pauline and I were able to share a room, which was great fun as we never argued. We had to wash our hair in the hand basins in our room, and dry it with a towel. "At least it's clean," Pauline used to say as we looked at the results. Pauline had naturally curly hair but I think it was almost as wayward as mine, with the horrid perm I'd had before term started. I never had a perm after that. Short straight hair was much easier to manage.

I did already know one other girl there. Cicely Wingfield, who had distinctive red, curly hair had been at the naval school too, in the same form and house. We weren't ever particularly friendly then, as she had started two years earlier, but we were glad to meet again. We shared a love of books. Cicely had the light blue eyes and very fair skin which redheads often have. She came from a close family and often talked about her mother and two younger brothers. Her father was in the Navy, like mine, but she didn't mention him as much. Her grandmother's sister, Cicely's great aunt, lived in Eastbourne in a flat which overlooked the sea.

Soon after we started at the college she invited Cicely to tea one Saturday afternoon and told her bring a friend, so I went along too. It became a regular occasion and we always enjoyed going there; she was so welcoming, pleased to see us, and interested in everything we were doing. She used to buy florentines for us, a treat which I'd not had before.

"Judy dear, do call me Aunty Doss, like Cicely does," she said one day. She was a very special person; I got very fond of her and loved going to see her. She had a cat called Monty and was a keen gardener. We corresponded regularly after I left Eastbourne, until she died some years later, when I was very touched to learn that she had left me a box of jewellery in her will. I still have some of her letters with her distinctive 'copperplate' handwriting, which was similar to that of my old teacher Miss Seller.

My parents came down to visit me every term, and I particularly remember one occasion. We were sitting on the stony beach having a picnic when a large seagull waddled towards us and suddenly pecked my mother's big toe...

"Go away, you horrible thing," she said, as Fish and I watched, helpless with laughter. She had to shout and flap her hands for a few minutes before it eventually flew away.

I wrote to my parents every week, and it was always lovely to get Mum's weekly news in return and hear how David was getting on.

There weren't many rules at the college but I soon came across one. I was sent for by the vice principal, a rather large, imposing, bespectacled lady.

"Take your earrings off, Judy," she said. "They are quite unsuitable to wear during lesson time."

"Yes, Miss Visick," I said. I had been wearing a pair of large white daisies. I took them back to my room and didn't wear earrings in class again. I was disappointed as I had quite a collection of them.

I enjoyed most of the lessons. We were taught everything to do with running a house, from plain cooking, sewing, and dressmaking, to laundry and housework. We had to sew with a very fine needle, size 10 between, which is minute, and we always used a thimble. This felt very awkward at first. We had notebooks in which we wrote all the theory, and we stuck sample patterns of seams and patches in it too. We made a 'housewife', known as a 'hussif', a small oblong of blue gingham lined with flannel. It had a pocket at one end, and was rolled up and tied with tapes. In this we kept a tape measure, tiny sharp-pointed scissors, a thimble, a reel of sewing cotton, and a few pins and needles. I have mine still. We made a pair of silk French knickers, with wide lace-edged legs, fastened with buttons. Mine were pale blue. We wouldn't ever have wanted to wear them, they were much too old-fashioned; something our mothers would have worn, but not us girls.

We made a silk petticoat too. One day I was trimming a seam in mine when I accidentally cut a hole in the middle, near the seam.

"Look what I've done!" I said, imagining instant expulsion.

"Don't worry, Judy," said the teacher. "We'll just add an extra piece of material, nobody will know."

Lastly we made a baby's smocked dress. Mine was pale yellow with white smocking. I was rather pleased with it.

In dressmaking we were taught to use a sewing machine. We each made a cotton dress, using a commercial pattern, altered where necessary. It would have been more useful to have learned to draft our own, but that is hindsight, of course. We did choose our own material and pattern.

We had cookery lessons in a huge kitchen with several ovens. There was always a stock pot, permanently bubbling with meat bones, carrots, and onions stuck with a clove, which made the room hot and steamy. We did food preparation and were shown how to 'draw' a chicken.

"Here come the intestines… the liver… and the heart," said Miss Crawford.

"Ugh, how disgusting," we whispered to each other as she did it. We were shown how to gut and skin fish too.

We also made short crust pastry.

"Half fat to flour, a tablespoon of water to each ounce of fat," said the teacher. "Rub the fat into the flour with your fingertips."

Puff pastry was an involved process of rolling out dough, putting cut up squares of butter on half of it, folding it edge to edge and rolling it out again. This was repeated several times and it had to rest in the fridge in between. I expect top chefs still make it but most people buy it ready made from the supermarket, which is far less trouble. You can buy short crust pastry too, of course. I recently tried it but it was difficult to roll out and didn't taste very nice. So I still make my own but using a mixer rather than my fingers.

I wouldn't buy white sauce in a packet either. We were taught to make it from scratch. First we weighed the margarine and melted it in a saucepan, then stirred in an equal weight of flour:

"Cook it until it honeycombs," said our teacher. "Now stir in the milk. Do it slowly, or it will go lumpy… don't have the heat too high."

We learned how to make soups and stews, bread, cakes, biscuits, and steamed puddings. And we had to roast joints of meat with the appropriate accompaniments, and to get it ready with everything cooked at the same time.

There were electric irons for ironing clothes but we had to use old-fashioned 'flat' irons heated on a metal plate; we spat on each to see if it was hot enough – it sizzled if it was. It was important to get it right as it scorched things if too hot. They cooled quickly so we'd put them back on the hot plate and get another. We sometimes ironed on a table, rather than an ironing board. If the cloth was too dry, we scattered water from a jug with our fingers to dampen it as we worked. Woe betide you if there were any creases. I've recently seen flat irons and a hot plate in the local museum.

"It beats as it sweeps as it cleans," said the housework teacher, demonstrating a vacuum cleaner, but we had to learn to clean carpets with a dustpan and stiff brush. The teacher would run a damp finger along the surfaces to check that we had dusted properly too. It was all to be done again if not spotless. It did teach me to be thorough, for a while anyway.

We had frequent written tests, and towards the end of our final term, practical exams on laundry, housework, and cooking. I used to get quite worried about the latter, but Pauline was great, she calmed me down. I was more academic and helped her with written work, and it was the mutual support which was one of the nicest things about our friendship.

After my parents got married, my mother had been 'presented' at court by her mother-in-law. This was known as 'coming out' in 'society', and traditionally occurred after girls left school and were officially 'grown up.' My parents decided to apply for me to be presented too, as this was the final time it was taking place, and an extra day had been added, which was when I was invited to attend. Several other girls at Eastbourne were going too, although none of my particular friends. We had had a few lessons in learning how to curtsey at college.

"Right foot behind left foot, gradually bend your knees… hold your skirt out… don't let your legs wobble… slowly stand upright again." We had to practice to make sure we could do it easily.

I went up to London by train, on the Wednesday evening. My parents met me and we stayed in a hotel in Knightsbridge. The next day I put on a pale yellow silk dress, which my mother had made for me. Long, above the elbow yellow gloves and a yellow hat completed the outfit. Mum looked gorgeous as always, Fish wore morning dress and a top hat. A chauffeur drove us to the mall, where we joined a long, slow queue of cars. We went through large gates, into the forecourt, and through an archway, and we stopped at the red carpeted entrance of Buckingham Palace.

Clutching my name card I joined several other girls I knew from Eastbourne, and we walked up a wide, shallow, red-carpeted staircase, with ornate pillared, gilded walls and wonderful paintings. Everyone was chattering in hushed voices, feeling somewhat overawed by the grandeur of the occasion. We eventually arrived in the throne room. The girl in front handed her card to a footman.

"Miss Sheena Smellie," he announced.

Then it was my turn. "Miss Judy Dalglish."

I curtseyed to the Queen then to the Duke of Edinburgh, who smiled at me. I thought he must have been amused at Sheen's name, but maybe he recognised my name because Fish had been in The Royal Yacht Britannia. I had to walk backwards for a few steps and then followed Sheena past the rows of proud parents. I spotted mine smiling broadly and I smiled at them. We waited in an anteroom until everyone had been presented, then we met our families and had tea and chocolate cake. It was over so quickly that I hardly had time to take it in, but it was very exciting if slightly unreal, and of course a historic occasion as it didn't happen again.

I was one of the last but wasn't really a 'proper' debutante as I didn't do 'The Season' which immediately followed the court presentations. This was because Fish was about to be posted to Malta, and my parents didn't have the money, or move in 'Tatler' circles for that matter. The season began with Queen Charlotte's Ball; the young men who were invited to partner the girls attending it were known as 'Deb's delights'. The person presenting the girl, usually their mother, gave a cocktail party or dance for their daughter, and everyone attended events such as Ascot, Henley, and Wimbledon. It was really an upper class marriage market.

I had to catch the milk train to Eastbourne very early the following morning to do my final cookery exam. This was to cook a three course meal which included roast beef and Yorkshire pudding, and it lasted two hours. I recall watering eyes as I grated horseradish for the sauce, but I did pass it despite shortage of sleep, and I was duly awarded my Housekeeper's Certificate.

Cicely and I still laugh about Eastbourne. It was so old-fashioned and no use for getting a job afterwards. It was probably aiming only to educate us to be housewives, although girls who stayed for a fourth term did get a catering qualification. Many years later my mother asked me if I would have preferred to go to university instead, but I told her I wouldn't. In those days going to university was an option for very few girls. As Cicely said,

"Most of us were just expected to become naval wives... yet we both went to university in our late fifties... both of us got a first... and we'd both left school at sixteen!"

I was very happy at Eastbourne and the skills I learned there stood me in good stead. I made my own clothes for many years, and my children's too. Eventually, readymade clothes cost less than buying patterns, material, etc. I was working and by then my girls wouldn't have been seen dead in anything made by their mother.

My enthusiasm for cooking didn't outlast the years of fish fingers and sausages for my children, and after I started teacher's training college, love of books quickly succeeded it. My girls both loved cooking though, and 'helped' in the kitchen from an early age. My then teenage son once said to me,

"Mum, please don't put a crease in my shirt sleeves."

"You'll have to iron your shirts yourself," was my reply. "What's good enough for your father is good enough for you."

He did learn to iron too. I now pay someone to clean the house for me, but do occasionally remember that vinegar and newspaper is just as good for windows as any modern product.

Pauline and I are still friends. She lives in Devon and has seven grandchildren, with whom she is very involved. She is a skilled needlewoman and is a leading light in the local Patchwork and Quilting Group. We don't meet often but it's always great fun when we do.

I see Cicely twice a year. She lives in Brighton, close to her daughter and two grandchildren. She was widowed very young and brought up her two children with her extended family nearby. Her great love is travelling. We both enjoy going to art exhibitions, talking about books, and reminiscing about school and college. I really appreciate having been friends with them both for such a long time.

Back to April 1958. College finished, I was ready for the next phase of my life. My parents had sold Frensham Grove and moved to Park Hall. Fish flew to Malta to undertake command of a frigate, HMS Woodbridge Haven, and two flotillas of eight minesweepers. My mother and I followed soon afterwards, and we lived in Malta for the next eighteen months.

Chapter 4

Malta

I stepped from the aircraft into warm, scented air. A bright blue sky… yellow and white stone buildings glinting in the sunlight… church bells clanging discordantly… even now when I get out of an aeroplane in the Mediterranean or Middle East, I remember the day when I arrived in Malta. I loved it.

Fish met Mum and I and drove us to the Tigni Court Hotel in Sliema, where we spent a few days while looking for a flat. Mum found one very soon, on the top floor of a newly built block at the corner of Tower Road, which ran alongside the harbour creek. It's only disadvantage was no lift, so we climbed a hundred stairs to get there.

"Did he escort you up the stairs or leave you at the bottom?" Mum would ask me the day after a party. It was a long way to go down to collect the mail too.

The flat was very spacious with tiled floors throughout, easy to keep clean but chilly in the winter. Fish's ship HMS Woodbridge Haven was moored at the far side of the harbour; we could see it from our balcony. Fish was taken to and fro by the ship's *dhaisa*, a small boat propelled with one oar by a Maltese boatman, Salvatore Zammit. Half of the inshore flotilla minesweepers were moored in the middle of the creek, the rest were usually at sea, patrolling off Cyprus. There was so much to look at with ships going to sea or returning. I knew most of their pennant numbers and waved at my friends as they went to sea or returned. At first I didn't realise how close to shore the ships came until someone said they had seen me in my nightie.

Malta was barren and rocky, with few trees, but there were carpets of flowers in spring. I'd never seen miniature irises and daffodils before. It was usually sunny and mild in winter; only a cardigan was needed, rarely a jacket. It didn't rain much but was often windy. Sometimes there was a *sirocco*, a hot sand-filled gale force wind when ships had to leave harbour in case their anchors dragged. Summer was very hot, although only less nice in August, when it was humid and mosquitoes abounded. I would hear their distinctive 'pinging' and squash them with a shoe, leaving small splats of blood on the walls.

There was a cinema on the ground floor and I could hear the soundtrack from my bedroom – *Titanic* became a bit monotonous after three weeks. We often went to the cinema. Fish was very tall and used to put his long legs over the seats in front.

"Do you mind? Your feet are in my face," said a man sitting below us.

Shopping in Sliema was quite an experience. You'd think it was your turn next and someone behind would shout for what they wanted. The butcher was the worst. We had to get used to metric weight too – things were sold in *rotolos*, which must have been kilograms. Some of the fruit and vegetables were new to us. We often bought *pomelo*, a large fruit with a very thick skin, a cross between a grapefruit and an orange. It was delicious.

Valletta, the capital, had many more shops, including ones selling fabric. I particularly remember buying some cotton with huge orange poppies on a white background; I made a straight knee length dress and was wearing it on board a ship on the way to Cyprus. Someone else had a dress in the same material and seemed somewhat put out, but I thought it was amusing.

The officer's club was on the coast nearby and we often walked there when we had finished our chores. It had a bar, showers, and changing rooms. There was no beach, we just jumped straight off the rocks into the clear blue sea not far below. It was wonderful. At other times we went by bus to St Paul's Bay, which had a long, long sandy beach. We took a picnic and sunbathed, cooling off in the sea at intervals, and getting very tanned. Meliha Bay was sandy too, but we had to clamber down a steep path to get there.

David (aged nearly fourteen) was still at school in England but flew out to Malta for the summer holidays. Just before we went to meet him, Mum rather hesitantly said,

"Judy darling, would you make sure that David knows the facts of life?"

He did of course, and we laughed about it. Being a boy he was able to stay on board Woo Ha, and was at sea with Fish when there was a sudden crisis in the Red Sea. Fish had to go there immediately with no time to put David ashore first. The Royal Navy always solves problems, though. David was transferred to another ship, looked after by a friend of Fish's, and arrived back safely in Malta some days later. The inshore flotilla was away for over three months after this, so it was a lonely time for Mum, who often got anxious phone calls from sailors' wives asking if she knew when the ships were returning. She didn't actually but was able to be of some comfort, if only as someone to talk to.

I was luckier as the service community was very social. The ships all had cocktail parties, dinner parties, and dances, both for those stationed there and others passing through. On my eighteenth birthday I was invited to a party on board HMS Cumberland, where I met a tall, fair-haired young sub lieutenant, Tim Woodward. He took me out to dinner afterwards and then we walked along a moonlit beach, beside the gently swishing sea. That was the occasion of my first kiss. His ship sailed soon after and we didn't ever meet again, but I never forgot him.

I went out with several young officers after this, in the Army and Royal Marines as well as the Navy, and went to equally romantic venues, but I didn't ever fall in love with anyone, or they with me for that matter. Before the pill, relationships between the sexes were quite decorous, in my experience anyway. I heard reference to girls who 'did' but I wasn't one of them.

I had one friend whom I saw a lot and was quite fond of; his name was Guy Liardet, a lieutenant in HMS Fiskerton. He was six years older than me. Tall, blue-eyed, with crinkly fair hair, and the proud owner of a new Volkswagen Beetle. Actually, he had a bad stammer, which hadn't prevented him winning the 'Sword of Honour' at Dartmouth, but I'm ashamed to say I did find it somewhat embarrassing at times. I met him again in England and stayed with his family near Arundel. He'd warned me beforehand that they all wore overcoats at home, and he wasn't joking. That was when he told me I was 'rather boring', and I wasn't surprised; I rather agreed with him. We drifted apart after that. Guy did well in the Navy and went on to become an admiral.

Another good friend was Kit Layman, a sub-lieutenant in HMS Walkerton; he was always someone I could ask to be my partner if invited to take someone with me. He asked me to the 'Families Day' in his ship – all the inshore flotilla had them – so I did get to spend some time at sea, which I loved. Back in England, I quite often went to stay for weekends with his naval family and became very fond of his mother. Kit went on to have a distinguished career in the Navy, including service in HMY Britannia. He was awarded a DSO in the Falklands War when his ship, HMS Argonaut, came under enemy fire. Like Guy, he became an admiral. Our relationship was never other than platonic and we both married other people even if our respective mothers wished otherwise.

I was friendly with some of the naval daughters in Malta; Sue Harrison I'd been at school with, Vicky Lee-Barber and I shared a birthday. Her parents were great friends of my parents, as were Sue Walsham's. I also remember Deidre Hamilton Hill, who later married Corin Redgrave. We met at parties and they came to boat picnics, but I wasn't particularly close to any of them.

On Sundays we went with Fish to the dockyard church on Manoel Island, Mum and I in our best dresses and a hat. Afterwards, we changed and set off in a motor boat for a picnic, taking several friends. The boat would anchor and we'd dive or jump straight in to swim. We sometimes took water skis. I always fell off before I got upright, but I could manage a water board, which was easier. One of the hazards of swimming was jellyfish, which were translucent with long trailing tentacles, and not easy to spot. I soon found that I was allergic to their sting, which felt like a burn, got very swollen, and blistered and left a scar. Horrid things. After that I was very cautious about swimming.

In winter, after church, we were often invited to 'curry tiffin' with Army or Royal Marine friends, in their mess. The curry was rather 'English', with side dishes of coconut, mango chutney, and sliced bananas. There was a particularly delicious pudding called *gulag Malacca*, a translucent tapioca with a sauce that might have been maple. I've never come across it since. On Sunday nights, a cinema screen was erected on the quarterdeck, with a buffet supper of local food before the film was shown. Another popular event was horse racing, which didn't interest me I have to say.

I was sometimes taken out sailing, but I never took to it as David did; he became very proficient and subsequently crewed for the Fastnet Race in the South of England. I didn't like being blown and tossed about in small boats. I loved bigger ships though, even ferries, and was never seasick however rough it was.

My parents loved exploring and often took me too when Fish had leave. We went to Italy; Naples with its wide bay and the ruins of Pompei nearby, Rome with its frenetic, horn hooting traffic and the Coliseum's huge amphitheatre. We threw coins in the Trevi Fountain to make sure we returned, which in my case was forty years later. We went to Libya, too, staying in Tripoli, and we saw the ancient Roman ruins of Sabratha and Leptis Magna with their amazing mosaics.

Another time, Mum and I went by sea to join Fish in Cyprus. We stayed in Kyrenia for a few days. The hotel had cockroaches which lurked in our shoes. I didn't like that much but the sea was directly under the hotel window and that was fabulous. We explored the huge, extensive ruins of St Hilarion Castle, built on cliffs high above the sea. It was very hot climbing up the steep, rocky paths, there was no shade at all.

Recently, David reminded me about something which happened during his Christmas holidays. A group of us went by boat round the harbour singing carols and were offered punch or mulled wine in every ship we visited. Afterwards, as our parents met us at the jetty, David was very sick over the side of the boat. Fish wasn't amused.

"You let the side down, cock," he told David the next day. "Don't bloody well behave like that again."

On another occasion, I'd had a few friends to dinner in the flat before we went off to a dance. I'd left the washing up in the sink and this time it was me facing my mother.

"Judy, do the washing up before you go to bed," she said, "or you won't be able to have friends here again."

One of the more memorable parties was the fancy dress dance on New Year's Eve, at the Phoenicia Hotel. Fish wore a red and white chequered *shamaag*, an Arabic headdress; Mum, all in black lace, was a witch. I made 'horns' to match my orange dress and was a devil; my partner, Kit (mentioned above), was a green stuffed pepper. Being tall, I'd had to take the man's part during ballroom dancing lessons at school.

"Mum and I are the dancers in the family," David told me, but I enjoyed it nevertheless, except Scottish reels during which I often turned the wrong way.

It was always lovely to get letters from England, and I spent a lot of time writing them myself. I wrote regularly to my grandmother, Ducky, in Yorkshire, to my friend Pauline from Eastbourne days, to my three aunts, Fish's sisters, and to my mother's sister Kate in Canada. I also corresponded with naval friends when they were at sea.

A feature of Malta was their frequent religious festivals. Processions of flower-bedecked floats displaying huge models of various saints were paraded through the narrow streets accompanied by a noisy brass band, and at night there were huge firework displays which filled the sky with noise and colour for quite a long time.

Fish's appointment ended in August 1959 and there were several farewell parties. I had one given for me by my godmother, Dot Lyddon, Mum's friend from Eastbourne days. She had met her future husband Bertie when his ship had visited Whitby; Mum met Fish at their wedding a few months later. The party at their house in the dockyard was a happy occasion to which I invited all my friends. Although shy, I seem to have been quite popular, but did think it had more to do with my being 'the captain's daughter' than me as a person. I don't think all the male attention went to my head though as I'd hate to have been thought a 'spoiled brat'.

I wouldn't have wanted to live in Malta permanently; it was an artificial life, but I was very lucky to have lived there for over a year, especially as I didn't have to earn my living and had nothing to worry about other than what to wear for parties. I was sad when we left and my life was never so carefree again.

I couldn't believe how green England was, seeing trees, fields, and cows as we came down to land at the airport. It was lovely to be back at Park Hall, next door to Ducky again. It wasn't for long, though. Fish's next job was Captain of HMS Excellent, at Whale Island, Portsmouth. Aged almost nineteen, a new chapter of my life was about to begin.

Chapter 5

Hawtreys

Fish started his new job in September 1959, soon after we returned from Malta. He had been appointed as the captain of HMS Excellent, the Naval Gunnery School situated at Whale Island, attached to Portsmouth by a causeway. Fish was very happy about this; as a gunnery officer himself it was regarded as a 'plum' job. The Captain's House had a staff, a cook, and two stewards, so my mother had nothing to do in the house other than choose menus; the wardroom kitchen provided our meals and the food for my parents' frequent dinner parties. As the captain's wife, Mum was involved in various local committees which soon kept her busy.

Portsmouth had a large naval population with the dockyard, other shore establishments, and of course ships of all sizes in the harbour. It was almost as social as Malta.

I started having driving lessons, and that was all right, but having to practice with my parents was another matter. Mum would sit beside me, pale and almost visibly shaking. Fish just shouted.

"Put the bloody brake on, woman," he'd say.

"I'm trying to," I would shout back. The worst time was driving behind a big lorry climbing a very steep hill in Yorkshire.

"How did you get on?" said Fish when I took my test.

"I failed," I said.

"I knew you would," he said, and so had I.

No more was said about lessons and it put me off learning to drive for quite a while. I finally passed it just before my fiftieth birthday and really couldn't imagine why I had found it so hard for so long.

I didn't much like being the captain's daughter at Whale Island; it was such a small place that I felt rather conspicuous there. I wanted some independence and to earn my own living too, although I did have some money as my parents had given me a clothes allowance when I was sixteen. I wasn't qualified apart from my Housekeeper's Certificate, and I'd always loved children, so thought I'd look for a residential job in a school.

I went to London to see a well known agency, Gabbitas Thring, who arranged an interview for a job as an assistant matron at Hawtreys, a boys' preparatory school on the edge of the Savernake Forest in Wiltshire. I was very excited when I was accepted, at the salary of £100 a term. I started just after Christmas at the beginning of 1960.

Hawtreys was housed in a huge stately home, leased from the Marques of Aylesbury. It was set in acres of grounds including a deer park. The house had a pillared, portico entrance. A wide, shallow staircase rose from the huge, pillared hall to the landing, with numerous rooms opening off on one side, a balustrade overlooking the hall on the other. My small room was up a further staircase to the floor above. It had a view of the deer park and I was very happy up there, relishing my independence, anonymity, and solitude. Next door to me was the junior master, Jonathan Joel. I used to listen to his gramophone playing classical music and loved it from that moment on, after a while beginning my own collection of records.

The matron of the school was a Miss Jenkins, a trained nurse who looked after the boys' health. She seemed ancient but probably wasn't; I was rather in awe of her. She was only there for my first term as she had to have an operation to fuse two vertebrae in her back. The other assistant matron was Joy Wynne; her father was vicar of the church in the nearby village of Great Bedwyn. I'd been born in a vicarage, so we had a similar background, but Joy was two years older than me and much more worldly wise. We got on well and I enjoyed working with her.

While Miss Jenkins was on sick leave, we had a temporary matron, Anne Dunn, also from Great Bedwyn. Her father was a retired naval commander so we had that in common. Anne had trained at St Bartholomew's Hospital in London, but hadn't had a lot to do with small boys; she said that I helped her to learn her job. She had recently finished a four year friendship with a doctor whom she realised was never going to propose marriage – and he'd then immigrated to Australia and married someone else.

The headmaster told us that Anne's younger brother, James, had disappeared several months previously, and it was six months before his body was eventually found in a sewer, chained to the railings. It was shocking hearing about Anne's brother, of course, but Joy and I were so young, I don't think the full horror of it really occurred to us, and Anne herself didn't mention it. She was a very cheerful, enthusiastic person, and we became good friends, especially after Joy got involved with the junior master. Some evenings we shared a bottle of wine and some cheddar cheese. We kept in touch after leaving Hawtreys, for a while each of us renting a bedsitter in the same house in Notting Hill Gate, London.

Some of the teaching staff lived in, some lived locally, but as there was no staff room I didn't really get to know them. The senior master, known as 'Walks', and his wife Peppa were kind and sometimes had me to tea; he taught Maths, she taught Music and played the piano for assembly and chapel services, held in the hall. The junior mistress, Jill, had a crush on the Classics master, Dick Frewen; she spent hours mending his academic gown – the male staff all wore them – but he didn't seem very appreciative. He used to coach some of the older boys in his room, and Mr Rappoport (who taught French) sometimes went there on some pretext or other, as he suspected that Dick wasn't just teaching, but he never found him doing anything remiss. We thought it was very amusing, not realising the implications.

The school had ninety-four boys aged from seven to thirteen years, who slept in big dormitories on the first floor. We matrons had to supervise the boys getting up in the morning, at bath times in the evening, and going to bed at night. We sat with them at mealtimes, too: breakfast, lunch, and high tea. We did have a couple of hours off in the afternoon, but were otherwise busy until the boys went to bed.

A big part of the job was looking after the boys' clothes. I had to unpack the trunks of the thirty-four youngest boys and pack them again at the end of term. We sorted the laundry and did the mending, which included darning socks for which my Eastbourne training came in useful. Joy and I worked together in the laundry room, chatting constantly about clothes, make up, and of course the boys; I recall us discussing their anatomy and which of them had been circumcised. We had a lot of fun together. During Lent we decided to give up taking sugar in our tea – Lent was taken seriously in those days. We looked forward to having sugar again at Easter, but by then tea tasted too sweet, so what were we to give up the following year?

Some of the boys seemed very young and vulnerable when they first came. I remember Alexander Sandberg coming up to me, holding the hand of his younger brother Patrick, who had just started that term and was looking very tearful.

"Please, ma'am," he said, which was how the boys had to address us, "my brother's homesick."

I hugged Patrick. "I'm so sorry, darling," I said. "It'll go away soon, I promise." They went off again, and Patrick soon settled down.

Hawtreys was one of the prep schools for Eton and many of the boys were from aristocratic families, although I didn't realise it at the time. We had to correct the boy's table manners, and one day I took Charles Brudenell-Bruce to task.

"Don't put your elbows on the table, Charlie," I said. "You can't do that until you're an uncle."

"I am an uncle," he said, "David is my nephew." I had thought they were cousins, a year apart in age, but actually Charlie's father was the Marques of Aylesbury by his third wife; his much older half brother (son of the first wife) being David's father.

"My parents are divorced," David said one day, looking rather sad.

"Never mind, darling," I said. "I'm sure they both love you."

He also told me that his mother was in the South of France with a well-known actor. Quite a few of the boys had similarly difficult backgrounds.

I also looked after Roddy Macdonald, a lively ginger-haired boy whose father was a racing manager. He later had a much publicised affair with Princess Margaret.

The boys were known by their surnames, to the teaching staff, anyway; we matrons didn't have to be so formal. In the case of brothers, they were Major, Minor, and occasionally Minimus, Min for short. There were three Richmond-Watson boys; the younger one of twins was gorgeous, he had big brown eyes and dark red, wavy hair. They were sitting near me at breakfast one Sunday morning.

"Eat your baked beans, Stuart," I said. "They're good for you."

"I don't like them."

"I know you don't, but you aren't allowed to leave food. Just have a few more," I said, and he reluctantly ate them.

Not long after, during Chapel, Stuart was very sick, and I had to get a mop and bucket and clear it up. Poor little boy.

Another time a particularly violent tummy bug did the rounds and even the older boys were sick wherever they happened to be, not able to get to the loos in time. We matrons were dashing upstairs and down clearing up after them. I then got it too. I was in the middle of packing trunks, so I put clothes in a few of them, and crawled into bed for a while. Then I was very sick again, felt a bit better, and packed a few more trunks. Luckily, the loo and basin were adjacent in the bathroom, and after a while I gave up trying to carry on, and stayed in bed.

Most of the boys were well-behaved, but occasionally one would be naughty – cheeky, usually – or maybe we'd catch two of them fighting. Once I sent a boy called Caldicott to the headmaster, Mr Goodeve-Docker, and he was duly caned. We thought nothing of it, but it does sound very strange these days. My brother was frequently caned at his school and said it never did him any harm.

We each had a day off during the week, mine was on Thursday. I often rode my bicycle to the station and took a train to Salisbury or Newbury for the day; I was very happy exploring places on my own. Sometimes I cycled through the Savernake Forest to Marlborough, a five mile ride and beautiful, especially in Spring and Autumn. Once or twice a term, Cousin Sylvia, a contemporary of my mother's who lived in Andover, came to pick me up in her car and take me home for the day, which I always enjoyed. I cleaned all their shoes for them.

Sylvia's husband, Fair, was a New Zealander and a lovely, gentle, kind man. He adored Sylvia and was heartbroken when, in old age, she became demented and no longer knew him. Sylvia had been married before, and her daughter Bunjie, eight years old, had died under the anaesthetic when having her tonsils out. She had a younger son too, Christopher, for whom she never seemed to have much time; he had the saddest big blue eyes I've ever seen.

In my free time I taught myself to paint, using oils on canvas boards. I painted a view of the front of the house from the carriage drive (which was about a mile long) and also a view of the back. My father framed them for me and they were a happy memory of those days. I did quite a lot of charcoal sketching too.

Jonathan (the junior master) and Joy saw a lot of each other and they quite soon got engaged. I was delighted when Joy asked me to be her bridesmaid. The wedding was in January and Joy wanted me to wear red velvet. I made a straight dress with a detachable, flared overskirt. It took hours to make as velvet isn't nice material to work with; it 'creeps' as seams are stitched and I had to keep re-doing them. Some years later I used the dress to make dresses for my two girls to wear for Christmas.

I stayed with Anne's parents the night before the wedding and went to the vicarage in the morning to get ready.

"Your dress is a bit tight, Joy," I said. "I can hardly do up the zip."

"Actually, I'm pregnant," she said, "but please don't tell anyone, my parents will be upset…"

"Of course I won't," I said.

Anthony was born in the summer and I was asked to be one of his godparents.

I was very happy at Hawtreys and thoroughly enjoyed working with the boys, but after four terms there I felt that the time had come to move on. The headmaster gave me a very nice testimonial and said that the experience of working there would stand me in good stead when I had my own children – I'm not sure that it did, though. I left at Easter, not quite sure what to do next, but in the meantime returning to Portsmouth for Fish's last few months at Whale Island.

Back to being the captain's daughter again.

Chapter 6

The Far East

It was strange being back with my parents again, and not working, but I soon settled and found plenty to occupy myself for the next three months.

I started having typing lessons at Whaley; the keyboard was covered and I had to remember where the letters were. I never achieved any speed, and felt slightly self-conscious being the only girl, but the sailors were nice to me and typing was a useful skill. I did a still life painting course at the technical college in Portsmouth; I enjoyed it very much and learned quite a bit. I painted a few scenes at Whaley, one of the row of redbrick buildings that included the Captain's House, looking through the arch in the rose garden towards green expanse of the cricket pitch and the athletic track. I sat outside with my easel on hot, leisurely summer days.

As in all naval areas, there were lots of social events including summer balls, always superb occasions, and I went with Fish and Mum to a garden party at Buckingham Palace, with crowds of people in their best clothes, balancing tea cups and eating chocolate cake. Finally there were several farewell parties before we left Portsmouth at the end of July and moved all our belongings back to Park Hall, where Fish had a few days leave.

Fish's next job was at sea; he was delighted to be appointed as captain of an aircraft carrier, HMS Bulwark, stationed in Singapore. He flew out there in August 1961, and Mum planned to follow him at the end of David's school holidays.

"Judy, would you like to go the Far East instead of a twenty-first birthday present?" my parents asked me.

"Yes please, I'd absolutely love to," I said. "Thank you so much... I remember us all being there when I was eight... it would be wonderful to go there again." I was very excited about it.

During that summer in Portsmouth I'd met a young man called David Mortimer, a naval lieutenant who was doing a course at HMS Dryad, the naval navigation school. He was six years older than me, tall, good-looking with fair hair and blue eyes, and quite serious, like me I suppose. He took me out a few times, I liked him, and we got on well. He knew that I was going away soon, so we probably got involved sooner than we might have done otherwise.

Anyway, he wanted me to meet his parents and one day he drove me to their house in Wiltshire for lunch. They seemed nice people, his father quiet and reserved, his mother very chatty, quite a forceful character. David was their only child; they hadn't been privately educated themselves but had sent him to Radley, and were obviously keen for him to do well in the Navy, as was David himself. That was the day I saw David use a small tray purse, which surprised me; I thought men used their trouser pockets for change. I didn't say anything to him, and I told myself not to be silly about something so trivial.

After we left Whaley I invited David to stay at Park Hall for a few days, so we could spend some time together before I went to the Far East. He arrived one evening and the next day we went to Whitby. It was a beautiful sunny day. We had just explored the ancient ruins of Whitby Abbey, and were sitting on a seat overlooking the sea when David asked me to marry him.

I was taken by surprise and without really thinking about it, I said, "Yes".

I don't know why I was surprised. I should have realised where our short relationship was heading; perhaps it was because I was flattered, and it was rather a romantic setting. I felt in rather a daze as we went back to Park Hall.

I found Mum in the garden.

"Mum, you do like David, don't you?" I asked her.

"Yes, very much," she said. "Why are you asking me?"

"We want to get engaged," I said.

"Oh darling, how lovely. What a pity Fish isn't here, I'll send him a telegram straight away... we'll have a special dinner tonight to celebrate."

At dinner we were talking about Fish's new job, and Mum said she couldn't wait to join him.

"You won't want to come, Judy, will you, now you've just got engaged?"

"I do want to, actually," I said. "I'm really looking forward to going. After all, we won't be getting married until Fish comes back to England."

"We won't announce your engagement yet, then," she said. "Let's keep it unofficial for the time being."

David did his best to be positive about it. "Hong Kong is a wonderful place for shopping, darling. I'll give you some money to spend for our future home," he said. "Things are much cheaper out there. You could get us some china, couldn't you?"

"Thanks very much, that's a lovely idea," I said.

It was sad parting when David went back to Portsmouth, but it was worse for him than me, as I was going away and our future plans were on hold.

I went to tell Ducky about us getting engaged. She was excited and began trying to tell me something, pointing upstairs to her bedroom. She'd had several strokes and couldn't talk but I eventually gathered that she wanted to give me a ring. I found it in her jewellery case; it had diamonds and rubies set in gold. I felt quite overwhelmed as I thanked her; it was a wonderful gesture and I felt I didn't deserve it.

Soon it was time for Mum and I to leave Park Hall and set off on our travels. The RAF sometimes had free seats on transport planes; Fish had applied for two of these 'indulgence flights' and at the end of August we went to stay at Yeovilton Naval Air Station in Somerset, to await an available flight. We were lucky and got one four days later.

It took twenty-eight hours to get to Singapore. We stopped three times en route: I awoke on my twenty-first birthday just before we landed in Aden, then we stopped in El Adem, and finally in Gan, a tiny island in the Pacific. The plane was small, crowded, and noisy, and at one stage the sailor sitting beside me fell asleep on my shoulder, but I loved the journey and didn't mind a bit. Each time we stepped out of the plane it was into wonderful hot, spicy air with blue sky and palm trees.

Fish met us at the airport and drove us through Singapore Island and across the causeway to Johore Bahru in Malaya, where he had booked rooms at the rest house. It was very comfortable there; the large rooms had verandas overlooking the lush, tropical gardens full of trees and exotic flowering shrubs. It was very hot and steamy; every day at two o'clock the sky opened like a tap and rain poured down for about two hours. I'd never heard or seen rain like it, it made such a noise. The humid tropical heat meant that we had to shower and change clothes at least twice a day and had to sleep under nets because of all the mosquitoes.

There was plenty to keep Mum and I occupied in the rest house. We washed and ironed our clothes, we read books, and, sitting on the veranda, Mum painted in water colours, while I did charcoal sketches of the view. We both wrote lots of letters, too. Mine were mainly to David, telling him all about what I was doing. At first I looked forward to the air letters with his familiar neat, slanted handwriting, but after a while I felt disappointed and increasingly irritated. We disagreed about when I was intending to return to England, where I would live until we could get married amongst other things. I didn't like his rather sanctimonious attitude, and I didn't think he had much sense of humour either.

One morning, Mum and I thought we'd go for a walk. We were soon dripping with perspiration.

"No wonder everyone goes by car or taxi," said Mum. "I'm worn out... walking isn't a good idea in this heat."

Fish was very amused when we told him about it.

We spent a lot of time in Bulwark, where Fish had a comfortable cabin made even nicer by lamps, photos, and cushions from Park Hall. Singapore was very social, and I helped my parents entertain visitors, always including two or more of the ship's officers. There was the familiar routine of Sunday church on board, taken by the ship's padre. This was followed by a boat picnic, but no swimming as there were poisonous snakes in the sea, which was cloudy and uninviting, unlike the Mediterranean. On Sunday night there was a buffet supper and cinema on the quarterdeck, always a lovely occasion.

Fish's officers were all very kind to me, and I made a few friends amongst the younger ones, especially John Ashworth, whom I got to know quite well.

"You're engaged to someone, aren't you Judy?" he asked me one day. "What's he like?"

"Oh yes... David Mortimer... he's in the Navy, doing the navigation course in Portsmouth... he's twenty-six. Actually, I haven't known him long... we only met in June. I'm not sure we ought to have got engaged so soon..." I said. "What about you? Lots of girlfriends?"

"I met a gorgeous girl called Mary just before I came out here," he said. "It always happens in the Navy… you change jobs at the wrong time… but I'm seeing someone out here too… see what happens. I'd like to see Mary again, I must admit…"

So whenever I saw John I asked about his love life, he asked me about David, and we talked about life on board Bulwark.

"Your Dad's pipe smells awful, Judy. Does he smoke old socks?"

John was a good friend. We corresponded after I left and met up again in London, which was fun. And in due course he married his gorgeous Mary.

My parents always explored wherever they were stationed. We went up country several times, staying in rented bungalows, with a local woman to cook and clean. Bathrooms had a huge Ali Baba jar to sit in, having first removed all the insects inside. Shoes had to be inspected too.

Port Dickson was a beautiful place with a long, white sandy beach, fringed with palm trees. One day it was cloudy as I lay on the beach wearing a two piece bathing suit. That evening my midriff was slightly red and by the middle of the night I was so stiff it was agony to move, and then I came out in huge blisters. It was certainly a lesson to me that the sun can burn even through clouds.

We stayed in Johore Bahru for two months, and then Bulwark went to Hong Kong to take part in fleet exercises. Mum booked a passage for us in SS Cathay, and we arrived in time to be on the jetty just as Bulwark came alongside. It was exciting being in Hong Kong again and I remembered a lot about it: the thronging crowded streets, the skyscrapers, the noisy traffic, the ferry going between Hong Kong Island and Kowloon, and the shops which sold everything you could possibly want to buy.

I had great fun spending the money David had given me. In one emporium I acquired a carved camphorwood chest – it smelt wonderful inside – with a matching set of three occasional tables;

some Japanese Noritake china which included a dinner service, an after dinner coffee set, and a tea set too. In the same shop were lovely open work china lamps with a bulb inside as well as under the shade; I bought two of them. Another time I got a wooden statue of a Balinese lady and a painting of a junk in Hong Kong harbour. I found a copy of a Singer sewing machine for all of £5 – I was thrilled with that – and a lovely little gramophone in a blue leather case. The last two became very treasured and much used possessions.

The shops selling dress material were amazing too; I got some dark blue, green, and purple checked Thai silk, and had some high-heeled, square-toed shoes made to measure in dark green silk to go with it, or rather to match the dress I made from it. I also bought a turquoise Chinese brocade *cheongsam*, a traditional straight, fitted Chinese dress with a high collar fastened with tiny buttons across the left shoulder and down one side; the right of the skirt had a slit to just above the knee. It was my favourite dress and I wore it on many occasions.

We had a picnic at Big Wave Bay and the waves were just as huge as I'd remembered them, and the peak of Hong Kong Island just as high. The car drove up and up round the hairpin bends, the boats in the bustling harbour looking smaller and smaller as we went.

Hong Kong was where I got to know Fish's young secretary, Brian. He was engaged to someone in England, as I was. I got very fond of him in that short time, and he of me, I think. We didn't keep in touch though, perhaps just as well. Hong Kong was such a beautiful, romantic place to be, easy to be tempted to form relationships even though yourself engaged or even married, an aspect of naval life which worried me a bit, especially as I'd met several of the wives left behind in England, looking after their children. I should explain that a post in HMS Bulwark was a 'sea job' and there were no accompanying allowances for families. We were lucky that Fish could afford to have us with him; most wives could only go out to Singapore for a holiday. Mum was once advised not to let Fish too far out of her sight, not that she need have worried; Fish only ever had eyes for her.

After a month in Hong Kong we went back to Singapore by sea, in time for Christmas celebrations. We joined the ship's company for midnight communion, and on Christmas morning the service of nine lessons and carols. It was exhilarating singing with all the male voices. Afterwards, Fish made the traditional captain's visit to the mess decks to wish the ship's company happy Christmas; Mum and I accompanied him. It took ages climbing up and down ladders as Bulwark was such a huge ship, with a crew of nearly two thousand men. We had to have a shower and change after that, before lunch in the wardroom, and presents for everyone from the tree. Mine was a very sharp paperknife in a wooden sheath – I have it still.

HMS Bulwark was about to leave Singapore to go to Fremantle, Western Australia, for an official visit, and Mum was flying there too. I'd had a wonderful holiday in the Far East, and enjoyed every minute of it, but now felt that it was time I returned to England and got a job. I wasn't eligible for an indulgence flight home, so Fish booked a passage for me on the Royal Fleet Auxiliary Bacchus, which was due to sail on December 30th. This meant that I'd miss the Bulwark New Year's Eve Ball, which was a pity. I was very sad to leave, and it's the only time I ever saw Fish with tears in his eyes. Mum and I cried too. It was almost a year before I saw them again.

RFA Bacchus was a tiny ship; there were only four other passengers, all much older than me. After dinner, some of us played Scrabble with the captain, but I was good at it and the captain wasn't happy being beaten by a girl, so the games stopped. After that I got friendly with a couple of the young officers and spent evenings with them. Soon after we left Singapore, Bacchus got engine trouble and we stayed in Penang while it was fixed. We were taken to see a snake temple, which was quite an experience – snakes were lying on picture rails and curled round light flexes, and there was an enormous python curled up asleep, thankfully behind bars.

A letter from Fish arrived while we were in Penang and brought tears to my eyes again.

Let us not dwell on that wretched Saturday when you left us. Seldom have I felt more miserable, but that is an indication of how much Mum and I love you, my darling. Suffice to say your time in the Far East with us has been a joy from beginning to end, except for the end…

We stopped in Aden, where friends of my parents, Nicky and Knocker White, kindly took me out for the day. We stopped in Gibraltar too. It was a long voyage and it was over a month after leaving Singapore that we crossed the Bay of Biscay, where the sea was very rough indeed; I tried to walk along the deck, going upwards one minute and running down the next, buffeted by the wind and wet with spray. I loved every minute of it.

When I got back to England in early February, my fiancé David was there at Chatham to meet me. But when I saw him again I realised that my feelings about him had changed. He must have guessed something was wrong because quite soon he said,

"What's wrong, darling? Aren't you happy that we are together again?"

"No I'm not, David. I'm very sorry but I don't want to marry you now."

"Why ever not? I thought you loved me… you said you did. "

"I thought I did when we were at Park Hall, but now we've met again I realise that I don't. I'm really sorry, I don't like hurting you but I don't want us to be unhappy. It's much better to call it off now."

"You shouldn't have gone to the Far East…" he said.

"It wasn't that… we shouldn't have got engaged so quickly… we hardly knew each other."

I'd had doubts at the time we got engaged, but pushed them to the back of my mind, thinking that marriage was a long way off. Actually, it was David's letters. We'd been corresponding for six months and as I got to know him better I began to think I didn't like him much, and seeing him again confirmed it. It was a difficult homecoming, and it was a relief when we said goodbye to each other.

A few days later his mother telephoned me at Park Hall.

"Judy," she said, "you shouldn't have broken your engagement to David. Grown up people don't behave like that. You shouldn't have gone off to the Far East either…"

"I'm very sorry, Mrs Mortimer," I said, when I managed to get a word in. "I realised that I didn't love David when we met again… we should never have got engaged… it was a big mistake." I was very glad I wasn't going to have her as a mother-in-law.

I wrote to tell my parents. They sent me a telegram to say they quite understood and their reassuring letters followed.

First Mum's:

…My poor poppet what an absolutely miserable time you must have had, if only I could have been there with you… Fishy and I weren't a bit surprised… though I would never have admitted it before, frankly I'm glad because nice as David was, he wasn't really good enough for you… I tried to think that his many advantages out weighed his lack of background but didn't really convince myself… and there were too many arguments about all sorts of things for us to feel that you were absolutely ideal for each other…

Then Fish's:

> *Poor old girl, what a wretched horrid homecoming you had. I'm afraid your news came as no surprise to either of us. I had formed my own impression that things weren't going too well and I suspect that was one subconscious reason why all of us felt so miserable when you left Singapore…*
>
> *I am absolutely certain that you were correct to come out to the Far East, I was a chance (sic) too good it be missed, an education, a safety valve, an added chance to grow up…*

I also had a letter from Kate, in Canada:

> *I thought I would write <u>at once</u> after getting your letter about David, as I expect you are feeling a bit flat and blue; but really darling though I didn't meet David, I am really rather glad that you are not being married at 21! I know that not many people want to wait as long as I did (although I think by doing so I had the best of both worlds – the married and the single!) but there are still so many people to meet and enjoy in this world and so many places to go and lets face it, in these days when most people haven't the money for servants, one is more tied down when one is married with children… so I should steer clear of actual engagements – especially long ones.*

What a lovely, uplifting letter – Kate really was the best aunt.

Once over the initial upset, and I did feel very unhappy about it, I was fine, happy to be home and looking forward to finding a job.

I never wore my grandmother's ring. I gave it to my brother David when he got engaged to Robina, some years later. Ducky had died by them, but I'm sure she would have approved.

More than fifty years later, I've just been staying with my dear friend Pauline from Eastbourne days.

"Pauline, did you meet David Mortimer?" I asked her.

"Yes, I did, I thought he was lovely. You seemed quite happy with him.... not over the moon though... why did you break it off? You didn't seem to want to talk about it..."

"It was his letters... I didn't like them. We argued," I said.

"Your parents seemed to like him."

"That would be because he was a naval officer."

"I got the impression that David was glad that you were a captain's daughter too."

"That's no surprise, but it's amusing to hear it after all this time."

Chapter 7

London

England was covered in snow when I got back in February, and it didn't thaw for about six weeks; pavements were slippery with impacted ice and it was very, very cold. People kept asking where I'd been as I was still tanned after my travels.

It was lovely seeing Ducky again, but even though I'd only been away six months, she seemed even frailer, though she was still her old cheerful self, smiling and very happy to see me, interested in all I was telling her even if not able to respond other than saying "yes" or "no." She just sat in her chair all day, and the only thing which ever seemed to upset her was if her watch or clocks were the wrong time, which made her quite agitated.

We were so lucky having Hilda looking after Ducky; she'd been with my family since she was a sixteen-year-old housemaid at the vicarage. She'd married a local farmer, John Marshall, while we were in Malta, and had a daughter, Gillian, now a few months old. They all lived at Park Lodge. I'd known Hilda all my life; she'd looked after David and me when we were young. She was always pleased to see me and loved having someone to talk to while she was cooking. She used to make jam tarts and cake for John's 'pack up' which he took to the farm with him.

"Ee, this knife is blunt," she said one day. "I could ride bareback to London on it." Another time she told me how busy she was. "I ran up those stairs so quick, I met meself coming down again"… "I read t' obituaries in't Gazette to see if I's still alive"… "Eee, I feel like two o'clock half struck today". That's such a useful expression, I always think. I sometimes feel like that myself and always think of Hilda coming out with it.

I was very happy being back in my own room at Park Hall. I wasn't alone in the house, not that it would have worried me, although I did think I'd seen ghosts one night, in the spare room, when I was younger. Mrs Cowburn, who was my parent's housekeeper, lived in the self-contained wing, with her daughter Barbara. Nobody seemed to know if there'd ever been a Mr Cowburn; we thought Mrs Cowburn was actually what was then known as an 'un-married mother'. She was a kind woman, somewhat deaf, but luckily for me was happy to cook for me, and my brother David too when he came up during his holidays. I think she liked having people in the house.

One of the first things I did was to go to see David at Sherborne (School) – as his big sister and with our parents away, I took my responsibility seriously. The headmaster was watching the rugger match.

"You must be David's twin sister," he said.

"Actually, I'm four years older," I told him.

"I'm so sorry," he said.

But I didn't mind at all, and nor did David; we thought it was very funny. It was lovely seeing David again, but I hardly recognised him as he had grown so much; he was inches taller than me, and would soon be as tall as Fish. He was in the middle of applying to join the Navy; he'd failed once and another interview was taking place in May, so it was an anxious time for our parents. Luckily, David was a great optimist and never let anything much bother him. I did tell him that our parents had spent a lot of money on our education and the least we could do was work hard to repay them. He didn't tell me to shut up – I must have been such an irritating 'bossy boots' – but neither did he take much notice.

I was getting long letters from the Far East, both my parents keeping me abreast of what they were doing. Soon after I left Singapore, HMS Bulwark had gone to Freemantle, Western Australia, for an official visit lasting ten days. Mum flew from Singapore to join Fish, and their letters were full of what a beautiful place it was, how they were welcomed and entertained, and how they wished I had been there too; *'you'd have loved it, darling'*. Bulwark went from there to Aden for several weeks, Mum following by sea, and then back to Singapore again. They were glad to have news of England too and pleased to hear that I'd been visiting local family and friends.

It was rather fortuitous that I was back, actually, as poor Ducky was taken ill again. The doctor confirmed that she had had another stroke and would need some nursing care. I wrote to tell Mum of course, and her reply came by return, dated March 28th.

> *I'm very sad to hear about Ducky, I did hope another stroke would be a big one, I didn't think it would be possible for her to have yet another small one. However I'm much less worried than in the past, it's wonderful having you in England darling, & you seem to have been so sensible & full of good suggestions & I'm sure must have been a great comfort to Hilda. Poor Ducky, what a misery it all is, but I was so thankful you said she was still happy. If Nurse Gamble would come for £10 either by day or night & Hilda could manage the rest I'm sure that would be the answer.*

Nurse Gamble didn't stay long, she moved to Scarborough and a better job, so I had to find another part-time nurse. The alternative would have been the Chubb Hill Nursing Home at £10 a week, but Hilda didn't want Ducky to go into one yet, while she still knew what was going on. A nurse came by taxi from Ruswarp for a while, but finally Ducky was a bit better and didn't need nursing so Mrs Nellis, whose husband drove the village taxi, came to bath her a couple of times a week.

Whilst in Singapore I'd met Gerry Slater, visiting her husband Russell, HMS Bulwark's doctor. She'd asked me to stay in London, so I took her up on it. They lived in a flat in Chiswick.

I registered with Universal Aunts, hoping to get a temporary job as a mother's help. Having helped with many younger cousins I reckoned I could do it. I was sent to Brixton to look after a toddler called Sarah whilst her mother was in hospital having a second baby. Her father, Anthony Eyton, was rather tall, with a shaggy beard.

"Look, Sarah, here's Daddy," I used to say when he arrived home in the evening. He looked as bemused as she did.

He didn't seem to be an involved father, but he did become a successful and well known artist; I used to see his huge paintings at the Summer Exhibition at the Royal Academy and always took an interest in his work.

Next I was sent to a Jewish family in Hendon, with a toddler and a new baby. I was happy helping Mrs Evans with housework, cooking, washing, and ironing, but I wasn't there for very long.

I went back to Gabbitas Thring to enquire if there were any available jobs as assistant matron to start after Easter. I saw Mrs Hudgell who'd interviewed me last time.

"Do you want a school job, Judy," she said "or would you consider a job in London? I'm looking for a clerical assistant."

"I'll have to find somewhere to live, but I'd love to do it," I said, and went off feeling very happy.

When I told Gerry about it, she said, "You must PG with me, Judy. I'd love to have you, stay as long as you like."

It was fun staying with Gerry. She was tiny, with unruly blonde hair scooped up into a bun. She was quite scatty, taking ages to get meals ready as she hardly drew breath, but she was very kind. I think she and Russell had been married for quite a while, but they didn't have any children.

I started at Gabbitas soon afterwards. I had to sort the post, write all the details of people job hunting onto cards, do the filing, and if Mrs Hudgell was busy, I interviewed people too. I shared an office with another girl, secretary to one of the directors, and really enjoyed it. The office was in Sackville Street, between Piccadilly and Regent Street, near Swan & Edgar, Fortnum & Mason, Hatchards, and not far from John Lewis. I earned £10 a week, £8 something after tax. I loved the job and I loved London too. Mrs Hudgell took me under her wing and was very kind to me. After a while she referred to herself "Uth Muth" and I'd go to her house for a meal, with her and her very nice husband.

My Eastbourne friend Pauline was living in North London with her husband Tony and new baby Edward; it was lovely seeing her again. Also in London was Anne Dunn whom I'd worked with at Hawtreys. She was working as a dental nurse and living in a bedsit in Notting Hill Gate. We met often. She introduced me to opera, although I never really liked it, and I went to hear her singing choral music with a Knightsbridge Choir. She took me to Portobello market, near her bedsit. There were numerous stalls selling fruit and vegetables and all kinds of other things, especially vintage clothing. A fascinating place.

Through Gerry's downstairs neighbour Maureen, I'd met a barrister, Jan Paulusz, whose family were Dutch although he'd been educated in England. He was kind, intellectual, and rather vague. He took me out a few times, and he'd kiss me goodnight and say "see you soon" but not get in touch again for two or three months.

"I thought you'd gone off with a blonde," I said once.

"No," he said. "I've been rather busy at work."

I didn't ever meet his family or know much about him, but he was a sweet man, I enjoyed going out with him, but wasn't too worried when I didn't see him – I wasn't smitten in other words.

I settled happily into the job, and then Gerry told me that she was going to fly out to Singapore to see Russell. There was only one snag – her dog, Judy, who happened to have the same name as me. She was an overweight poodle that was blind and had only three legs, but Gerry assured me that she was perfectly happy.

"Judy, you can stay here while I'm away, but could you look after Judy? She won't be any trouble. I'm only going for about three weeks."

"That's fine, Gerry, I'll be happy to do that. I'll find somewhere to live when you get back."

I was invited to Portsmouth for the Whitsun Bank Holiday weekend, to stay with Margaret Eldin-Taylor, whom I'd met in Singapore. Her husband Alastair was a Royal Marine officer serving in HMS Bulwark.

"I'd love to come, Margaret, but I'm looking after Gerry's dog while she's away. Do you mind if I bring her too?"

"No, of course not. I love dogs." So off we went on the train together, Judy huffing and puffing as the weather was hot and sunny.

"Judy… that poor dog… I've never seen anything so shaggy and neglected. Why ever hasn't Gerry had her clipped? We can't possibly leave her like that in this heat – I'll trim her. I'm used to dogs…"

So I held Judy, who I must say was very good, and Margaret cut her coat off – both of us quite helpless with laughter. Judy was unrecognisable she was so much smaller.

"I wonder what Gerry will say when she sees her?" I said to Margaret. Mum said in her letter:

'*We did laugh about you clipping the poor hot poodle, I'll remember not to mention it to Gerry.*'

Soon after this, Anne told me that there was an unfurnished bed-sitter free in the same house as her. This was too good to miss, and I paid a deposit.

I wrote to tell my parents about Pembridge Square, and a letter from Fish came by return:

We're very thrilled to hear of your bedsit though I think Mum has expressed the hope that it might have been bigger to include her! Ha ha! How excited you'll be to be on your own & independent & you'll probably want to stay so even if we get one or a flat ourselves depending on the future. How happy you sound darling & well done finding your own feet like this.

The only problem was that there was no sign of Gerry coming home again; from the sound of things in Mum's letters she was having a very good time out there. A further complication was that I didn't get any letters for about three weeks, as the postman in Bulwark hadn't sent them off; I didn't get the furniture list and I couldn't find out Gerry's plans.

"Anne, I hate to ask but could you possibly lend me some money? The rent's due, I'm stuck in Chiswick with the dog, and I don't know when Gerry's coming back, she said she was going for three weeks and it's already six or seven…"

"Don't worry, Judy, you do seem to be having a difficult time… you can have ten pounds…"

"Thank you so much, Anne. I'll pay you back as soon as I can – I hate borrowing money…" It was frustrating; I was cross with Gerry and longing to get on with finding out what furniture I could have, and moving into my own place.

In the meantime, Kit, my naval friend from Malta days, was back in England and he came to see me in Chiswick.

"You're looking very well and happy," he said.

"I am. I love living in London, and I like my job at Gabbitas too. What about you? Have you heard about your next job?"

"Yes… I'm going to HMY Britannia."

"That's wonderful – well done! Fish was in her, as you know, he loved every minute of it. I bet your parents are pleased."

"They are. When can you come and see them?"

We discussed dates, and he also asked if I'd like to go to the Whaley Summer Ball with him.

"Yes please I'd love to go to Whaley again. It's a good excuse to make myself a new dress. Thank you so much for asking me."

John Lewis never failed to have something I wanted, and sure enough there was the perfect fabric for the strapless, long straight dress pattern I'd found, slit to the knee on one side. I'd have to bone it, but that shouldn't be too difficult. It was lurex jersey, with fine stripes in emerald green and gold.

I knew I didn't have much time to spare on the day of the ball; even though it was Friday there was no question of sneaking off early, so on the dot of five I dashed out of the office, got the train, ran home from the station. Ten minutes later I was all ready when Kit came to collect me.

"All ready to go? You must have had quite a rush…"

Kit drove us to Portsmouth and over the familiar causeway onto Whale Island, past the Captain's House where we used to live, to the parade ground, where we parked. It was really exciting being back there, seeing so many people, the men in black ties, the girls all in colourful long dresses.

"Judy! Good to see you, how's old Fish / your father?"

"Did you have a good time in the Far East?"

"What are you up to now?"…

We had drinks and dinner, before dancing to the excellent naval band. I loved it and was sad when it was time to leave. Fish reported by letter that a friend of his had said I looked very soignée.

When I finally moved into Pembridge Square in late July, I was really happy; it was great being in my own little home, especially after all the to-ing and fro-ing with Gerry's plans, the lost mail and being tied to Judy.

The room was on the fifth floor, square, with two dormer windows and sloping ceilings. It had a tiny bathroom in one corner, but the lavatory was on a half landing below, shared with other tenants. The bath had a shelf over it, hooked up to the wall when not in use. This served as a work top and also a draining board for washing up. A square of blue carpet covered the middle of the wooden floor, the rest being polished stained boards. I had a single bed in one corner, and a bedside table on which stood my precious gramophone, a round table in the middle with four upright chairs, a double sofa and a large armchair, a mahogany roll topped desk, and a chest of drawers. Lastly I had a white painted Formica-topped cupboard in which I kept china, etc, with a Baby Belling cooker – oven, grill, and hot plate – on top.

People asked me, "Where do you live?"

"Notting Hill Gate; I've got a bed sitter with a roof top view."

"Where did you say? North of the park?"

I loved being in my very own unfashionable place. My parents had lent me good, antique furniture. I bought some dusters and some Antiquax polish, and frequently polished it all, giving it plenty of 'elbow grease' as Hilda would have put it; the desk was particularly rewarding, the roll top gleamed and my room generally had the comforting smell of polish – it reminded me of Park Hall.

I caught a 12 or 88 bus two minutes away, which went along the Bayswater Road, along Oxford Street, and down Regent Street to Piccadilly Circus, two minutes from the office. My bus fare was sixpence each way. I used to buy a cheese sandwich for lunch, for a shilling. Pickle or tomato cost threepence more, and I couldn't afford that. I was paid in cash fortnightly. The night before pay day I sometimes had one and tenpence for fish and chips, otherwise I had beans on toast or a boiled egg. I did my shopping in Portobello Road on Saturday mornings. The other thing I always did was have ladders in my stockings mended at the cobblers, which was cheaper than buying new ones.

My life was quite well-organised. My fortnightly budget allowed for either a weekend away, or a dinner party, including a bottle of wine for one and sixpence to accompany my rather limited cooking. I used to visit my aunts, Fish's sisters, each in turn: Alison, and the twins Val and Marie. They all had children much younger than me, and I loved helping to look after them, and being part of their family lives.

Not long after I moved into Pembridge Square, my Aunt Kate, Mum's sister, moved into a flat at the bottom of Putney Hill, while her husband Rick was serving with his Canadian Army battalion in Vietnam. Kate didn't like living in Canada and had always returned to England whenever she could, staying at Park Lodge with Ducky, so I'd known my cousins since they were tiny.

Richard was now nine and away at prep school, Anne, seven at school locally, and the twins, Rory and Patricia, were three. I often looked after the twins at weekends so Kate could go away to stay with friends, taking Anne with her. I really enjoyed that. Tricia used to sit on my knee and undo all my cardigan buttons, then do them up again. She was the lively, boisterous one, Rory much quieter. Gorgeous children they were, but then I loved children. Mum, on the other hand, didn't. I learned from Mum's letters that Kate had wanted to borrow Park Hall when she came over that summer, to which Mum reluctantly agreed, with conditions. '*I simply hate the thought of Kate's children rampaging around my poor house*', she wrote, so she was relieved when Kate decided to live in London.

HMS Bulwark had begun to make her way back to England, her last port of call being Aden. Mum, who had followed the ship everywhere she went, flew back from there in November, landing just before a pea soup fog closed the airport. She stayed with me at Pembridge Square for two nights. We had some sweet, dark sherry before dinner; I don't think I'd tasted it before, I rather liked it. Mum looked well and very tanned. It was lovely to see her again and we had lots to catch up on before she went back to Park Hall.

HMS Bulwark came into Plymouth on December 17th. Mum, David, and I were on the jetty as she came alongside – an emotional moment, as it was her last voyage. I'd bought a new coat for the occasion, emerald green with black fur collar and cuffs. Then we all had a happy Christmas at Park Hall and Fish finally left the ship in mid-January.

We were all waiting anxiously for news of whether Fish was to be promoted to admiral. He'd talked to various friends who had rated his chances as 'fair', but although Fish had been put on the 'short list' he was up against some very able people and vacancies were limited. The expected letter soon came; '*I am more than sorry that I have to tell you that the Sea Lords… have been unable to include your name in the final list for promotion to Rear Admiral…*'

Fish was initially disappointed, not least because my mother wasn't to be 'Lady Dalglish', but he accepted it very philosophically. He knew he was outspoken, not to say tactless at times, but most of all he wasn't a 'desk man' and promotion would have taken him further away from serving with people, with whom he was always happiest, especially at sea. A consolation was his being appointed a Commander of the British Empire; we three accompanied him to Buckingham Palace to receive this honour from the Queen, which added to the Commander of the Royal Victorian Order he had been awarded after his service in the Royal Yacht Britannia ten years previously.

Fish wanted to get a job after leaving the Navy, and London was the best place to look for one. I was commissioned to find somewhere for my parents to live. I looked in the Evening Standard and saw one available in the End House of Coleherne Mews, not far from Earl's Court Station. It had a large sitting/dining room, two bedrooms, kitchen, and bathroom. They had hoped for Kensington but as the flat was ideal in every other way, they took it.

Fish soon got a job, as welfare officer for the Metropolitan Police. He took to it very happily; the problems he had to deal with were so similar to his naval life, and many policemen were ex-service. It was harder for my mother, who missed the Navy, especially the social life, although they had quite a few friends living in London too. I didn't see much of them as they went up to Park Hall every fortnight in summer, once a month in winter, mainly to see to the garden.

In August 1963 my Uncle Rick returned from Vietnam and he and Kate had a farewell party in Putney, before they all went back to Canada. They invited me to it, a chance for me to wear my Chinese *cheongsam*. Also there was Peter King, an Army friend from when they were all stationed in Tokyo.

"Do bring your nice friend John Corry," Kate had said to Peter.

"Thanks very much, I will," he said.

Peter had met John on an Army exercise some years earlier. I was duly introduced to John.

What a good-looking man, I thought; not quite my height, he had iron grey wavy hair, thinning on top, bushy eyebrows above big green eyes, and a thin, serious-looking face which lit up when he smiled. He was well built with broad shoulders, but quite thin.

A week later a few of us met Kate and Rick at a local restaurant, for a final farewell. I sat next to John at dinner and had such a nice time; he was so easy to talk to. I learned that he'd been a professional soldier for twelve years, serving with various battalions, and had retired from the King's Shropshire Light Infantry as a captain eight years ago. He was now a chartered structural engineer with George Wimpey, a building company. His father had died some years ago, and John was living with his mother and much younger brother and sister.

We talked about religion. John had been brought up a Methodist and was now being instructed in the Catholic faith by the abbot of Ealing Abbey.

"I find Catholicism very logical," he said. "After all, the Catholic church was founded first. All the other churches are just splinter groups. They only came into being after Henry VIII took a fancy to Anne Boleyn. What about you? Do you go to church?"

"Yes I do, I go to St Matthew's Bayswater, near where I live," I said. "I was born Catholic, but my father changed to the Church of England when I was a baby, and he's very anti-Catholic now."

I'd always found this rather puzzling, as his siblings were all Catholic and I loved my uncles and aunts. But Fish had always said that one shouldn't talk about religion, so I enjoyed being able to talk about it with John, although I didn't then know enough to argue the point about the Church of England being a mere 'splinter group'.

John asked for my phone number but didn't actually contact me until a couple of months later. I was buzzed in my room.

"Telephone call, Judy," said the housekeeper. I dashed down five flights of stairs.

"Hullo, Judy," said a deep voice, "it's John Corry, I don't know if you remember me, we met at Kate and Rick's farewell dinner."

"Of course I remember you," I said. "How are you?"

"I was wondering if you'd like to come to a bonfire party at Lasham, the airfield where I'm learning to fly gliders," he said.

"Thank you very much, I'd love to," I replied.

"I'll pick you up at three o'clock on Saturday week," he said. "Peter King is coming too, and Douglas Bennett, a friend of ours who was in the Navy."

"I'll look forward to it."

What shall I wear, I wondered. I'd just made a straight skirt with a matching waistcoat in Douglas tartan, which I wore with a black silk shirt, and a navy wool blazer. It wasn't the most suitable outfit for a November night in the country; not for the first time, vanity did me no favours and I was very cold, shivering actually, except when I was near the huge bonfire. I had a lovely time though, they were all so nice to me. They were all older than me: John was nearly thirty-nine, Peter and Douglas over forty; I was twenty-three, but I always got on well with older people, and was more at ease with them than with my peers.

Soon after this, I had John Corry and Peter King to dinner at Pembridge Square. I asked Fish and Eve too; they had already met Peter. The evening went well, conversation flowed. I saw John quite regularly after that, enjoying his company and also struck by his beautiful manners. He was very well-informed on all kind of subjects, always interesting to be with. He sometimes took me out to dinner at a local bistro, and one evening we went to see the film *Zulu*, which was a treat, as I loved going to the cinema.

I found out more about John; he and his brother Norman were born in Iraq and had been taken back to Darlington aged six and four, to be brought up by their father's eldest sister, Gina, and her husband Harry. After that, those little boys only saw their parents when they returned to England on leave every two years. They met their new baby brother Gerald in the summer of 1938, their parents' last visit before the war. Norman died of pleurisy when he was eleven, the following February. His Uncle Harry had just said, "You haven't got a brother anymore." I felt so sad when John told me that; it explained his being so serious, having been bereaved of his beloved brother when their parents were so far away.

It seems that soon after this, Aunt Gina thought John was lonely and would be better at a boarding school than being a day boy at Darlington Grammar School, where he'd won a scholarship. He was sent to St Peter's School, York, just after the war started.

"It's the oldest school in England," he told me.

"Were you happy there?"

"Well, at first the other boys thought I was a 'swot'… and of course I'd come from a Grammar School… so they looked down on me."

"Did you get used to it? Did you like it eventually?"

"Oh yes, I did, I got very fond of it. I enjoyed rugger… and cross country running… I was good at that. I wanted to join the Army and knew I'd have to be fit."

"What else did you do?"

"Well, there was a 'Dig for Victory' campaign. I used to help Uncle Harry in the garden, so I'd learned a bit about growing things and I grew some prize marrows… the boys said, 'Oh no, not Corry's marrows again'… we all got a bit sick of them…"

In March 1943, John, aged eighteen, volunteered to join the Army, doing officer training at Dehra Dun Academy in India, which was equivalent to Sandhurst. For a while he served in No 1 Army Commando, and after the war ended in the SAS. Then he was posted temporarily to Iraq; it was nine years since he last saw his parents, and now he met his new baby sister Gloria. Gerald was at school in England. Sometime after that, rather than take up at place at Cambridge, John became a regular soldier, joining the 1st Battalion of the KSLI, and amongst other postings, he spent time in Germany. He retired from the Army in 1955 to train instead as a chartered structural engineer, deciding that his by then widowed mother needed his support at home.

"John would have done very well if he'd stayed in the Army," a friend of John's later told me.

Now John's sister Gloria was a very pretty, bubbly girl of nineteen, like John to look at, with a mass of thick, curly brown hair; she and John were close. I got on well with her, and she came with John to have tea at Pembridge Square. John gave me the book *Three Men in a Boat* for Christmas, which was a nice surprise; I wasn't expecting a present. He invited me to attend the ceremony at Westminster Cathedral when he was received into the Catholic Church, with Gloria and John's sponsor, a Polish man called Michael Wojtaniewski. I felt privileged to be included in such an important occasion, but I didn't much like the cathedral. It was huge and very dark, with lots of people milling around. The service was unfamiliar and quite unlike Anglican churches, where no one ever genuflected.

It was one day in the office in early February when I heard John's voice on the phone – although we weren't supposed to have personal calls – and my heart gave a funny lurch.

Must be getting fond of him, I thought, but all the same I was surprised a week later when he told me he loved me.

"Will you marry me?" he said. He had traces of ash on his forehead, as it was Ash Wednesday and he'd just been to church.

"Yes, I will," I said.

"Don't you want to think about it?"

"I don't need to," I said. I felt happy and safe with John, so agreeing to get married felt right, however unexpected the question.

"We'll have to get married in a Catholic church, darling... our children will have to be brought up Catholics..."

"Yes, I know. Mum had to promise that too, but it didn't happen because Fish changed... he won't like our wedding being Catholic..."

"Do you mind, darling?"

"No, I don't, as long as I don't have to change myself. I love my church... I don't think I want to be a Catholic."

"No, of course you won't have to change, but I'm afraid you'll have to have some instruction before we get married."

"That's ok..."

The next morning before I went to work I called in to see Anne, just across the landing.

"John has asked me to marry him, and I've said yes."

"That's wonderful news, dear. I'm so pleased... I hope you'll be very happy." Anne was laughing with pleasure, and I went off to work feeling very happy and excited.

I happened to be meeting my mother for lunch, which we sometimes did. As we walked through Fortnum & Mason I said,

"Mum, John Corry has asked me to marry him."

"I thought you were getting fond of him," she said, "but you'll be a widow in your sixties." That was all she said, and I felt rather upset and deflated.

"Can I bring John to see you and Fish tonight?" I asked her.

"Yes, that will be all right," she said, rather stiffly. I was very glad when it was time to go back to the office.

When John arrived that evening, he'd made other plans, so I had to phone my mother.

"So sorry, Mum, John's arranged to take me to meet some friends of his. Can we come tomorrow night instead?"

She didn't sound very pleased.

John gave me a ring which he said his mother had kept for the girl he married – it had five Burmese pink rubies, set in gold, and fitted perfectly. It was lovely but secretly I was a bit disappointed that I hadn't been able to choose it.

John took me to meet his friends John and Maggie Rinfret, who lived in a large flat in Chelsea. John Rinfret and my John had been at college together, and Maggie was a trained nurse. They hadn't been married long. They were full of questions about me, and how long I'd known John.

"Have you met John's mother?" John R asked me.

"No, not yet," I said, wondering what he meant.

My parents were welcoming and we talked about the announcement of our engagement in the Telegraph and Times. I was aware that they weren't ecstatic about our engagement. They didn't voice any objections, but I sensed that they were putting a good face on it – that they had agreed 'a party line.' I can see their point now; after all, John was sixteen years older than me, a Roman Catholic, ex-Army (a ruddy 'Pongo' said Fish, the Navy's nickname for the Army), an engineer (not quite socially correct), and half French to boot. At the time though I think I was too happy to take much notice.

Everyone in the office was happy too. My photo was published in the Evening Standard. '*Yacht Commander's daughter gets engaged*' said the caption. I had lots of letters following the announcement in the Telegraph and Times. I kept them all and stuck them in a scrapbook, having first answered them.

"You are a dark horse, Judy," said my friend Cicely from Eastbourne days.

I met John's mother the following weekend, at their house in Ealing. John had told me that she was ex-patriate French. Her name was Anastasia, 'Anas' to her sisters, and in due course she became 'Grandmama' to our children.

Only once did I say "Hello Grandmama," on the phone.

"I'm not your grandmamma," she snapped; I always called her 'Mrs Corry' from then on.

She had lived in Iraq where she had met John's father. She and John were close; she'd been widowed suddenly when John was only twenty-one, and she had had little support from Cyril's family in Darlington, who had regarded her as a foreigner.

Mrs Corry was small, overweight, and she looked foreign; she had dark eyes, and thick black hair confined by a net. She had a strong accent, and laughed as she chatted. She was friendly and seemed happy about our engagement. There was no sign of Gerald, which John said wasn't unusual, but Gloria was there and excited as I'd asked her to be one of my bridesmaids. I was relieved when the visit was over, as I'd found my future mother-in-law slightly intimidating, quite unlike anyone I'd met before.

I went to church as usual the following Sunday, and spoke to the vicar afterwards,

"Mr Yale, I've just got engaged."

"Congratulations, Judy," he said. "I hope you'll be very happy. When are you getting married?"

"We haven't arranged a date yet, but I'm really sorry, I won't be able to get married here as my fiancé John is a Catholic."

"I'm sorry too… I expect you realise it won't be easy for you, belonging to different churches? You'll be expected to bring your children up as Catholics."

"Yes, I know I will, we've already talked about it."

"Well, you can always come and talk to me, Judy, and if you like I'll have a Communion Service for you on your wedding day."

"Thank you so much, Mr Yale, I'd love that. I'll let you know the date."

We went to Park Hall for Easter. The view was shrouded in a thick fog and the mournful tones of the fog horn at the Whitby Lighthouse were heard all that weekend, but subsequently John loved Yorkshire as much as I did. He met Ducky, bedridden and barely conscious, not long afterwards. David was with her when she died on April 13th. I was very sad, but happy for her, as her life had been pretty miserable during her long illness.

We discussed wedding plans.

"It's a pity John is an RC, you won't be able to get married in Aislaby," said Fish, "the wedding will have to be somewhere in London. Do you have any ideas, John?"

"What about Ealing Abbey? It's where I go," said John.

"Too far from central London… but I think we might be in the Oratory parish… I'll make some enquiries. If it has to be RC at least it's convenient and my grandmother donated the Dome in memory of her husband – that might be a help…"

"The Hyde Park Hotel is near there too – how about there for the reception?" said Mum. "Judy, let's go to John Lewis next week, we can look at patterns, and there's a shop in Davies Street which specialises in wedding fabrics."

"Thanks, Mum, that sounds lovely. By the way, I've already asked Gloria to be a bridesmaid. I thought I could have my cousins too?"

"Yes… that's a good idea… you were bridesmaid to Marie and Val, and they and A were my bridesmaids… this will be the first wedding in your generation." Annie and Amanda Marie's daughters were seventeen and eight, Val's daughters, Liz and Caroline, were sixteen and nine, while Marybell, A's daughter, was thirteen; they were all very excited about the wedding. Annie was especially pleased; we were close and had often spent time together.

Events moved quickly after that. The Oratory agreed to let us be married there. Fish's brother and my godfather, Douggie, who was stationed in Muscat, Oman as military adviser to the Sultan, wasn't due back until early July, so we opted for July 4th rather than June, which my parents would have preferred. In the midst of all the wedding plans came a letter from Kate:

"…I am having <u>another</u> baby probably due about mid August!! I feel all the family will simply scream (I must admit it was not <u>planned!</u>) but I am pleased… and so are the children… Do break the news to Mummy and Fishy and David… Now the invitation to your wedding came today and <u>how much</u> I wish we could all be there, I simple <u>hate</u> to miss it as do Rick and the children… even if the airlines flew me there I doubt if they would fly me back afterwards! I look vast already…

I expect my mother did scream, I don't remember. I was pleased about the baby as I loved all my small cousins, but very sad that they wouldn't all be with us for the wedding.

John had good news though. The abbot of Ealing Abbey, who had instructed John in the Catholic faith, had agreed to marry us; he'd also given John some advice.

"Don't pressure Judy to become a Catholic, will you?" he'd said.

I liked Father Rupert when I met him, he seemed a kind, gentle man, and I could see why John was so fond of him.

My parents arranged the reception at the Hyde Park Hotel and organised the invitations.

"We'll just invite our friends who know you, Judy," they said, "and of course you must have your friends too. Get John to give us his list, won't you?"

We chose John Lewis for our wedding list; we selected various household items and some glass. Of course I already had the china dinner and tea set which I'd bought in Hong Kong. I was kept very busy writing thank you letters for everything we were given. To this day I still use three lovely crystal flower vases.

Mum took me shopping in the West End. The dress pattern we chose was Empire line; long and straight, with a band under the bust, a wide round neck and long sleeves, coming to a point over the wrist, and it had a detachable train behind. Mum bought cream-coloured silk for me, to match the family wedding veil, and we got white *Broderie Anglaise* for the six bridesmaids. Their dresses were straight too, but had short sleeves.

Next was a visit to a bridal shop to find a headdress; I tried several, and ended up with an unusual gold and pearl crown that suited my hair, which I usually wore in a French pleat. We also found some gorgeous shoes with a small heel, in gold mesh.

I cut out my dress, and Gloria's, on the floor of my bedsit and made them on the sewing machine I'd bought in Hong Kong. I also made my going away outfit in cream linen, a sleeveless dress and jacket, and I bought a cream, flowered hat to go with it.

Father Peter Bentley instructed me in the Catholic faith at the Oratory, and I attended six sessions.

"Don't you want to ask any questions, Judy?" he said.

"No thank you," I answered, "you've explained everything."

John found us a flat in Barnes, just over Hammersmith Bridge. One Sunday afternoon not long before the wedding we'd gone there, and I was going to do some cleaning. However he'd omitted to tell me that his mother and Gloria were coming there too – so I was totally unprepared when the doorbell rang, I opened the door, and there they were. No kettle to make tea for them, no blueprint for

how one behaves on such occasions. Somehow I managed to offend
Mrs Corry who, after this, never would come to our home. Not that
anything was said at the time, but I was beginning to discover that
one didn't only marry one's husband, one was stuck with his family
too, and maybe that was what John Rinfret had implied when he
asked if I'd met John's mother.

I had intended to work until the wedding – but Mrs Hudgell
told me to take the Friday off. That was the day that Mrs Corry
phoned me.

"I give you my son, Judy," she said. I thought it was a bit odd.

I'd moved out of Pembridge Square a fortnight before the wedding
and stayed with my parents at End House – except for the night
before the wedding when David came home, and I stayed in our new
flat in Barnes. I was sad to leave the bedsit where I'd been so happy,
but excited about the future too.

My wedding day was bright and sunny, not too hot. My parents
picked me up and we went to St Matthew's for Mr Yale's communion
service. It was a lovely start to the day.

I got dressed at the Hyde Park Hotel, joined by my bridesmaids,
who all looked gorgeous. Mum was glamorous and elegant in a white
lace dress and matching hat, but she wasn't very pleased that I chose
to wear a lovely gold cross, lent to me by Mrs Hudgell (my boss at
Gabbitas Thring) rather than pearls, and that I'd asked Gloria to be
my chief bridesmaid and not my cousin Annie.

We had lots of photos taken before we set off for the Oratory. The
bridesmaids went first, Fish and I followed in a white be-ribboned
Rolls Royce. We went past some roadworks; all the workmen waved
at me and I waved back, feeling just like a princess. I wasn't nervous,
just excited. But it did feel a bit unreal, as if it was happening to
someone else.

We arrived at the Oratory – the name for the huge Catholic
church in Brompton – early, Fish's naval planning having gone very

smoothly. There were lots of people waiting outside. The church felt strange; it was so huge, dark, full of ornate statues and paintings, full of people too, turning to smile at me. I saw David, one of the ushers, with Peter King and Douglas Bennett and my cousins John and Michael (Aunty A's sons). Then the organ started playing Jeremiah Clare's *Trumpet Voluntary* and we all set off; I was holding Fish's right arm, the bridesmaids, two by two, behind us, a solemn black-robed official led the way and the aisle was so long that it took ages to get to where John was waiting with his best man, Crick Grundy, an Army friend.

I'd mostly been to Church of England weddings, and the Catholic service was different, but I did manage to repeat the vows all right – including promising to obey. Had I been Catholic we would have had a wedding mass, but ours was a short service with only two hymns. As we went to sign the register, my mother said,

"They got the hymns wrong. We should have sung *O Perfect love* at the beginning…"

I still love to hear Mendelssohn's *Wedding March*, which was played as the service ended and we slowly walked down the aisle, everyone smiling, and I was grinning from ear to ear. Photographs were taken of us standing on the steps, cameras flashing, passers-by looking on. Uncle Alec had a cine camera too. Then there was a chance to say hello to a few people, before the car arrived to take us for the short journey back to the Hyde Park Hotel.

My parents didn't have a receiving line, I suppose because they didn't want to meet John's relations and friends. It was so exciting seeing my uncles and aunts, and my grandmother Gar, too, Fish's mother; it turned out to be her last outing, as she had a stroke not long afterwards. Lots of naval friends too: Kit Layman from Malta days, John Ashworth from Singapore. My parents had paid for Hilda (who'd looked after Ducky) and John, also Mum's hairdresser from Whitby, Madge, and her husband Fred. It meant a lot to me that they had come, and I believe they had a wonderful weekend in London. I talked to Pauline & Tony, various girlfriends, office colleagues, and of course John's family and friends.

The speech was given by Bertie Lyddon; his wife Dot was my godmother. Bertie said that I was the nearest they had to a daughter of their own, and I was most touched by that. Time went very quickly and it seemed much too soon that Fish was telling me it was time to get changed.

Lots of farewells outside the hotel, then we were whisked off in the Rolls, to Riverview Gardens, our new home. My parents took a party to Quaglino's that evening, and they had a great time. I felt as if the party were going on without us, which it was, of course.

I really enjoyed my wedding day, it all went so quickly though. I was still sad that Kate couldn't have come; her baby was born on August 23rd and was christened Robert. The other absentees were Aunt Daphy, Fish's sister, who was a nun in the Order of the Holy Child Jesus, and couldn't go to social events, and Uncle Douggie who didn't get back from Oman after all.

In spite of a few tense moments, mostly to do with my mother, and slight regret that the Oratory had felt so alien, it had been a wonderful day and I felt a bit flat now it was all over.

Judy Dalglish no more... now I was Mrs John Corry, and married life had begun.

Chapter 8

Newly Married Life

The day following the wedding we drove to St Ives, Cornwall, where John had booked a cottage for two weeks.

"You'll rather be thrown back on yourselves, won't you, Judy?" Peter King said when he heard about it.

I wasn't quite sure what to make of it at the time, but of course he was right. John and I hardly knew each other; meeting daily was very different from living together. John liked to sleep late, but I always got up early, and had to amuse myself for quite a while before he stirred. He used to take a thermos of tea to bed, and smoked, too – which I didn't – he'd light up first thing in the morning as well as puff away all day. And he ate a raw egg with tabasco sauce for breakfast. Ugh!

John knew St Ives well; he and Peter used to go down there for holidays. It was a pretty little town, much like Whitby. We walked all over it, looking at all the shops and artist's studios. We went for lovely walks on the cliffs above the sea, too. Usually we had dinner out, but one night we collected lots of mussels and tried cooking them in the cottage. Not one of our better ideas, they were inedible so we had to go out to eat after all.

Sometimes we lay on the beach reading.

"I never get sunburnt," said John, so I took him at his word and didn't wake him up when he fell asleep one afternoon.

That night he was in great discomfort and the next day we went back to London a few days earlier than planned.

I was happy to be back at work again, at least that was one thing that hadn't changed. I met Mum for lunch at Fortnum's and we were talking about the wedding.

"I had a long chat with Elizabeth Layman," she told me. "We were saying what a pity that it wasn't yours and Kit's wedding."

I felt downcast by this, but didn't say anything, there wasn't much I could say really. But Kit and I had only ever had a platonic friendship, and he was soon due to get married himself.

Mum was also very annoyed that the best man, Crick Grundy, a friend of John's from Army days – had given the remains of the wedding cake to Mrs Corry instead of to my mother.

"We were going to send pieces to people who couldn't come," she said. "How could he have been so stupid?"

I was glad it hadn't been my mistake. I think it was John who instructed Crick, but I didn't tell my mother that. It was a relief to get back to the office.

It was a bit strange being married, at first. John often went to see his family in the evening.

"You can come too, darling," he said, but having come from a family who only went to see people when invited, I didn't feel comfortable just going.

"Let's not have a television," John had said before we got married, and as I wasn't used to having one, I didn't demur. However, knitting, reading, and listening to music did pall after a while, and I couldn't just go and see my family.

"You made your bed, Judy," I said to myself. "You must just get on with it."

During our engagement, John had come over to see me every evening. Now whenever we went anywhere, John always wanted

Gloria to come too. That was OK, I did get on well with her, but I did find it a bit galling that my company didn't seem to be enough. Not that I said anything.

In the days before vending machines, the office had a 'tea lady' who brought her trolley round twice a day, in the morning and afternoon.

"Good morning, Mrs Leaworthy," I said, not long after I'd returned from my honeymoon. "Please could I have Bovril instead of coffee?"

"Of course, dear," she said, giving me a knowing look. I had been feeling a bit off colour and lacking in energy, so I did realise what she was thinking.

Sure enough, a visit to the doctor confirmed that I was expecting a baby.

"You'll have to have a home birth," he said. "Hospitals only take people who may have complications, and there's nothing wrong with you." Then I had to break the news to my mother.

"That's very soon," said Mum. "You haven't been married for long."

I told her what the doctor had said about a home birth. "Why don't you have the baby at Park Hall? It would be much nicer for you than being in London."

"Thank you so much, Mum. That sounds wonderful." I was somewhat surprised by this, as being a grandmother obviously wasn't on Mum's 'wanted' list, but it seemed a lovely idea.

John's family were very happy.

"My first grandson," said Mrs Corry, firmly, never mind that the baby might be a girl.

I was happy too; I'd taken for granted that we'd have children, but maybe not so soon. I didn't much like feeling sick, tired, and tearful, although that didn't last for long and I was actually in very good health.

In October, two of Mrs Corry's three older sisters, Daisy and Eva, arrived in England from Iraq, and they moved into a house near

Ealing Common Station. The eldest, Pauline, was already in England with husband Walter. They lived in Kent with their daughter Dolly, son-in-law Patrick, and their four boys. Daisy, the second, was the bossy one. Eva, the third, with a cigarette always hanging from her lips, was very easy going.

"What for, Daisy?" she'd say, with a shrug of her shoulders.

Small, dumpy, and foreign-looking, with dyed hair, Daisy and Eva wore shapeless skirts and endlessly re-knitted, equally shapeless cardigans. Eva hadn't been to England, Daisy had, and they both enjoyed London. The annual Ideal Home Exhibition was a favourite expedition and they always came back with the latest kitchen gadget. They were great cooks and loved entertaining; we always ate too much when we went there. I got on well with Daisy and Eva, particularly Aunt Eva. None of the tensions of my relationship with Mrs Corry, thank goodness.

Nowadays girls seem to work until the last minute before giving birth, but seven months was the norm then, and I left Gabbitas Thring around the end of January. I'd enjoyed my job, but was glad not to have to stand in the tube.

I was quite happy at home, getting ready for the baby. We had a nice spacious flat, with big rooms and high ceilings. It had two double bedrooms and a small back room for the baby. I made my maternity clothes: loose tops worn over a skirt with a U-shaped gap which tied over my 'bump'. Mum made nighties for the baby too, and I knitted some tiny jackets. I was lent the family basket crib, used by all my cousins; I made a 'skirt' for it in pale yellow spotted muslin. I also made a pale yellow quilted detachable lining for a rush Moses basket.

I wasn't at home that long, as the doctor said I shouldn't travel too close to the birth. I went to Park Hall in the middle of March, about three weeks before the due date, which was early April. I saw Dr Lyne, whom I already knew, and met Nurse Bretherick, the local midwife. I'd been going to classes in London and had been doing breathing exercises, and I knew something of what to expect during the birth.

Now here was Hilda looking after me as she so often had at the vicarage when I was a child. After Ducky died, Mum had asked Hilda if she'd like to housekeep for her and Fish, so the three of them had moved to the wing of Park Hall. Gillian, now almost five, was very excited about the baby. Amongst other things we washed all the new terry nappies. I was on my own for a while, which I never minded, and Mum came up about a week before the baby was due. A few days later I woke up early with feelings of discomfort.

"Mum, I think the baby must be on the way. I'd better phone Nurse Bretherick."

Mum was a bit flustered. "Are you sure? It's not due for another four days," she said.

"It won't be here until the early hours," said Dr Lyne. "I'm going to the races."

Nurse Bretherick examined me and said she'd be back later. I rang John, who was still in bed. Mum rang Fish who was on his way to the Army Navy rugger match at Twickenham.

I was quite happy doing my breathing exercises, but Mum was anxious and, as much to keep herself occupied as me, she had me hold the scissors as she re-covered the bathroom windowsill with sticky-backed plastic. I didn't feel like lunch but in any case Nurse Bretherick came back and told me to get into bed. It was getting quite uncomfortable by this time. I did have an injection in my bottom but very soon afterwards I was told to push... and push... but not that long, because there was a 'whooosh', then a wail...

"It's a boy," said Nurse Bretherick.

She washed him in the bedroom basin and put him in a yellow, flowered nightie. Dr Lyne was summoned away from the races and that was the worst bit, all three stitches of it. I was sure he'd used the same rusty-looking needle as he had when my brother David was born twenty years earlier.

"What do I do about feeding the baby, Nurse?" I asked.

"Give him a damn good suck," she said. "I'll see you tomorrow morning." I think Edward was the two thousandth baby she had delivered.

It was only mid-afternoon.

"What big feet he has," said Mum. The baby weighed 8lbs 4 oz so was quite big. He had a very red face and black hair.

Fish had a splendid time at the match.

"I'm a pregnant grandfather," he told all his friends, accepting yet another gin and tonic. My mother eventually reached him on the phone.

"Judy's had the baby."

"Female did you say?"

"NO, Fish. It's a BOY!"

He was rather pleased, as was David, on guard duty at the Bank of England. By this time he had joined the Army and was a subaltern in the Scots Guards. John came up from London that evening.

"He's gorgeous, darling. You are clever," he said. "Was it painful, the birth I mean?"

"Yes, but not unbearable... I was lucky, he came quite quickly... but being stitched up was horrible and I feel really sore now."

The following weekend Fish came bounding up the stairs, three at a time.

"Where's my grandson?" he said. I'd never seen Fish so excited; he loved babies, all the Dalglish's did, and I'd taken after them.

I had to stay in bed for a few days and sit in a salty bath to help healing. I was glad to be up and about again. My parents soon returned to London, and Gloria came to stay for a few days. She didn't want to be alone the first night.

"The house is creepy," she said.

"Don't worry," said John. "You can borrow the baby."

But she locked the door and I hated that.

We had a problem finding a name; Mrs Corry said he should be called Cyril, after her husband. I flatly refused. Poor John was stuck between a tearful wife and a rather forceful mother. John wanted a saint's name and my cousins already had quite a few of the best ones; eventually we decided on Edward John Cyril, but I think my parents thought he should have been Edward James (Fish's name).

We all went back to London when Edward was about three weeks old, and I began the next phase of my life, a mother as well as a wife.

Chapter 9

Motherhood

Once back in London, we soon settled into a routine. Edward was a good baby, I enjoyed looking after him, and I had a good health visitor to advise me about his progress and help with any concerns. We had good doctors too. I had a big Silver Cross pram, with plenty of room for shopping in a tray underneath, and I often went over Hammersmith Bridge to the open air market which sold fruit and vegetables. I used to do our washing in the bath, put it through a spin dryer, and hang it on a collapsible airing rail on the balcony outside the kitchen. I sent sheets to the laundry.

I had a sling to carry Edward in, and I took him in it to the office to show him off to my erstwhile colleagues. I took him to Buckingham Palace to watch my brother David taking part in the changing of the guard. He was a subaltern in the Scots Guards, doing a short service commission in the Army. He'd been accepted soon after leaving Cothill House, the prep school where he'd been a junior master.

"Look, Edward," I said, pointing. "There's Uncle David, doesn't he look smart in his bearskin?" And then, to a bemused stranger, "That's my brother carrying the colours."

John worked at George Wimpey, an engineering firm in Hammersmith only ten minutes away, so he got home nice and early. Sometimes I took Edward to meet him. John then relaxed in the bath, while Edward was in his cot in the room nearby.

"Oooooooo-oh," sang John.

"Ooooooooo-oh," sang Edward.

This went on for quite a while. John came to fatherhood later than most of his friends, but was very happy that we had a baby son.

When Edward was about six months I phoned John in the office; we often spoke during the day.

"Darling, Edward's got a tooth! I heard it clink against the spoon." I'm not sure which of us was the more excited.

At weekends we often saw John's family, sometimes going to Pett's Wood in Kent, to visit John's cousin Dolly, husband Pat, and four boys, Bernard, Leonard (both teenagers), Robert, and David, the latter being sweet playing with Edward. They were always very hospitable and had a lovely garden to sit in. We went for walks along the tow path towards Putney, especially when Edward was big enough to sit in a push chair. He'd laugh, pointing at the ducks, saying,

"Wa wuck…"

We went to Park Hall for Easter, and in the summer we joined my parents there for a weekend and stayed on by ourselves for the rest of our two week holiday. My aunt Kate, Mum's younger sister, had come over from Canada for the summer and was staying next door at Park Lodge. It was lovely having her there, not least because Kate had not got married until her mid-thirties, and her youngest child was only seven months older than Edward. Kate and Mum were very different. Mum was tall, slim, blonde, elegant, very well-organised. She was a reserved, private person. Kate was taller, quite well-built, with long brown hair which she usually wore in a bun. She was friendly, outgoing, and laughed a lot. Mum loved formal entertaining and she was very good at it. Kate was informal and welcoming whatever time of day.

"Come in, darlings, have some coffee," she'd say, and she was quite happy to rustle up an impromptu meal late at night. And of course Kate loved children, having five of her own, whereas Mum just tolerated them in small, well-behaved doses.

We used to put Robbie and Edward together in a playpen in the garden, and on nice days we'd take all the children to the beach, including Gillian. Hilda was there to listen for Edward, so we often went over to Kate for the evening. Sometimes Rick was there too, and we'd have a drink together in the pub opposite.

I always went to the village church for the Sunday morning service. Kate used to arrive during the first hymn, very smart, wearing a large hat, and with the five children trailing after her.

"However do you manage five children, Kate?" I asked her.

"Well, darling, I did have them one at a time, except for the twins..."

I was sad when the summer ended and they all went back to Canada. Before she went back she always had a few days in London, distributing the children amongst me and various friends.

We'd arranged to spend Christmas alternately with our respective families, and this year it was to be with John's family. We went to midnight mass at Ealing Abbey. The music was glorious, and unlike Anglican churches, it was crammed full of people with standing room only. It was the first Christmas I had ever been away from my family, and I was VERY homesick, unexpectedly so, although John's family, particularly Daisy and Eva, were very kind to me, and were thrilled to have Edward with them. He was nine months old and a very happy, engaging baby.

Not long after this, a visit to the doctor confirmed that I was expecting another baby.

"My second grandson," said Mrs Corry.

I wasn't at all daunted by the thought of two babies in nappies, and John was so happy that he was telling people before the conventional three months.

"It's very soon after Edward, isn't?" said Mum. "How are you going to manage two babies in your flat?"

"I'll be fine, Mum," I said. "I'm really pleased, and so is John."

"Would you like to have it at Park Hall again?" said Mum. "And I wonder if your friend Anne could come and help look after Edward?"

"I'll ask her," I said. "Thanks, Mum."

I started having driving lessons again, having failed the test when I was nineteen.

"Not yet, Mrs Corry," said my nice instructor as I overtook a car rather too widely, just near Roehampton Hospital. By now I was having difficulty fitting behind the steering wheel, so I decided to resume lessons after the baby was born.

We had two weeks at Park Hall on our own in the summer, as we'd done the previous year; the weather was glorious and Edward was very happy. I remember him going towards the sea with a determined stride, looking every inch the miniature of the policeman he became in the future. We explored the moors too; John always liked going there more than the beach. He then had to return to work, planning to return for the baby's expected arrival in early September. Mum and Fish came back in good time, and Anne Dunn (my friend from Hawtreys days) came to stay.

This time the due date came and went.

"Any sign of the baby, darling?" said John on the phone, ringing up to wish me a happy birthday.

"No, darling, I'm sorry, there isn't."

"When's that baby coming?" said Fish. "Let's try some cross cut sawing. I think that might do the trick." So after lunch Fish and I did loads of clearing amongst the overgrown rhododendrons, Mum and Anne carting wheelbarrows of stuff to the bonfire, Edward in a playpen on the lawn.

"I'll give you some castor oil," said Anne, after tea. "That sometimes works. You'll either sit on the loo all night or go into labour." It tasted disgusting but I managed to get it down, and before dinner Fish gave me a gin and tonic for good measure.

I woke at one thirty am with familiar pains and phoned Nurse Bretherick, who'd delivered Edward. She came very promptly, examined me, and said,

"This won't take long, you're well on the way." Less than two hours later, with a whoosh and a wail the baby arrived...

"What is it, dear?" called Anne, waiting on the landing.

"It's a little girl," said Nurse Bretherick.

I could hear Anne and my parents saying, "How lovely."

The next thing I knew, Mum was drawing open the curtains, letting in bright sunshine.

"How are you, darling? The baby came very quickly, didn't she?" She and Fish had already dressed Edward and brought him in to sit on the bed beside me. Then Fish brought in the Moses basket, and Edward leaned forward to look inside.

"It's a baba."

"Kiss the baba, darling," said Fish, and Edward gave his new sister his, and her, first kiss. "Look what the baby's brought you."

"It's a book," said Edward, laughing as he grasped it in his chubby hands.

"What a determined little chin she has," said Fish, looking fondly down at the baby. She was lovely, not at all red as Edward had been. She had dark hair and blue eyes, and I needn't have worried that I wouldn't love her as much as I did Edward.

As the baby had come four days late, and so quickly, again John wasn't there for the birth, but he arrived the following evening and was very excited, not least to see Edward, whom he'd missed, and me too, come to that.

"She's beautiful, darling," he said, as he held his new daughter. "Well done. How are you feeling now?"

"Fine thanks, just a bit tired. I was lucky though, she came even quicker than Edward."

The next day, Anne had to go back to her job in London.

"Thank you so much for coming to help, Anne," Mum said. "What a pity the baby was born late… but it's lovely that it was a girl." Later Anne told me that Mum had also said, "Let's hope Judy stops at two children."

We had decided, before the baby was born, that we'd call her Clare Anastasia.

"You can't call her Clare, it's a Jewish name," said Mrs Corry on the phone.

"Why not?" I said to John. "It's nothing to do with your mother what we call our daughter. We're using her name too, aren't we?"

Gloria had something to say about that, too.

"You can't use Mummy's name as a *second* name," she said. "You should call her Anastasia."

Once again I was in tears. "She'll get teased at school," I said. "Imagine calling AnasTAAAAAAASIA across the playground."

Back in London, life was pretty busy, as Edward was very energetic and Clare was a difficult baby. She didn't sleep well at night, and got frequent colds, it being winter. When old enough to have solids, she spat out most foods and then yelled, very loudly, as she was hungry. I ended up giving her scrambled egg most days, which I should only have given her once a week. She was a gorgeous baby though, with big blue eyes and curly, dark hair.

The flats had communal gardens opposite, backing on to the towpath and river. In the afternoon I used to go out there, armed with tissues, drinks, toys, and my knitting. Quite a few other young mothers used to come out too, so we chatted while the children played. I was so lucky to have that, as otherwise I'd have been quite isolated. Helpful too, as when Edward started having tantrums, Abigail's mother was able to give advice, having older children herself.

"It's when children are at their most unlovable that they most need loving," she said. Easier said than done, I found.

Edward loved Clare and she hero-worshipped him.

"Boy," she called him.

One day he held out an apple. "Say apple, Clare."

"Appu," she said, laughing happily.

Clare broke all the norms of child development. She cut her first teeth at five months, and at about a year, she cut three in just over a week. She walked at ten months.

"Why don't your children just sit on a rug, like your friend Caroline's baby?" said my mother.

Clare had talked early too, a little chatterbox she was.

Kate was over for the summer again, always such a special time. "Why don't I look after Edward and Clare for a couple of days?" she said. "You and John could go away by yourselves." It was the first time I'd left them, and I did enjoy it, but I was very, very happy to see them again.

A while later the doctor came to the flat to see the children, who had some ailment.

"Dr Docherty, might I be feeling sick for any other reason than having a baby?" I said to him, a bit anxiously.

"I think you'd better come and see me in the surgery, my dear." Sure enough, our third baby was due at the end of the following March, when Edward would be three and Clare eighteen months. John was delighted, and told everyone. I was slightly embarrassed, though. The birth rate was rising and to have more than two children was somewhat socially frowned on.

We had a very nice milkman who delivered to the flats.

"Mr Stanley, please can I order an extra pint of milk? I'm afraid I'm expecting another baby."

"Never mind, dear, they bring their love with them," he said, which was so comforting.

"I thought you'd have another," said Mum. "All your friends seem to have three…"

Mrs Corry was pleased and equally predictable. "My second grandson," she said.

The next few months passed busily and happily. I still did quite a bit of dressmaking, clothes for the children and myself. I made a camel cloak which comfortably hid my bump and was warm too. And of course I met my friends in the gardens, and sometimes some of my relations came over too. We saw a lot of Gloria, who often baby sat; lovely for the children to have a young pretty aunt to spoil them, and a help for me too.

No Yorkshire birth this time. We were at home in Riverview Gardens at around eleven pm, four days past the due date, when my waters broke. Two midwives soon arrived, as my previous births had been so quick. Not this time however; it was soon after eight the following morning that the midwife called John.

"The baby's almost here."

John came to hold my hand. "I could feel Clare's soft little face as I closed the door," he told me later. Very soon the baby arrived.

"It's a girl," said the midwife.

The next moment, Edward came running in. "Mummy, you've got blood on your bottom!"

Nothing like an impromptu introduction to their new sister, as she was washed in the baby bath, alongside Edward's car and Clare's doll.

"She's perfect," said Dr Kinsey, normally taciturn, smiling at her.

The baby was smaller and fairer than the other two, weighing seven pounds ten ounces, they'd both been eight pounds four. I was tired, but happy, especially that John had been there this time.

Aunt Eva came to look after me for the next few days, and it was the most peaceful, happy time. No drama about names; Gabrielle first, the name of the lovely wife of the headmaster at Cothill, the prep school where David had taught, and Evelyn after my mother.

Now that we had three children under four, John's converted Catholic principles deserted him, and he suggested a visit to the family planning clinic. Just as well really, I had no regrets but had conceived rather easily. Mrs Corry was not to have her second grandson. She loved them all, but especially Edward. The other two became known as 'the girls'.

I was busy, of course. Mum kindly paid for a nappy service for the first three months, which was a great help, and Lucia, a schoolgirl who lived opposite, took Edward and Clare out in the afternoons during her holidays, so I could rest. Gabrielle was a good baby, luckily. Edward was at playgroup three times a week, not that he liked it much. He cried wanting to come home, Clare cried wanting to stay but she was too young. I had to help regularly too.

One day the supervisor said, "Oh Judy, I didn't realise you were here today – Edward hasn't been shouting." It must have been hard for Edward, having two sisters so close. He was fine with them but had begun being difficult with me.

All three children fitted in the big pram, the girls inside and Edward on a child seat. The worse thing was coming home with the shopping. I had to take two children up two flights of stairs and come back for the shopping and last child, the others wailing outside the front door. The man in the ground floor flat regularly came out and shouted, "SHUT UP." I just said "Sorry," and dashed upstairs as quickly as I could.

We continued to stay at Park Hall for two weeks each summer. I recall Clare at twenty months, shouting "It's a Moo!" as we passed a field of cows on our way to Sandsend, the nearest beach, Clare lying on her tummy beside me, sunbathing, Edward and Robbie busily digging in the sand nearby. The following year there's Gabrielle bending over Fish as he lay dozing on a rug.

Kate was usually at Park Lodge too. John and I would go ahead to Sandsend first with our lot, Robbie, twins Rory and Tricia, and Hilda's Gillian, all of them in the back of the car in the days before seatbelts. John sang *Waltzing Matilda* and they all joined in. Kate came down later with a thermos of tea and some lemon buns. She'd join the children in the sea, long hair flowing, laughing as she swam. Later Tricia would come over to Park Hall and help me showering our lot and putting them to bed. It wasn't that long since I'd been putting her and Rory to bed.

Another summer there had been a fatal car accident; two elderly women from Aislaby had been killed in a head on collision with a lorry, outside York. A pall of sadness hung over the village. Their funerals were on the same day, Kate and I went to both of them. Later we took all the children down to the beach. At first subdued, they began playing together. Rory lay down on the beach, and the other six children began piling sand on top of him, right up to his neck. They all collected shells and stones, laying them around the mound. Then they danced round him chanting, "Rory's dead! Rory's dead!" After that another child was buried, until one by one they drifted away. Such a lesson in how children deal with such events.

When Gabrielle was about a year old, I received a letter from my mother, and I phoned John straight away.

"Darling, you'll never guess what's happened. Mum has given me a cheque for two thousand pounds."

"Goodness, how kind. What made her do that?"

"Apparently she sold a Chelsea china tea pot she found at Park Hall. We can start looking at houses now, can't we? I'm so excited… can't believe it really. David's got a cheque too, of course…"

We looked at a few cottages near Barnes Pond, but they were smaller than our flat, only two up, two down. Mrs Corry looked at houses too. One afternoon John phoned;

"Darling, can you get someone to look after the children, and meet me at the office? Mummy has found a house near Ealing Common. We can go straight over and see it."

I phoned to give my parents the good news. "Mum, we've found a lovely big house, and our offer has been accepted."

"That's good, darling. Is it in Barnes?"

"No, actually, it's in Ealing. It's much bigger than the Barnes houses, lots more space. Would you and Fish like to come and see it?"

"Where's Ealing?" said Mum.

"About four miles from Hammersmith," I told her. "The house is huge, it's on three floors, it's got six bedrooms, and a garden and a garage."

"It sounds ideal… we could come on Sunday afternoon." They did come, but didn't say much. I don't think they approved of the area.

I had reservations about living near Mrs Corry, but the house was so suitable in every other way, that hardly mattered. John did agree with me that our respective mothers could be equally difficult; Fish wasn't very nice to John either. I'd mentioned it to Kate.

"Don't worry, darling. It's the old bull resenting the young one."

The house wasn't far from stations and shops. The front had a view right down the road and over the railway and school playing fields at the back. It had been empty for quite a while and needed re-wiring. John's brother Gerald told John how to do this, so John got all the materials, and he and I went over at weekends and did it together. It was great fun actually. The children were very excited about the house.

"Stairs, Mummy… can we go up?" They were excited about the garden too, but at first they all came running in when a train went past.

Mrs Corry organised for the back door to be moved from the side to the back of the house, and for access from the house to the downstairs lavatory, which only had an outside door to it. She also asked for bars to be put across the large window of the side room, for the children's safety. I'm sure they were a good thing but they were very tedious to paint.

Just before we moved, Gloria came to see us. "John and Judy, I've just had a terrible argument with Mummy. I'm sick of being at home with her and Gerald. Can I come and live with you instead?"

"Of course you can," we both said. "It'll be lovely for us to have you."

The move went well. There was only one snag: no electricity; it was getting dark, we were unpacking by candlelight. Gloria took charge and phoned the Electricity Board.

"Why haven't you been to connect us?" she said. "Yes, it IS an emergency. We've got three children under five here, and it's snowing outside. Please send someone immediately." Luckily that did the trick, although it was quite late when someone finally turned up.

We moved into 1 Oakley Avenue, Ealing, on March 10th, 1970, and that was the start of a whole new life. It was an exciting prospect.

Chapter 10

Oakley Avenue

"Judy, how can you bear living without a stair carpet?" said Caroline, one of my friends from Barnes who'd come to visit us.

"It doesn't bother me at all," I said. "I'm so happy having all this space... and the garden."

The house was large and shabby; it needed a lot doing to it, and we didn't have much money. We had some carpets and mats from Barnes which were fine for a start. John put up shelves in the children's bedroom, and we soon settled down, re-decorating what needed doing most. I enjoyed being John's 'plumbers mate' and we were a good 'do-it-yourself' team.

I was soon busy dressmaking. My cousin Annie, one of my bridesmaids, as I was to her mother and her mother had been to mine – wanted Edward to be a page and Clare a bridesmaid at her forthcoming wedding to Rufus. I made Clare's dress, a long one, in blue silk, and Edward's shirt too. For myself I made a flowered, long-sleeved dress with a plain sleeveless coat, and I bought a large matching hat.

On the day of the wedding we had to leave a disconsolate Gabrielle behind with Gloria, and Clare managed to get mud on her blue shoes just as we left the house.

"Clare is much too young to be a bridesmaid," said my mother.

In fact, Clare behaved beautifully, albeit carefully pulling her flower posy apart during the rather long Catholic service. During the reception, Edward was overheard speaking to a waiter.

"Please would you bring my sister some coffee?" he said, and the kind waiter duly did so.

Family weddings were a lovely opportunity to see my relations, especially my aunts.

"Judy darling," said Auntie Val. "Richard has just got a job in London. Do you think you could have him to stay for a week or two until he gets settled?"

"Of course, Auntie Val," I said. "We'd love to have him, and we've got plenty of space."

Soon afterwards, Richard arrived, and we put him in the double bedroom at the back. In the event, Richard stayed with us for three and a quarter years. It was such a happy time. He got on well with Gloria, who was with us still until July. He was very good with the children, being the second of five siblings himself. He ate everything I put in front of him, and we enjoyed the same programmes on television, particularly the long-running 'Family at War'.

"Not that again," John would say. "Do you have to watch such depressing things?"

"We like it," we both replied.

Richard usually went home to Wiltshire at the weekend, preceded by several phone calls to arrange lifts, which I found rather amusing. Sometimes he was there when I gave the children their tea.

"What do you say?" I said one day as I handed out some bread and marmite.

"Thank you, Judy," he said, laughing.

"So sorry, Richard, I wasn't thinking…"

Edward had his fifth birthday soon after we moved, and after Easter he started school at St Saviour's, about a mile away on the far side of Ealing Common. It was Church of England as we weren't in the catchment area for a Catholic School, and our parish priest said it would be all right, even though I'd promised to bring the children up as Catholics.

Come the first open evening we both went to St Saviour's, John somewhat reluctantly it has to be said.

"Good evening, Mr Matthews," I said. "We're Edward Corry's parents."

"Oh my God," he said, obviously dismayed. "Edward sits under the table eating the dog biscuits which are meant for weighing!" I was taken aback by this, but lacked the confidence to challenge him. I should have said, "How is he getting on otherwise?"

In September, Clare started going to playgroup. Gabrielle and I took her there after taking Edward to school and collected her at lunch time. For the afternoon session we collected Clare first and then went to get Edward. I often stayed for a bit, playing with the children, and in any case mothers had to help regularly.

The year soon passed, and then it was Clare's turn to start school and Gabrielle's to go to playgroup. It was a happy year with just Gabrielle at home during the day. She talked non-stop, without her noisier siblings competing for attention. We used to look in all the gardens as we went to and fro. I had her friend Josie to lunch, too, or she'd go to Josie's house.

It was that year, before Gabrielle started school, that we went to France during the summer holidays. Gloria was working there and had rented a house for us to stay in. We went on the overnight ferry to Cherbourg, John driving us through France to Jarnac, near Cognac. The house had a large garden and we made full use of their barbecue. My schoolgirl French was adequate for local shopping, to my surprise. We spent a day at Royan on the coast, with a long, long sandy beach, and we collected huge pinecones from beneath the trees fringing the shore.

Unfortunately, after ten days there, the rain descended heavily, and the locals said it would last for the next week, so we decided to go home early. Cooped up inside, the children amused themselves drawing, but to my horror I found traces of felt-tipped pens on the immaculate white leather sofa. What were we to do? Gloria came to the rescue, being fluent in French, and bought a product which removed most of it. It was quite a relief to get in the car for the homeward journey, but we'd all enjoyed most of the holiday and Gloria had been happy having us there.

Whilst still in Barnes, John had bought a book in the 'For Sale' bin in WH Smiths. Entitled 'The Art of the Silversmith', he showed it to me, saying "This is something I'd like to do sometime." He started collecting tools and bought a small piece of silver with which he made a pendant for me, and a ring of twisted silver wire. After we moved he went to an evening class in East London and made bigger items, which he had silver-plated. Using our kitchen as a workshop, he made napkin rings for the children, mugs, a salver. He made gold wedding rings for most of my cousins, as well as other items which he did as commissions for friends. He even learned to cast gold, using a cuttlefish bone as a mould; I always wear a small gold signet ring which he made. He had all his work hallmarked at Goldsmith's Hall, where his own Makers Mark, 'JPC', was kept. I always enjoyed seeing him with his blow torch and hammers, admiring his practical skill and how he used it so creatively.

John's best creation of all was a chalice with an ivory knop, made of silver, which he had gold-plated and engraved with the children's names. He gave it to St Saviour's Church of England School, with thanks for educating our Catholic children. It has to be said that the priest who received it wasn't particularly enthusiastic. But my friend Marion, who'd taught Clare, later told me,

"It was a wonderful gift, Judy, and it is always used at the weekly school mass."

We saw my brother David quite frequently, which I was always happy about. For some years he'd been friendly with Robina Redway, or 'B' as she was usually known, whose parents lived in Aislaby too, and socialised with our parents. She and David had come to Gabrielle's baptism, which made my day as Fish and Mum had made an excuse not to come. Anyway, one evening he came upstairs as I was putting the children to bed.

"Judy, I've got something to tell you," he said. "I've asked Bina to marry me and she's said yes. I haven't told the parents yet though, so don't let on, will you?"

"How exciting, of course I won't tell them. I'm really happy for you both. I'm very fond of 'B', and I can recommend being married… David, I've got the ring Ducky gave me when I told her that David Mortimer had asked me to marry him. Would you like to have it?"

"That would be wonderful, I'm a bit hard up at the moment… are you sure you don't want it?"

"Yes, quite sure. I never wore it, and I'm sure Ducky would approve of you having it instead, if she were still with us."

"Thank you very much, Judy. I'm sure B will love it."

I was pleased that David and B were getting married, and that he'd told me first. We often confided in each other, as our parents weren't easy to communicate with. Mum adored David; he could do no wrong, but Fish was often cross with him, and I guess I was the opposite. I got on well with Fish but often irritated Mum.

I got the impression our parents weren't all that pleased about the engagement. They didn't have much in common with Paul and Jackie Redway, who were very informal, sociable, and gregarious, and they had a houseful of dogs too. Most of all, they weren't ex-Royal Navy, and David had gone out with several naval daughters in the past.

The wedding took place on October 7th, at St Margaret's church in Aislaby. David and B had met for the first time on that date seven years earlier. To be honest, I was slightly envious that they were getting married there when we couldn't. The reception was held at the Redway's house; Edward was a page boy, and the girls were bridesmaids. I made their outfits of course, in mauve, and I wore a mauve suit, not homemade this time. Gloria came too; she'd come to live with us again after she left her job in France.

The night before the wedding, Gabrielle kept us awake with a bad, rasping cough. Aunt Val came to the rescue – she and Uncle Tony were staying at Park Hall too.

"It sounds like croup, Judy," she said.

Tony took me to Whitby to buy a wool vest, and Val sat Gabrielle by a bowl of very hot water with a towel over her head, and by the afternoon she was all right. It was a lovely wedding, and we all enjoyed the weekend, apart from the worry about Gabrielle's croup, that is.

Now the children were all at school, I had a bit more time to myself. I started to do the playgroup leader's course, one day a week. It combined lectures with making things: a drum out of a coffee tin, some sticky back plastic and a car inner tube, and some maracas from washing up liquid bottles. I enjoyed it very much, and the following summer was awarded my Playgroup Leaders Diploma.

"Did you know about the teacher's training college in Acton, Judy?" said the course leader. "It caters for mature students. You should apply for it, you're good with children."

I talked to John about it.

"Go for it, darling," he said. "You should get a qualification of some kind. I'm so much older than you, it would be a really good idea. If anything happens to me, you'd be able to earn a living."

The big advantage of teaching rather than a secretarial job was that I'd be at home during school holidays. I'd have hated not being at home then, but I did want to use my brain for something more than running the house.

I got an application form from the college. I already had seven O-levels, and my playgroup involvement was relevant experience with children. When I went for an interview, I had to do a written test about an inspirational teacher. I wrote about Miss Seller, whose small school I'd attended in Yorkshire until I was twelve. Then I met Miss Carter, the principal.

"How do you think you'll get on in a state school, Mrs Corry?" she asked me. "After all, you've been privately educated, and you'll find it's very different."

"I don't know, Miss Carter. I love children, and I'll do my best."

I was very excited to be offered a place to start a year later, and accepted straight away.

In the meantime, I became the supervisor at the playgroup, for which I earned £5 a week. I saved it up, and at the end of the year I was able to pay for a fitted carpet for the stairs, landing, and our bedroom, which was very satisfying. My years at the playgroup stood me in good stead; after I qualified as a teacher, for all except the first year, I taught nursery children.

Fish had much enjoyed ten years as welfare officer for the Metropolitan Police. It was an interesting, challenging job, and he was very well thought of, but having reached sixty in October 1973, he decided to retire for good. He and Mum were going to live permanently at Park Hall. I was sad that they were leaving London, but we didn't see them all that much, they had busy lives and so did we. We had a farewell dinner party for them.

Fish was sitting beside me and we chatted about this and that. Then I said,

"Fish, I've got something to tell you. I've been accepted at a teacher's training college in Acton, and I start next September."

Fish then practically choked over his soup. He turned away from me, and talked to whoever was on his other side for the rest of the meal. So naturally I said no more about it, and they moved to Park

Hall soon afterwards. They were looking forward to living next door to Kate, now permanently at Park Lodge.

Later John and I were talking about the evening.

"I tried to tell Fish about college, but he didn't want to know about it…"

"Never mind, darling. I'm pleased about it, and that's all that matters."

"I know you're right, but I still mind about Fish… at least your mother is pleased I'm going to college… I was very surprised about that."

"Yes, Mummy is happy about it… she tried to get a job herself when Gloria went to school, but they said she was too old… so you are lucky to have this opportunity…"

One evening not long after they'd moved to Park Hall, Fish phoned.

"Judy darling, I've got some terrible news. Kate has had a car accident. She and Rory are in hospital, badly hurt; Tricia just had a broken finger and she's at Park Lodge with Anne."

"That's dreadful, Fish… poor Kate… whatever happened?"

"Apparently Kate was in a collision at a crossroads on the A1, taking Rory back to school after half-term."

"How are they now?"

"Kate has a broken pelvis and broken ribs; Rory has had his spleen removed. They are both making good progress."

"How sad this happening when you'd just moved… I'm so sorry…"

The children made get well cards, and I put a note in my card telling Kate about college. It was ten days later when I heard the phone ringing as I got home from collecting the children. It was Fish.

"Bad news, Judy… darling Kate died this morning."

I was shaking, and could hardly believe what I heard.

"But I thought she was getting better?"

"She was, but apparently she had a massive embolism which stopped her heart. The funeral will be next week."

Those poor children, was my immediate thought. Robbie was only nine, Rory and Tricia were thirteen, and Anne was seventeen. Richard was nineteen, and at Sandhurst, the Army officer training college. An additional sadness was that Rick had been living in London for quite a while, and had to be tracked down by the police.

Gloria came to stay to help John look after the children, a friend of mine taking them home from school until John got back from work. I got a lift up to Yorkshire with a friend of Kate's.

"Don't cry at the funeral, Judy," said my brother. "You'll upset the children."

"Mr Moody has had a terrible time digging the grave, the ground is so stony. It took him half the night," the churchwarden told Fish. There was no space near the rest of her family, parents, grandparents, and sister, so poor Kate had to be put in another part of the churchyard. Somehow it made it all the sadder.

"It's the first time Kate's been on time for church," said Fish as the hearse arrived.

We walked behind the coffin into the full, hushed church. After the service, it was a really awful moment watching the coffin being lowered into the ground, listening to the words, "earth to earth, ashes to ashes, dust to dust…"

Poor Rory was still in hospital.

"I'll wheel my bed there," he'd said. He was the closest to Kate of all her children.

A lot of Kate's friends had come to the funeral, and we all went back to Park Lodge. It was actually quite a party, everyone talking about what a character Kate was. She'd have loved it and would probably have been surprised to realise how well-loved she was. The next day I went back to London. Fish took me to catch my train at York and very sweetly gave me £5 for the fare.

"Would you like us to come to Park Hall for Christmas, Mum?" I'd said to Mum before I left.

"No thank you," was the reply, and I felt rather sad.

Many years later I heard that when Kate died, Mum had shut herself in her room and cried for three days. During the war, when I was a baby, Mum's youngest sister Joan died, aged nineteen, and Mum had taken the death of her father hard too, but she was always a very private person emotionally, with a 'stiff upper lip' approach to life.

Kate's death left a big hole in our lives; it was a terrible shock, having been so sudden. I was talking to Hilda, my mother's housekeeper, about how sad it was.

"Kate was only fifty-three. It's so young to die, and so awful for the children."

"She'd never have made old bones," said Hilda, who'd nursed Ducky, my grandmother, until she died. I found this comforting; Hilda was so wise.

I had an email from Tricia recently telling me how much Hilda meant to them all.

(without Hilda) we might have gone off the rails. She was unfailingly kind, very supportive in all sorts of practical ways and kept us amused and laughing with her funny stories. It was to Hilda that I used to run in after school, with Gillian, after Mummy died and often had tea there (her lovely little icy cakes that she used to make for John's "pack-up" lunch). We were always welcomed into her little house and ran in there at any time of the day or night, which we would not have dared do with your parents.

When Rory had recovered, he and Tricia got places at Ripon Grammar School as boarders, and Robbie joined them there when he was eleven; Anne boarded with friends locally until she finished her A-levels and went on to university, and she looked after her siblings at Park Lodge during the holidays. Kate would have been proud of how they all coped without her. They all did very well in later years; all of them went to university, Richard and Robbie had successful careers in the Army before going on to become tycoons in the City of London, Tricia works as secretary and researcher in the House of Commons, Rory has a chateau in the South of France. Kate would have had nine grandchildren. Rick eventually returned to Canada and had a few happy years there before he died.

Robbie had godparents in London who were good to him, and he often stayed with us too. He and Edward explored London on buses and tubes, and had a week in Paris while Gloria was working there, which was a great experience. Latterly, Edward told me that they'd played on the railway embankment too, luckily unscathed. In the summer I used to take them all to Richmond Open Air Swimming Pool, a favourite expedition.

Richard moved out in the summer of 1973; we were very sad to see him go, he'd lived with us for three and a quarter years. He'd recently become engaged to Victoria, and their wedding was the following March. Our three were again page and bridesmaids, and I made their outfits.

Richard and Victoria subsequently had a son, Jonathan (my godson) and daughters Rosie and Lucy. In March 2014, Richard and Victoria celebrated their Ruby Wedding. Gabby and I were very happy to be invited to attend, an excuse for a night away in Solihull.

In the summer of 1974, we were staying with my parents at Park Hall and were having a drink before dinner, when Fish said,

"Judy, I believe you are going to teacher's training college soon. Val and Tony were talking about it when they stayed here recently; they think it's very enterprising."

"Yes, I am. I'm really excited about it. The college is very near home, and I'll have school holidays so it will fit in with the children. If I pass the certificate well enough I can go on to do a fourth year and get a B.Ed."

"What on earth is that?"

"Bachelor of Education, it's quite a new degree qualification."

"Are you sure you can do it with running the house and looking after the children?" Mum said. "It sounds a lot to take on."

"I think I'll manage all right. By the way, have you still got my old bicycle here? It would be really useful to have in London."

"Yes we have, I'll get it sent down to you."

"Thanks very much, Fish. I'll be able to take the children to school, and then just get on my bike to go to college. It will only take about ten minutes to get there."

"It's funny that my parents have finally asked me about college," I said to John later. "I tried to tell Fish months ago… I suppose they forgot with all the trauma of Kate's death."

"Yes, they might have done. But maybe Val and Tony's approval has changed their minds…"

Mum never had a job; her role had been to support my father, especially entertaining his naval colleagues, which she'd loved and was very good at. My life was very different; I'd have hated being a naval wife. I must have been a disappointment to Mum, although she never actually said so.

In September 1974 I had my thirty-fourth birthday. It was eighteen years since I'd left school, and now I was about to become a student again. It was an exciting, if daunting, prospect.

Chapter 11

Teacher Training College

I can remember sitting in the garden one afternoon thinking, *I wonder if I'll ever be this free again, once I start college?* I was looking forward to it, but at the same time I was rather apprehensive.

The day finally arrived. Edward was now nine, and at Christ Church, a Church of England junior school in Ealing Broadway. He went to and fro by himself. The girls were eight and six, still at St Saviour's, and I took them there first. A neighbour was going to take them home on my late days, but not for long, as I'd be home by 4.30.

It didn't take long to get to Thomas Huxley College. Like anywhere new it all seemed confusing, lots of women milling about, just a few men, and they all seemed to know each other, just like they had when I first went away to boarding school.

We were given a lot of paperwork which included a timetable, and found out which of four groups we were in, each of twenty or so students. I was in Early Years, those who wanted to teach children under eight years old. All mature students, my group contained several girls in their twenties; the rest were older, most like me in their thirties, a few in their forties.

Lectures began the following day. There were new subjects that I'd never heard of, such as Sociology; I didn't know that there was a science about people in everyday life, and I found it fascinating. The lecturer was Fred Murphy; over forty years later, I am still in touch with him, and we sometimes meet for coffee. One of the first books I read, recommended by Fred, was *Invitation to Sociology* by Peter Berger, and I could hardly put it down.

The experience of lectures seemed a bit like the children's television programme *Playschool*. Each day the presenter would say,

"Let's go through the round window" – or the square or the rectangle – the camera would zoom through and there was some exciting scene. Academic work opened so many windows for me; it was very exciting and I was so happy that I'd begun my course.

We visited St Mary's Parish Church, which college overlooked. There had been a church on the site for a thousand years, the present huge building being Victorian, with beautiful stained glass windows. We then had lectures on the history of Acton, which had been known as 'Soapsud Island' because of the many laundries there. As the railways expanded, many houses were built in the area from late Victorian times onwards.

Our house, dated 1919, was on the borders of Ealing and Acton. I discovered that we'd been only the third family to live there, preceded by the Smith's Crisp family.

"This was a very grand house," said the gas man, installing our meter. "The family had a chauffeur-driven car."

The Corry family clearly weren't up to the mark.

As part of my coursework, I wrote and illustrated a short book for children entitled *The Story of a House*. As if told by the house, it related how our family had come to live there. Recently I found that I'd given carbon copies of the text to Edward, Clare, and Gabrielle, and they had each illustrated it. I was happy that they were all interested in what I was doing.

On a long, narrow piece of hessian, I made a collage using different fabrics. It depicted part of our road; in the centre, our house and number 3, its 'other half'. To the left, the block of flats which had been built in part of the garden, before we moved there; to the right, our neighbouring house numbers, 5 and 7, architecturally different from ours. I put three small faces looking out of our windows, Edward upstairs, Clare and Gabrielle downstairs. Lastly I inserted a dowel rod through the top hem, so it could be hung up.

About half our timetable consisted of lectures on aspects of education, and we had to choose one other curriculum subject to study in depth. Although I loved History I thought it would be better to do Art; a practical subject with less reading, and one which I also enjoyed. I'd taught myself to paint while I was at Hawtreys and had done quite a lot of drawing with charcoal, pastels, and pen and ink.

We did a block of time on each discipline: painting, clay, and printing. Painting was too modern for me, I didn't relate to abstract work. Clay was good fun; I made a couple of figures which were fired, and I still possess, but fabrics, printing, and batik became my main interest, and that was what I specialised in. I especially enjoyed batik. Using a metal container with a fine spout, I poured hot wax onto a piece of cloth, following pencilled outlines of houses and/ or churches; I then dipped it into a succession of different coloured dyes, adding further detail with the wax. It was great fun to do. When finished, the wax was removed with a hot iron and blotting paper. I made hangings of the best ones, using dowel rod. I did screen printing too, using similar images, including arches.

Local history became the basis of written, illustrated work for my finals; I did two volumes entitled *A Personal View of Ealing and Acton*, and *Churches*. The first consisted of a history of the area, with pen and ink drawings of our and others' houses; I drew barge boards (the gable by the roof) and the stained glass in front

doors using water colours too, and I drew tiled floors, like our hall.
I bicycled round the local streets looking for different images to
draw. The second volume contained drawings and a brief history of
some of the local churches.

In addition to our main subject there were several other extra
courses available. I chose to do Maths, which I'd never been
much good at, although I did pass O-Level. The course was quite
a revelation and the subject came alive for me. I'd never heard of
negative numbers, or binary numbers either, the basis of computer
operations. We learned about tessellation too, such as used in tiled
flooring. Religious Studies was another 'through the window'
experience – finding out about Islam, Hinduism, and Sikhism. As a
regular church goer, and a vicar's granddaughter too, I found other
religions fascinating, especially the similarities between Judaism,
Christianity, and Islam, 'children of the Book'. Years later, I became
Religious Studies co-ordinator at the school I taught at and went
back to university after I retired from teaching to study it further.

Music was another discovery; I still remember the shame of
clashing the cymbals at the wrong time during a percussion session,
but singing in the choir was great fun.

Each year we had teaching practice, when we were assigned to
local schools for a few weeks. I was sent to three different local first
schools. I didn't much like the first teacher I was assigned to, and I
don't think she liked me either, as she gave me a group of the most
difficult children. That was the school where you'd be told, "That's
Mrs Jones's mug," and "Don't sit there – it's Mr Smith's chair."

The other two schools were friendlier. My finest hour was giving
the children some broad bean seeds, blotting paper, and a jam jar.

"Can I really take this home, Miss?" said Hazel, holding the
resulting plant, her face shining with joy.

On the whole though, I struggled with it, and was very relieved
when practice finished. Handling the children was no problem, but

I found the lesson planning difficult, and it was tiring too, being full time at school, and a lot of preparation in the evenings.

I was busy with a house to run as well as my course, but fitted it all in somehow. I used to go home at lunch time to wash the floors while there was no one there to walk on them. There was a playgroup at college at half-terms so I could take the children with me. I became quite good at reading while they were watching television, so I didn't need to shut myself away to study. And often, when I was having a bath, one of them would say,

"Can I come and talk to you, Mummy?" as I was a captive audience. The girls had always been fine about me being at college, unlike Edward who was always more of a handful.

"What's the matter, Edward?" I said during one of his tantrums. "My being at college doesn't affect you that much, does it?"

"Are we going to have an au pair?"

"No, of course not, darling… whatever gave you that idea? I've never even thought of it. Now go and finish your homework…"

It was John who'd encouraged me to go to college, and although he didn't do much about the house, he was always interested in my work and encouraged me when I sometimes found it hard going, so I was lucky. But of course, John himself was very clever and interested in all sorts of things; our house was already full of books. John had to put up extra shelves to accommodate all the extra ones I was acquiring.

One of the unexpected joys of being at college was being just Judy, no one's daughter, wife, or mother, and it was liberating. I did love my family, but also my independence. Another joy was making friends; for the first time in my life I felt fully part of a peer group, rather than an 'onlooker' as I'd felt myself to be at the naval school. I got on well with most of my fellow students; in particular I was very fond of Gill, who was younger than me. She used to come and help when I took Edward and his friends out for his birthday; one time we took them swimming, and another we went to HMS Belfast, moored on the Embankment.

Happy memories of the Royal Navy for me and the boys loved it. Gill also stayed in our attic bedsit during final teaching practice.

Joyce, in her late forties, was a great character, as was Pat, of similar age. They had both left school at fourteen and had quite recently got their O- and A-Levels at night school. I'd taken my education totally for granted, so I really admired them working so hard when they were older. One day we'd watched a film about a family living in poverty.

"She shouldn't be smoking," said Joyce.

"Surely she needs some pleasure?" I said – smoking being less frowned on than now.

"No, she shouldn't, not if they can't afford it," said Joyce. She'd experienced poverty, I hadn't, of course. I learned a lot from knowing Joyce.

The three years passed very quickly, and all too soon it was near the end of the course. Half of the course marks were awarded by continuous assessment, and I'd had good marks for my essays. In addition we had to do an education study of 10,000 words. I chose the topic of 'Bereaved Children' having some experience of them when my Aunt Kate died not long before I started college. I also remembered Joy, my fellow assistant matron from Hawtrey's. She'd died eight years earlier, of cancer, leaving four children under eight. I'd been terribly upset about that, not least because my girls were much the same age as her two younger ones. There were many books and articles about bereavement, and I found the research fascinating. My interest in the topic has continued ever since.

I've already mentioned the largely visual study of local history which I'd done for my art finals. In addition, we had to arrange an exhibition of our practical work and talk to an examiner about what we'd been doing. It was an anxious time, but fun afterwards showing off my work to visitors, including my own family and friends.

Lastly we had two final examination papers on consecutive days. I felt quite sick afterwards, thinking of everything I'd forgotten to write. Six weeks later the dreaded brown envelope arrived. I'd passed, with Distinction in Education, which I was thrilled about. But best of all, I had passed well enough to be eligible to go on for a further year, and study for the Bachelor of Education. Of course I accepted straight away.

One Saturday evening not long before term began, the children were in bed and we were relaxing watching television. Edward came downstairs several times wanting things until John finally said to me,

"Can't you control your children?"

"They're yours too," I said, equally irritated. "For heaven's sake go back to bed, Edward."

Edward said something rude; John stood up, shouting,

"Don't talk to your mother like that," and Edward ran back upstairs with John in hot pursuit. The bathroom door banged, and then I heard another loud crash.

"MUM, COME QUICKLY! Dad's hurt himself!" I rushed upstairs to find John lying on the floor clutching his leg, and groaning.

"I can't stand up."

"What happened?" I said.

The girls had got out of bed too, wondering what all the commotion was about.

"Dad tried to kick the door down," said Edward. "Sorry I was rude, Dad."

"Bit late for that," I said, helping John up.

To cut a long story short, John had ruptured his Achilles tendon. He had to have an operation to repair it and was in plaster for six weeks. I moved our bed downstairs, as John couldn't get up them, and of course had to wait on him, which entailed coming back from college to do his lunch, and I went to the library several times a week to get him books to read. CS Forrester, as I recall. Come to think of it now, I shouldn't have done so much for him, he could easily have got around on crutches.

I loved my B. Ed year. We studied the impressionist period in History of Art. I read everything I could get my hands on and went to see paintings in the National Gallery, the Tate Gallery, and the Courtauld Institute; the girls often came with me. During the Easter holidays there was a study tour, a week in Paris, which was magical. We had meals at pavement cafés; we went to the Louvre and the Jeu de Paume. It was so exciting seeing paintings I recognised, such a surprise when some were huge, and some minute, you can't tell their size from books. I particularly enjoyed seeing The Bar at the Folie Bergere by Renoir, but Edouard Manet was my favourite artist, and I saw several paintings of his, including Dejeuner du l' Herbe.

The three art lecturers were fun to be with, too. John Langley used to write our food orders on napkins and autograph them for our scrapbooks. It was the best of times, only slightly marred by coming home with a French cold, even worse than an English one.

One evening in early December of that year, I'd been visiting a neighbour. When I got home John greeted me, looking very serious.

"What's the matter, darling?" I asked him.

"Fish phoned with some very sad news. David and B's baby William has died."

This was such a shock, as he was only three months old and hadn't been ill. Apparently they'd arrived at Park Hall for the weekend, with James too, aged almost two, and when they took the carrycot out of the car, realised something was very wrong. It turned out to be a 'cot death' with no known cause.

The funeral was awful, the tiny white coffin, and my aunt's beautiful voice filling the church with, "There's a home for little children, above the bright blue sky". Earlier in the year, dear Aunt

Eva had died, equally suddenly, and I was sad about that too. I'd always wished she'd been my mother-in-law, she was so easy going.

Finally Fish's brother Douggie died, at only sixty years old, just as the course ended. My artwork reflected my feelings. I did a batik based on a painting by one of my favourite artists, Caspar David Friedrich, which depicted three crosses on a hilltop.

One summer Auntie Val and Uncle Tony lent us their house in Bradford-on-Avon while they were away, and we looked after their dogs, and spent a particularly memorable day in nearby Wells. Val and Tony were a great help when my finals approached. They had our children to stay so I could get on with preparing for exams and my final exhibition. On another occasion they took Gabrielle with them to Wales, where she had a wonderful time by the sea.

I had six final exams, three hours apiece, for which I had to travel by tube to the University of London. I didn't usually mind exams, but one paper had only one question to answer, and I hadn't fully revised any of the topics. For half an hour I watched the other candidates busily filling their answer books, and I was feeling scared and helpless, before I got on with it and did what I could. The other papers weren't so bad though. Robbie was staying with us when the results were posted at the university; he and Edward went up there to see how I had fared. The phone rang;

"So sorry, Mum, you've failed." It was Edward, but I could hear laughter in his voice.

"You horrible child, how DARE you pull my leg like that…"

I had passed, but didn't get honours, so I was a bit disappointed. It didn't really matter of course, it was still quite an achievement. It reminded me of getting my O-level results, and being upset that I'd failed French rather than being happy I'd passed six other subjects.

The following January, I went to the Albert Hall for the award ceremony. There was an amazing procession of academics in flowing robes, two by two. Finally there was the Queen Mother, the

Chancellor, who went to sit on a gilded throne-like chair. Meanwhile, rows and rows of black-gowned, mortar-boarded students were filing silently along the balconies, making their way down to the ground floor, ready for the ceremony to begin. Finally, my row was told to rise; we amongst the last of the sixteen hundred students there that day.

"Bachelors of Education," intoned the official. I handed him my name card. "Mrs Judith Corry," he said.

I curtseyed, and the Queen Mother gave me a dazzling smile, as if she realised how hard I'd worked to get there. I could see John amongst the audience behind her, smiling proudly.

"Your curtsey was the best," he told me afterwards. It was one of the most exciting, memorable days in my life.

I'd loved most of my time at college; I rediscovered my enjoyment of learning, it widened my horizons, and gave me tools to continue my own education as well as hopefully the ability to instil in my future pupils a love of learning. I read loads of books, keeping a record of them. I'm sure I read many more than I needed to, but it was such a pleasure. I particularly enjoyed History of Art, and visiting art galleries and exhibitions. It's something I continued to do in the holidays. But what I gained most was a bit of confidence in myself and what I'd achieved, in addition to running our home. Ironically, by the time I finished my course, I think Mum and Fish were quite proud of me too, and certainly John was. He'd been encouraging throughout, and it had given us a lot to talk about.

The next step was to find a job, and I was lucky. There was a vacancy in a primary school with a nursery attached, just two miles from our house. I applied for it, had an interview, and was accepted, to start in September 1978. Doing a full-time job was going to be very different from being a student. I was about to find out just how different.

Chapter 12

St John's School

"Good Morning, Mrs Corry, welcome to St John's," said Mrs Broadbent, my new head teacher. "And happy birthday... it's thirty-four years today since I started my teaching career... I hope you'll be as happy as I've been."

"Thank you, Mrs Broadbent."

I'd been appointed to Year 1 in an open plan classroom. There were sixty children in the year, my group of twenty being the youngest children. Joyce Ade had the oldest group and Wendy Savage the middle. There they were, twenty of them, sitting on the floor near my desk.

How could I have been frightened of them? I thought, as they looked so angelic. They weren't. I'd also been told that the job was 'Team Teaching.' It wasn't. All that meant was that I sometimes had half of Wendy's group for hall periods and story time.

"What should I be teaching these children?" I asked Joyce, who was Head of the First School.

"It doesn't matter what you teach, dear, it's how you teach it." So, no curriculum.

"Teaching is a basket full of tricks," said Mrs Broadbent, very kind and encouraging. "It takes about five years to collect one."

Somehow I muddled through that first year, greatly helped by Marion Beasley, the teacher at St Saviour's (where our children had been) with whose class I'd done creative activities whilst I was at college. She gave me ideas for lessons, and every Sunday night checked up that I was prepared for the following week. I was also helped by the 'comfort room' staff, just opposite my classroom. It was where the non-teaching staff did First Aid, amongst other things. I used to take the odd uncontrollable child to them, which was a great help; they were such kind women. Even so, I often used to bicycle home with tears streaming.

"Don't be silly, Judy," I'd say to myself. "You mustn't give up. It will be all right in time."

I think the worst thing was no doors anywhere; I felt just like a goldfish in a bowl. And having Wendy nearby; she was so efficient, she just had to walk through my class and the children would be quiet. I felt really ashamed that I was finding it so difficult, especially as I was some years older than Wendy.

Come the summer term, the other teacher who'd been appointed at the same time as I was came to see me.

"Judy, do you feel like swapping with me next year and teaching in the Nursery instead? I do like it there, but feel I'd like to do some proper teaching."

"That's fine by me, Caroline," I said. "We'll just have to ask Mrs Broadbent's permission." I was very happy to be returning to being with small children rather than five- to six-year-olds.

By this time I was fond of my present class, and had had some good times with them. I did a project on wild flowers and took the children out, two by two, at lunch time for a walk round the local streets. We picked what we could find and took them back to the classroom. I'd taken my own flower books there, and one child in particular, Caroline, who couldn't read, would happily pore over the pictures trying to identify flowers. I did a flow chart to show the curriculum areas covered by the project and volunteered to talk about it at a governor's meeting.

It was a few weeks into the autumn term, after I'd moved into the Nursery, that Rita Mould, who'd 'inherited' my former class, came up to me in the staff room.

"Judy, I don't know how you managed that class last year. They're a real handful, aren't they?"

"Yes, they were difficult," I said, feeling vindicated that an experienced teacher was finding them problematic too; it made my day, actually. But I always felt that most of the staff thought I'd been 'relegated' to the Nursery and wasn't really a 'proper' teacher; not that I minded. I loved the Nursery from the first moment I got there, and that was where I stayed for the next seventeen years.

The Nursery was a large open plan classroom, run by two teachers and two Nursery nurses. Each 'end' had a 'Home' and a 'Book Corner'; we shared the separate kitchen, where the parents gathered to collect their children at the end of the session. My end also had a small room with a door known as the 'quiet room'. Carpeted, it had three steps and could accommodate both classes. Usually though, it was where I did the register and had story time. Each class organised our own activities, and the children were free to play where they wanted. I was working with Betty Tidy, a Nursery nurse whom I'd already met several times; she was very experienced, and I couldn't have been luckier. We got on very well and became great friends, having outings together during the holidays.

There were a hundred and twenty children, divided into four classes of thirty children, two classes in the morning, two in the afternoon. It was a lot of children, but I quickly got used to them, and after a while the numbers were reduced to a hundred. It was lovely being with little ones again, getting to know their parents, siblings, and some grandparents too.

Jo, the teacher in charge, was doing a course and was quite often absent. One morning a replacement teacher came bustling in, a handbag on her arm.

"Where's the blackboard?" she asked me.

"We don't actually use one down here," I told her.

At the end of the day, said teacher went to see the head.

"Please don't send me to the Nursery again," she said. "I didn't go to college for three years to wipe noses and bottoms."

Jo left at the end of my first year, to be deputy head in a nursery school. In September, Caroline started, and Betty moved to the other end. I had a new Nursery nurse, another Jo. We teachers just had responsibility for our classes and did the paperwork. Otherwise, we all washed paint pots, changed wet knickers, mopped up sick, and worked with the children.

Just before Christmas I had a formal interview with Mrs Broadbent and a school governor, and was appointed as the teacher in charge of the Nursery. I was very happy about this, especially as I hadn't been teaching long. My colleagues were happy too and told me that Mrs Broadbent had asked them about working with me before the interview.

I was so lucky to work under Mrs Broadbent. She was great with the parents, some of whom could be difficult.

"People are never rude to me, Mrs Corry," she once said to me. "That's because I'm never rude to them." This was after an interview I'd sat in on, when she was talking to a particularly aggressive parent. I was amazed at how quietly and easily she got information out of her, and how quickly the parent calmed down.

I was re-doing my notice board one weekend, and Mrs Broadbent found me there.

"I love your enthusiasm, Mrs Corry, but don't let school take over your whole life, like I have." We were all so sad when she retired, not long after this; she was always concerned for the welfare of her staff as well as the children.

We had an interim head for a year, and then Pam Peck was appointed. Just before she started, the school had a terrible fire, on Christmas Eve 1980. The centre was gutted, and our Nursery, some distance away, was badly smoke damaged; the goldfish died in the heat. It was a devastating sight; we were all horrified and wondered if we would still have our jobs. Luckily, we did.

When term began, the first and middle school were squashed into two other local schools. In the Nursery we spent two weeks washing our toys, helped by parents; we spent a term in the separate huts, normally used by the middle school, while the nursery was re-decorated, then we moved back there, with the school office next door. A year later the school was re-united, and there was a large fancy dress party to celebrate.

Life in the Nursery was never dull. One afternoon I heard a child shouting,

"Mrs Corry, come quickly!"

I rushed round to the toilets to find Karen standing in a pool of diarrhoea.

"Don't move, darling," I said, filling the sink with warm water. I undressed her and lifted her into it. The other children crowded round as I washed her.

"Look, you've missed that bit."

Karen wasn't a bit fazed, bless her, I think she enjoyed all the attention.

Another time there was a yell from Theo.

"Mrs Corry, come and wipe my bottom."

"I'm not your mummy, Theo. Just try and do it yourself." It was hard to keep a straight face.

I especially enjoyed the babies; it wasn't long before parents used to hand them to me for a cuddle, saying, "Here you are, Mrs Corry. He'll soon be coming to you."

It was Betty's idea to ask mothers if they'd be prepared to bath their baby in the Nursery for us all to watch, and it become a regular and popular activity.

As I was playing a game with her, Joy said,

"Mrs Corry, Mummy's got a baby in her tummy. When it comes out, can it have a bath in the quiet room?"

"Of course it can, Joy," I said. "That will be lovely."

A few months later Mrs Hague brought baby Luke in. Betty brought the baby bath from the shed and got everything ready. Joy sat on the floor by her mother, holding the soap ready, and the children watched, fascinated, as Luke was undressed and put in the bath. He was very good, smiling at us all, and splashing vigorously.

Three years later, Joy's mother brought Luke to see us, just before he was due to start at the Nursery.

"Hullo, Luke," I said. "Last time I saw you, you were having a bath here."

"Was I really, Mummy?" he said, looking rather puzzled.

"Yes you were, darling," she said.

"Joy was so proud of you, especially as none of her friends had a baby brother," I told him.

During my playgroup years I'd learned the importance of parental involvement and encouraged it in the Nursery. Some of the mothers, and the occasional father, did help regularly. Young mothers can be quite isolated, so it was lovely too to see friendships developing. I always used to tell parents that I was there for them too; as a parent myself I knew a bit about problems with small children and was able to be of help.

Some of the children could be very difficult; I had one who bit other children with no warning and another who hit me as well as fellow pupils. Both of them were boys, but sometimes girls were a problem too. I often taught twins, which was interesting, and once I taught quads: one girl, three boys. One of them bit people, all of them got into all kinds of mischief, like putting a paintbrush in the goldfish tank, and if one was rebuked, all four cried very loudly indeed. I recommended that they be split into different classes in their next school.

There were very few children I didn't love though. Most of them were a joy, and when first in the Nursery, I thought I was lucky to be paid.

We didn't just have children in the Nursery. We had goldfish, and then we were given two guinea pigs, and we called them Toast and Marmalade. Marmalade got rather fat, and one day we came to school to find four tiny, perfect, noisy babies. We easily found homes for them, and after that, kept Toast and Marmalade in separate hutches, only putting them together when a litter would be born in term time. I took them home for weekends and holidays, unless one of the children wanted to 'borrow' them. Guinea pigs are clever; they quickly got used to knowing who would give them a piece of cucumber, and squeak loudly when they heard friendly footsteps. John's weren't amongst them. Our cat Tiger didn't like the guinea pigs either; she would turn her back on me when I brought them home.

We were given a rabbit, too, called Benjie. Caroline usually took him home but one holiday Jo took him instead.

"Jo, don't put him with your female rabbits, will you?" said Caroline.

"Mrs Tidy, why is there a baby guinea pig in the rabbit hutch?" asked a parent."

Betty went to look, and saw a baby RABBIT, and there were three more, hidden in the hay; Benjie obviously wasn't a male rabbit. It was so exciting; baby rabbits are very engaging. After that we borrowed the head teacher's rabbit, Sugar Puss, and let Benjie have babies at suitable times.

One summer term Caroline borrowed an incubator and we put ducks' eggs in it. They had to be turned several times a day, and at weekends one of us would come in and do it. They began to hatch when the children were there; a tiny tapping sound, a tiny hole getting bigger, then a bedraggled little bird struggled out, shaking itself. After a while more of them hatched and grew. Soon it was hard to imagine how they had ever fitted into an eggshell. Baby ducklings are adorable; we all loved watching them splashing around in a large tray of water.

Another year we couldn't get ducks' eggs, so got chickens' eggs instead. Equally fascinating to watch as they hatch, chicks aren't as attractive as ducklings; they get proper feathers very soon. I took two older chicks home for weekends for a while; they used to sit on John's knees, opposite each other.

One of the comfort room staff had 'rescued' a duck, called Jemima, and used to bring her to the Nursery for the day. She'd wander around quacking. If she saw two adults talking to each other, she'd peck their feet, and quacked very loudly when we had story time too. Caroline put her in the big sink, normally used for washing paint pots. The children would cluster round to watch, giggling and laughing as she splashed us all. Jemima's visits were always a highlight and no one minded mopping up her messes.

The Nursery had a separate kitchen and we each had a day during the week when our classes cooked. The Nursery nurses usually took small groups, but sometimes Betty would co-opt me to do something.

"Judy, you're good at yeast cookery, aren't you? Why don't you do hot cross buns with the children?"

I duly bought the ingredients, took a group of children into the kitchen, and made some buns. I put them in a warm place to rise, intending to cook them before the children went home at lunch time. I kept checking them.

"Look, Betty," I said, "Nothing's happened... the buns haven't risen!"

"Never mind, Judy," said Betty, but I was mortified.

After lunch I looked again, and they HAD risen after all, and were ready to cook. The next year I made dough at home first so it had time to rise, and we could eat the buns the same day. The dough made by the morning children was ready for afternoon buns, and I took the afternoon dough home. Quite a performance, but it worked well. We made a harvest loaf too. The children rolled out long thin pieces of dough for stalks and snipped round the edges of oval pieces to represent ears of corn. We laid them on a long piece of flat dough, to represent a sheaf of corn. The aroma of baking bread was lovely and it tasted good too.

Creative activities figured large in the nursery day; we did lots of painting, printing, and collage. One of my favourite activities was to make a chicken-wire 'skeleton' of an animal, or a dinosaur, or a person – a character in a story or song. We'd cover it in papier mache and paint it, then put it on the top step in the quiet room. Or I'd make an empty fridge carton into a 'house'. Or we'd transform a carpet roll into a maypole, fixed to the ceiling with crepe paper streamers for the children to hold when dancing round it. Once we had a Father Christmas coming out of a 'chimney'.

Music was an important part of Nursery life; singing gave the children confidence as well as vocabulary. As well as her school job, Betty was a Brown Owl, running a Brownie pack. She was a fund of songs learnt around campfires, with accompanying actions. One of them was a music hall song.

A mother was bathing her baby one night
The youngest of ten, a poor little mite.
The mother was fat and the baby was thin,
Only a skeleton wrapped up in skin.
The mother turned round for the soap on the rack
She weren't gone a minute, but when she got back
Her baby had gone, and in anguish she cried
"Oh where is my baby?" the angels replied:
"Your baby has gone down the plughole,
Your baby has gone down the plug
The poor little thing was so skinny and thin,
It should have been bathed in a jug,

In a jug:
Your baby is perfectly happy
He won't need no bathing no more
He's working his way through the sewers
Not lost, just gone before
Just gone before!"

Of course the words were inappropriate, which is why it was such fun singing them, and none of the parents ever complained.

"You wouldn't really lose a baby down the plughole, would you?" I'd say to the children. "It's just a silly song."

I thought it would be good if I could accompany singing, so I began learning to play the guitar. The tutor at evening classes went too quickly for me, so instead I joined middle school children in a lunchtime guitar class, much to their amusement, and I learned to play a few chords. Then I heard about a Japanese instrument, a chromaharp, which had pre-set chords, so I bought one and learned to play it, once going away for a weekend course. In time I became reasonably proficient and loved playing it.

I collected song books and I built up a large repertoire of action songs, dancing songs, and those related to the themes we did: farm animals, zoo animals, transport, mini-beasts, and favourite of all, dinosaurs. My colleagues were equally enthusiastic and we used to have both classes together for a sing-song on Fridays. Every term we had an open day for parents when we sang our current repertoire of songs, and had a cake sale to raise money for extra toys, and to feed the animals.

There were quite a few musicians amongst the parents, who brought their instruments to show the children, and we'd have an impromptu sing song. On one occasion we had three dads, playing the piano, guitar, and violin. Other parents played a saxophone, a clarinet, and some African drums. Sometimes a parent would accompany our singing on open days; otherwise it was me and my harp.

One year a BBC parent recorded our songs and made a tape for us, which I copied for parents. After that we recorded a tape ourselves. I must confess I shuddered when I heard my voice announcing the songs.

"Jo, I sound so fraffly well-spoken," I said to my colleague Jo Chambers.

"That's why the parents send their children here, Judy," she replied. Another time I overheard one of the comfort room staff talking to a parent.

"Mrs Corry sounds posh, but she isn't really." It made my day.

The children kept us amused. I was telling my afternoon class about Christmas.

"I've been there before," said Carmen, jumping around with excitement.

"I love parties," said Jessica, throwing her arms round me. Another time Betty Tidy and I were washing up paint pots.

"Is Mrs Tidy your mummy, Mrs Corry?" Daniel asked me. We both laughed.

"No, darling," I said. "Mrs Tidy is just a friend." Betty was actually only eight years older than me.

We always had a Christmas party and one at the end of the Summer Term for which we all dressed up. Betty was full of ideas; never to be forgotten was a 'Mini-beast Party'. Betty was dressed in a black bin bag, sewn with yellow crepe stripes, 'wings' suspended from her shoulders, two 'antenna' waving on an Alice band. We were all helpless with laughter when this 'bee' appeared, none of us were ever so inventive. I have to say that some of the parents were somewhat bemused when they saw us staff all dressed up, but most of them entered into the spirit and dressed the children up too, and we'd make party hats so no-one was left out.

I'd found the time when our own three children were small were especially happy years, so was very sad one year when two sets of parents separated; even sadder was a house fire in Southall. Two small children died; Saahil was only three, Sumair eighteen months. Shariq, the eldest, was able to jump out of the window. On the fortieth day after the accident, their grandmother brought sweets for the Nursery children; it was part of the Muslim tradition following bereavement. Saahil's father came to collect his plimsolls, burying his face in them; I just hugged him, tears flowing. For some years I visited the family on the anniversary of the fire, and on open days I told parents about the importance of smoke alarms.

A school colleague once said that the happy atmosphere in the Nursery spread into the school. I worked with Caroline for ten years, until she moved into the First School. Jo Chambers succeeded her, fitting in happily for the next year. Betty was our mainstay, quietly working away organising things.

"Judy, shouldn't we start thinking about Christmas?" she'd say to me, keeping me up to the mark in the nicest possible way.

We didn't have a lot to do with the adjoining school, mainly because our times were different; we didn't have a mid-morning break and our afternoon nursery started earlier than the school afternoon. For several years I was the team leader for Early Years, in addition to being in charge of the Nursery. Actually, I hated this. It meant management meetings with the head, and taking Early Years assembly, and arranging supply teachers for absent colleagues. The only nice bit was a combined Christmas show.

As well as us four regular staff, we had a succession of Nursery nurse students, some of whom were excellent, and in more recent years, we had school 'work experience' students too, for two weeks during the summer term. The boys were particularly good playing with the children. A few times I'd taught a student when they were three, amongst them Nicola; she was a kind, thoughtful four-year-old, and was now a capable, helpful student, who went on to do Nursery nurse training. Rewarding times, they were. I was in the

Nursery for so long that people used to say, "Mrs Corry! Are you still here?", but I think being part of the furniture, so to speak, was a good thing for the local community. I taught three or four children in many families, even five sometimes.

The end of the Summer Term was an emotional time, when I had to say goodbye to children and their parents. Nursery education was like the foundations of a house. After a year with us the children were ready for formal learning. Six weeks' summer holidays, always such a bonus in teaching, and then another year began. There were new children, new parents, sometimes new staff.

The years passed by quickly and, gradually, less happily. Betty's husband Ron was taken seriously ill with cancer, and she had to give up the job she loved to look after him. The Nursery was never the same after she left and I found running it much harder work without her. We'd worked together for fourteen years and were friends out of school too, as I was with Caroline and Jo.

The school was in a social priority area, surrounded by high-rise flats, many occupied by deprived families. When I was first there, ours was one of the few with an attached nursery, so quite a large portion of our intake served schools in middle-class areas, and four church schools too. This mixed intake was much to the advantage of the children; the less able were stimulated, and we benefitted greatly by parental involvement. Gradually other schools acquired nurseries of their own, and our nursery intake changed to having many more single parents and children with English as their second language. I had my handbag stolen from my cupboard one open evening, and a large bar of chocolate disappeared from the Harvest donations.

I did get on well with the colleagues who worked in the Nursery latterly, but they each had problems of their own so the team became less harmonious and supportive. One colleague had depression and another had a daughter in a violent relationship so quite often took time off and was unable to 'pull her weight'. The other teacher was very confident, and as my own confidence evaporated, she tended to 'take over', so that I felt even more isolated and inadequate.

Finally, one Monday morning, I just sat in the comfort room, unable to speak. Someone got the head teacher.

"You're worn out, Judy," she said. "I'll take you home. You must have a week off… go and stay with your mother in Yorkshire."

I did this, and returned for two days the week following. On the Friday, I couldn't even go through the door to the Main School, and that weekend I knew I couldn't go back. I was off sick for many weeks and had to see the health team at the council. I decided to take early retirement, which was agreed. I did want to go back at the end of the summer term, but wasn't allowed to on health grounds.

It was a very painful time. The classroom which had been my second home seemed an alien, unsafe place. I missed the children and felt I had let them down. Suddenly my world seemed to fall apart; it seemed a bit like falling off a bicycle and being unable to get on again. I could no longer do the job which I'd been so successful doing, for so many years. I completely lost my confidence. It was like bereavement, waves of sadness kept washing over me. I went home sick in January and I officially retired on September 1st.

Just before Christmas, Caroline phoned me. "Judy, you won't want a farewell party, will you?"

"No thank you," I said. "Actually, I'd hate it …"

"That's what I thought… but we've had a collection for you and wondered if you'd be able to come to assembly on Friday week?"

"Thanks very much, Caroline, I think I could manage that… see you then." So I went, and the children were lovely. I was still pretty tearful though. With the money I bought a garden seat and a set of huge plant pots.

It was more than a year after I went off sick that I finally started feeling better, and the bad days were less frequent. I gradually picked myself up again and found great comfort in doing things in the garden, re-decorating the house, and tidying out drawers and cupboards, long neglected.

Recently, I was in the doctor's surgery when a voice said, "Excuse me, are you Mrs Corry? I'm Jessica Brooks…"

"I remember you very well… you once threw your arms round me and said 'I love parties'… how is your mum? And Tamsin?" Then I turned to John, sitting near me. "Darling, I taught this girl in the Nursery, thirty years ago! Can you believe her remembering me after all this time?" The other patients in the waiting room were taking quite an interest in this.

"Mum would love to see you again, Mrs Corry," said Jessica, as we left the surgery. "Here's their address."

I wrote to Judy Brooks straight away. '*It made my day, seeing your lovely Jessica again…*' I met Judy and Tamsin, Jessica's sister, who hadn't changed a bit, and heard about their life in rural Herefordshire.

"Jessica loved the nursery," Judy told me. "'Big' school was a disappointment, and she didn't really enjoy school again until she was in the sixth form."

I quite frequently bump into parents whose children I taught and hear how well they have done. It's very rewarding to have that as well as all the happy memories of my teaching career.

During my last year of teaching, I'd been accepted for a course in Religious Education. All staff had to be responsible for a curriculum area and that is what I chose. I'd been to many after school courses, visiting Gurdwaras, temples, churches of different denominations. I'd found the visits fascinating.

"Would I be eligible to do the education course, as I'm so near retirement?" I'd asked Roger, the borough RE specialist.

"Certainly you are, Judy, I'll give you an application form. I'm very pleased you want to do it."

The course involved a week of lectures at St Mary's University College, Twickenham, and then one day a week for several weeks. I really enjoyed it, and I straight away thought, *I'd like to come here when I retire.* My retirement happened sooner than I expected, of course.

When I felt better, I applied to St Mary's for a part-time place at a course leading to a Bachelor of Arts degree in Theology and Religious Studies, and was very excited when I was accepted. Eighteen months after having to leave teaching, I was about to become a student again, and was much looking forward it.

Chapter 13

The Cottage

This chapter I'm going back in time, back to when I first met John, and writing about Yorkshire, always a large part of my life, where I was born and where my parents lived full-time when Fish retired.

We were quite an unusual couple, John and me, with him being sixteen years older than I was, and we had some fairly unusual friends. Not long after we got engaged, John came over one evening and we were chatting.

"Darling, I've just met an interesting man," he told me. "His name is John Cottell, and he told me he was a colonel in the Army Intelligence Services during the war. He was taken prisoner and spent time in Buchenwald."

"Goodness," I said. "Wasn't that a German concentration camp? I'm surprised he survived it."

"Well, he did, although he lost his sight for a while. Anyway, he seems OK now and I want you to meet him."

John Cottell was a tall, good-looking, dark-haired man with a moustache, and he wore square, black-framed glasses. He was much the same age as my John. Over the next few years he often came to see us, we got to know him quite well, and after our daughter Clare was born, we asked him to be her godfather. We gradually heard about his life; once he told us,

"I'm the man John le Carre wrote about in *The Spy who came in from the Cold*." In those days it wasn't socially 'done' to ask questions and I took my cue from my John, who didn't quiz him.

John Cottell met my parents, with whom he got on very well, and he sometimes stayed with them in Yorkshire. They introduced him to all their friends, so within a few years it seemed that 'everyone' knew John Cottell. He let it be known that he'd been injured in the war and couldn't have a conventional marriage. It seemed plausible, and a convenient reason to ward off the persistent attentions of several of my parents' widowed friends. Gloria was smitten with him too, although he was a good twenty years older than her. As a small boy, Edward was particularly fascinated with John Cottell, and we were talking about him recently.

"I often used to listen to him talking to you both," he said. "I remember him taking a small handgun out of his pocket and saying to Dad, 'Can you get rid of this for me, old boy? I shouldn't have kept it'."

"I remember that," John agreed. "I think I sawed through the breech so it couldn't be used, then threw it away."

"Once I went into the bathroom when John was having a bath," Edward went on. "He showed me a long scar on his abdomen. 'A German bayonet did this when I was a prisoner in Buchenwald', he told me. Dad, didn't John say he was at Arnhem in the war?"

"Yes… he was involved in the assassination of the German General Kussin… he showed us a photograph of it."

Once after John Cottell had been with us I asked my John, "Darling, are the things John tells us really true?"

"I've no reason to suppose otherwise," he said.

We were staying at Park Hall when the conversation turned to John Cottell.

"Have you seen John Cottell recently?" said Fish. "I wonder if he's told you his news. He's going to rent one of Mum's cottages. It needs modernising, and he's offered to do it up at his own expense."

"The one Mrs Cowburn lived in? Goodness, what a surprise! He does love Yorkshire, of course…"

Later John and I talked about it. "I wonder how it will work out, him living so near my parents?" The road to Park Hall's garage went past the back of the cottage, rather close quarters for someone unused to village life.

"It will be interesting to see, won't it?" he replied.

John duly modernised the cottage, one of the oldest buildings in the village. He knocked down the narrow passage by the front door to make a large open plan room, with a coal fireplace and a curtained-off kitchen area. In the other room he left one stone wall bare, making a feature of it. It was a light room, with windows at each end. We were intrigued by some of his innovations. The big room had a trap door in the floor; when lifted it exposed a deep rectangular space beneath. There was a 'hidey hole' under the winding staircase, and a sliding door hiding extra space in one of the cupboards upstairs.

"I might need to hide if anyone comes looking for me," he explained, and we just assumed that it was something that might happen to spies.

At first it was all OK, John living near my parents, but after a while they voiced irritation.

"John's always disappearing, going away without saying a word."

We did know what they meant; sometimes several months elapsed when we didn't hear from John either. Then David came to stay, and told us that John wanted to leave Aislaby.

"I wonder if your mother would let us have the cottage now John's going? It would be lovely for holidays. It's not that easy staying at Park Hall with the children, is it?" John said. My mother only liked children in small, well-behaved doses.

"I'll ask them for you, Judy, if you like," said David. "I think it's a great idea."

A few days later David phoned. "They are quite happy for you to have it, but John wants to be reimbursed for what he's spent on the place."

"That's all right, I could use my trust money if they'll let me… after all I've got my salary now, I don't need a private income."

When Ducky (my grandmother) died just before we got married, my mother had generously set up a trust fund so that I had a small income of my own. I asked John what he thought.

"You can, but ask them," he said.

So that is what I did, and they agreed; I think they were rather relieved to have solved the problem with John Cottell so easily. I paid John £2000, although I expect he'd spent more than that, and there was some money left over for us to buy furniture for the cottage. After this I gave Mum an annual 'peppercorn rent', to pay for a ton of coal, and she told us that she would leave me the cottage in her will. I should explain that Mum had inherited the cottages and two farms, along with Park Hall, from her mother's brother, Uncle Clifford. This was in 1955, when I was away at school.

We went to our lovely cottage for Christmas 1979, the first of many happy visits, and, rather magically, it snowed. It was easier being independent of my parents; not least I didn't have to nag everyone into punctuality or keeping the place tidy.

After this we went as often as we could, for two or three weeks in the summer and sometimes half terms too. Gradually we made a few improvements; John put up shelves for china and glass, and we bought a freezer and a washing machine. Outside in the half-walled back garden, we had a sycamore tree felled and paving stones laid to make a patio.

It was always a social time, between us in the cottage, my parents at Park Hall, and my Constant cousins at Park Lodge. Cousins Sylvia and Fair Fenwick, who'd been so good to me at Hawtreys, had retired to live in the village; David and B lived near York, with baby

James, and we often saw them, as we did Jackie and Paul Redway, B's parents. They were lovely people, very hospitable and kind to us, on one occasion looking after our three children for the weekend so John and I could go to a wedding. They were very supportive grandparents too, to David & B's children as well as those of their sons, Marcus and Hugh.

One summer we had a wine and cheese party, and the children had an impromptu 'disco' afterwards. Another summer we were there for my cousin Anne Constant's wedding, which took place at Park Hall. The children were page and bridesmaids and I was busy making the girls dresses as I hadn't had time to do it in London.

"I thought I'd be following the girls up the aisle, finishing their hems," said my mother.

The beach at Sandsend was still a favourite place to go, weather permitting. John used to love the moors too. We went to Wheeldale, and to the remains of a Roman road nearby. The children paddled in the beck, and we took a picnic, as well as a car full of children. Sometimes we walked along the banks of the river, in one place clambering precariously over boulders onto the opposite side.

Nearby was a wood, full of trees and also huge boulders. John led the children to believe that one of them was the gravestone of Zoltan, Count Dracula's hound. Bram Stoker's horror story was hugely popular in Whitby. In the eighteenth century, the count's ship had run aground on the rocks below the cliff-top ruins of medieval Whitby Abbey; the count ran up the ancient 199 steps to the churchyard, where it is alleged he kissed a young woman, and she became a vampire. The children were very excited by John's intention to engage a local stonemason to carve '*Here lies Zoltan…*' on the boulder.

"One of Dad's wackier ideas," said Edward, laughing when I reminded him of it. It didn't actually materialise though.

Another adventure was driving in the car down a rutted track beside the old vicarage and parking it beside a farm gate halfway down the valley. There we walked down a couple of fields and climbed over a fence to part of the River Esk, known in my family as 'Grandpop's Pool'. On the flat pebbled foreshore, John made a stone 'fireplace' and had the children collect sticks. He then lit a fire and we cooked sausages, impaled on a toasting fork. They were more than somewhat charred, but in a bread roll they made a delicious picnic.

One day in Whitby we went out in a boat for a day's fishing. Edward was very put out when Clare and Gabrielle both caught some whiting and he didn't manage to. I got a fishhook caught in my finger; the next day it went septic and I had to go to casualty at Whitby Hospital. The fish were very bony when we cooked them, not easy to eat, but most of us had enjoyed the day out.

That same holiday the children were playing in Park Hall Garden while we were having dinner with my parents and Val and Tony, who were staying. Edward came rushing in.

"Mummy, come quickly… the girls got stung by wasps in the wood… Clare's crying…"

There were several wasps caught up in Clare's long, thick hair, so it was off to casualty again, and they had tetanus injections. My mother was somewhat displeased… and poor Clare was quite unwell the next day.

Alec, Fish's youngest brother, closer to me in age than Fish, lived in Yorkshire too, near Thirsk. He and Jean had two small children, Charles and Alison. Later on they had my god-daughter Marie-Sophie, and then Sandy. All of them were very talented musicians, like their parents. Although my first cousins, I was forty when Marie-Sophie was born. We sometimes met them for a picnic at a reservoir near Thirsk, or they came to Sandsend. One beach picnic included my cousins John and Eileen Goldschmidt, with small daughters Sophie, Rebecca, and Alexandra. It was lovely belonging to such a large extended family.

Gloria often came with us to the cottage. Her relationship with John Cottell hadn't prospered, but she had met another

John, ten years older, a colourful character who had served in the Colonial Police in Kenya during the Mau Mau and was now in the Metropolitan Police. They'd stayed together in the cottage a time or two, 'chaperoned' by Edward and Gabby, and a few months later, had got engaged, but hadn't set a wedding date. She telephoned me one Monday morning.

"Judy, are you doing anything on Friday? John and I are getting married."

"How exciting," I said.

Gloria was a great organiser, and by Friday everything was ready. The wedding was at Chelsea Old Church. Gloria looked beautiful in a white lace dress; I helped her to get ready beforehand, my John (her brother) gave her away, and afterwards there was a wedding breakfast at a London hotel, for us two, Edward (aged sixteen), and just a few friends. Gloria and John went to the cottage for their honeymoon.

Two days later we had a phone call from Gloria in the middle of the night.

"John has been rushed to Scarborough Hospital… he's got a perforated appendix."

"You poor things," I said, "what a thing to happen on your honeymoon."

Luckily, John made a complete recovery after the operation.

Five months later in January, I was at choir practice at church, and the last hymn was,

Lead kindly light, amid the encircling gloom
Lead thou me on;

It wasn't just gloomy in the choir stalls, it was freezing cold; I couldn't feel my feet and was glad to get home afterwards. John was on the phone, looking very serious.

"Goodbye, old chap… let me know what happens…"

"Who was that, darling? What's the matter… you look very worried…" I said.

"That was John Gwynne-Jones. Gloria collapsed and she's been taken to hospital... she's unconscious." We did know that John's sister had had flu, but had no idea that she was so ill.

"I'm so sorry, that's awful news... poor John... poor you... which hospital is she in?"

"Chelsea and Westminster. I said we'd go and see her in the morning."

I don't think either of us got much sleep that night; the hymn *Lead Kindly Light* went round and round in my head. I was in the bath early next day when John opened the door.

"John just phoned... Gloria has just died... she had a massive cerebral haemorrhage."

My mouth went dry and I started shaking; this was devastating. Gloria was only thirty-six, newly married, John's baby sister, twenty-one years younger than he was. I hadn't always got on with Gloria myself, she could be difficult, but she was the nearest thing I had to a sister, and she was a very loving aunt. The children were terribly shocked.

"Mum, I feel as if someone has punched me..." said Gabby, in tears.

I went with John to tell his mother and her sister Daisy, who lived nearby. That was awful... and then we went to see Gerald, John's brother.

"Oh no!" he said. "Gloria was going to buy me a fridge-freezer on Monday." I should explain that Gerald had long-term mental health problems; he lived in a council flat just round the corner from school.

Later that morning John Gwynne Jones came to see us, with a large bottle of whisky; I'll never forget his desolate face. I just hugged him as I couldn't think of what to say. He and my John spent all day drinking.

Very early on the morning of the funeral I was in the kitchen preparing the food for later on. Gerald appeared, looking sheepish, in his hand the chain of the upstairs loo.

"So sorry, Judy, I've broken this…"

"Never mind, Gerald, it can't be helped. We'll just have to use a bucket to flush it." We were expecting quite a lot of people to come back to lunch. Luckily we had a downstairs loo as well.

There was snow on the ground when we drove to Kingston. It was the first cremation I'd been to, and I hated seeing the curtain creeping round the coffin, the noise of the rollers taking it away. I felt empty inside, had a knot in my tummy, and silent tears rolled down my face. Gerald cried during the service, but John was very calm. The girls were upset, especially Gabby.

"What happens when people die, Mummy?" she'd asked me.

Now, thirty-three years later, if I ever hear that hymn, *Lead Kindly Light*, it takes me back to that terrible January evening. Gloria's death had a bad effect on our family. I wish now that John and I had been able to talk about it, but we didn't.

As related in an earlier chapter, John had already lost a sibling when his younger brother Norman died in 1939. Now he had lost his young sister. After Gloria's death, John went off every weekend, shooting at Wembley Rifle Club. I 'inherited' John's mother and Aunt Daisy, who needed a lot of care, and I had school and involvement in church activities too.

We did still sometimes see John Cottell in Yorkshire; he rented a cottage about a mile away. One day he came to see us in London.

"I'm going to America be ordained as a priest," he told us.

"Gosh, John, you are full of surprises, aren't you? Whereabouts are you going in the States?"

"Baltimore," he said. "But I'll keep in touch and I'm sure I'll return to England sometimes." He left some silver forks in our keeping.

A year or two after this, in 1985, David sent us an article from the Sunday Times entitled *Colonel Cottell's I Spy Tales*. It seemed that everything John had ever told us was complete fabrication. He had been in the Army, an officer in the Royal Army Service Corps, but not in the SOE, not in Buchenwald, not at Arnhem. He wasn't a colonel with decorations after his name; he'd been living in Devon, running a café there with his wife. They were both now in America, and John was earning a fortune lecturing about his wartime 'experiences'. He hadn't been ordained as a priest either; the church had never heard of him.

This was really sad. We'd been so fond of John, as were many other people, and most of us had taken his tales at face value. It wasn't until he tried to publish a book in the USA entitled *Codename Badger* that some enterprising journalist followed up his claims and exposed it all as fantasy. John also figured in Rupert Allison's book *Counterfeit Spies*. Funnily enough he'd named the cottage 'Badgers Retreat'. It was thanks to him that we now had it. It was also quite something to have known a real counterfeit spy.

We rather lost the enthusiasm for going to Yorkshire after Gloria's death, and went to it much less often. Friends used to borrow the cottage for holidays, but now we decided to let it through the Ingrid Flute Agency, just reserving it for ourselves for a couple of weeks in the summer, and sometimes at Christmas. Clare lost interest too but Edward and Gabby still came as they had both enjoyed riding lessons. Edward had an air rifle and used to go out in the local fields in the late evening and very early morning to shoot rabbits. I went with him once and much enjoyed it, apart from seeing the rabbits shot, that is. Edward hung the rabbits on our washing line ready to be skinned. Mum loved to have some to put in her freezer.

At other times, during school holidays I used to stay at Park Hall by myself. I always particularly enjoyed weeding the vegetable garden, and in the spring, helping Fish to plant potatoes, onions, and leeks, and dig a trench for runner beans. I'd join him for a lunchtime drink at the pub over the road; Mum thought it wasn't a suitable place for the vicar's daughter to frequent. The vicar's granddaughter had no such worries though. I'd play games with Fish, too, cribbage or vingt-et-un, Fish's pipe clicking against his teeth as he contemplated his next move. He usually won.

In his seventies, Fish taught himself to use a computer and began to write his autobiography, *The Life Story of a Fish*. When I went to stay he would present me with the latest chapter; I did know quite a lot about his life, and had been with him in various places he'd been posted, particularly Hong Kong as a small child, then Malta after I was grown up, a brief time in the Far East, and lastly at Whale Island, Portsmouth. It was very interesting to hear about his Dartmouth days, his travels before the war, and then his wartime service. At the end of each chapter he'd write about his parents and siblings, what was happening to them, and then about Mum, her parents, David, and myself. The book included a chapter written by Mum, 'The Captain's Baggage' about being a naval wife. And now here I am, in my seventies, writing my own life story, *Fish's Daughter*.

It was such an exciting day when Fish's book was published, we were all so proud of him. It came out just in time, actually. Fish had already had a mini stroke in the summer, and just before Christmas, he had a proper one and I went up there to help Mum. The doctor said Fish should be in hospital, so I went with him in the ambulance as Mum didn't want to. I took her down to Whitby later.

As we went into the ward, Fish held his arms out wide, saying "My beautiful darling."

He had another stroke nine months later, each one leaving him more disabled, although luckily his speech wasn't affected. Mum did a wonderful job looking after him, and I went up there as often as my job allowed. Spending more time together, Mum and I got on better than we'd done for years, and enjoyed each other's company.

I left the village one Sunday evening, after Evensong, with a premonition that something was going to happen; I cried for the first few miles of the journey home. Sure enough, not long afterwards, Fish collapsed and was taken to hospital with his final stroke; this time there was no question of his going back to Park Hall, as he could no longer walk, but was paralysed down his left side.

It was so fortunate that it was the summer holidays; I stayed at Park Hall with Mum, we visited him daily. We also went together to visit a nursing home in a converted country house, a beautiful setting, halfway down the valley about a mile from Park Hall. Then full, we hoped there'd be a place when Fish was due to be discharged, and luckily in October, this happened. He was in Woodlands for a year, which included another summer when I was at Park Hall for about a month and saw a lot of him. He was well looked after; one of the staff, a pretty young nurse, used to call him 'Captain Darling' and Mum went daily to see him.

It was very sad seeing how thin Fish became; large and six foot three, initially he had to be moved in a hoist. A year later, two people could lift him easily. Never a patient man, during his illness Fish was usually very stoical. Then on Christmas Eve, I was with him, on my own, when he suddenly starting sobbing. I rushed to find a nurse.

"My father's crying, I think I've upset him… I don't know what to do…"

"Never mind, dear, it often happens at this time of year. Don't worry, he'll be all right."

I went back to Park Hall feeling awful, but didn't tell anyone about it, not wanting to upset them too. The next day Fish quietly said,

"Darling, I'm so sorry about last night… I don't know what came over me."

I hugged him. "It doesn't matter a bit… I'm just sad that you were so upset… I hope you're feeling better now."

Fish was eighty-two the following October 1st 1995. The next day, Mum phoned me at school.

"Darling Fish has been taken to Scarborough Hospital… I'm not sure what's wrong…"

"I'll come at the weekend, Mum," I said.

"Don't be silly, Judy," said my Nursery colleagues. "You must go tomorrow… we'll manage without you."

I set off at seven o'clock on Friday morning; the traffic wasn't too bad and I played a tape of Mozart, over and over again. Arriving at Park Hall at noon, I drove down the drive, seeing my mother through the hall window, just replacing the phone; at once I knew she'd been talking to the hospital.

"Darling Fish has just died," she said, and we both cried, on the doorstep, hugging each other. I could hardly have arrived at a more opportune moment.

David came over later, via the hospital, having gone through the formalities. We made lots of phone calls, arranged for the announcement in the Times and Telegraph, and talked about the funeral, which was to be the following Wednesday.

On Monday, letters started to arrive; lots and lots of them. We read them aloud in turn, often through tears as his friends said such moving things. I'd always known that Fish was very popular in the Navy; the tributes we received confirmed that.

The day of the funeral was one of those clear, crisp Autumn days; brilliant sunshine, blue skies, a light breeze stirring the fallen leaves. The phone kept ringing; one call was for me.

"Mum, it's Gabby," said a tearful voice. "My motorbike has been stolen… I won't be able to come to Fish's funeral…"

This was such a shame. Gabby had recently started a degree course at Manchester University and she'd really wanted to be with us all.

The rest of Fish's grandchildren were present; Edward and Clare (ours), James, Ben, and Emma-Rose (David's). We walked together through the village, following the hearse; Edward represented the Metropolitan Police, immaculate in his uniform. Fish had been their welfare officer for ten years.

The church was full. Fish had been involved with the British Legion, the Lifeboat Society, and the local Rugby Club, as well as being treasurer and churchwarden, and local organiser of the Best Kept Village Competition.

The vicar, David Prout, gave an inspiring address, and we sang the naval hymn *Eternal Father*, which always brings tears to my eyes. After the service we walked out to *The Arrival of the Queen of Sheba*, Fish's favourite music. There were lots of people outside the church too. A place had been found in the churchyard just behind other members of Mum's family. My abiding memory is of the clergy surplices billowing in the wind as the coffin was lowered into the grave. I always hate that moment, it's so final.

We had got the local club to lay on food at Park Hall, and as Fish himself used to say, "One always feels better once the funeral is over." Fish's twin sisters were there, his youngest brother, several cousins of mine. All the Constant cousins came, and friends, many of whom had travelled a long way to be there. It was a lively gathering, and Fish himself would have loved it.

I stayed at Park Hall a few more days, but then had to go home. I did hate leaving Mum, but knew she was strong and would cope all right; Fish hadn't been at Park Hall for fifteen months, so she'd had time to get used to being alone. I knew too that her garden would provide great solace.

I'd been bereaved before, quite a number of times, but Fish was the closest person I'd lost; often critical and crabby, he was never cross for long, and he had a great sense of humour. I loved him, I always felt that he was on my side, and I was special to him. Losing him was the end of an era, his passing left an enormous gap locally as well as to us, his family. He was a 'larger than life' character.

"Mum, I'm surprised you've taken Fish's death so hard," said Edward, who'd been close to Fish himself.

I felt conflicted, actually because I felt lucky to have had a father until I was in my mid-fifties and I didn't think I was entitled to be upset. One evening though I should have gone to an evening class but instead lay curled up on my bed and cried and cried.

"I feel awful," I said to John, "it really hurts."

"I know it does," said John, "but it will pass." Not much consolation at the time.

After Fish's death I always stayed with Mum, and as a family we rarely used the cottage. I went to Park Hall every holiday; it was two hundred and fifty miles away and took about five hours to get there. With going to Yorkshire, my school job, and home to run, life was pretty busy. As related in the previous chapter, about eighteen months after Fish died my job came to an abrupt end. I faced another life change, another challenge: to continue to support my mother, to get well again myself, and to find a new direction in retirement.

St Mary's University College Twickenham, here I come.

Chapter 14

St Mary's College, Twickenham

I'm sitting at a table outside the refectory, during the lunchtime break, with several other mature students, and we are chatting to each other in the autumn sunshine. This is only the second time in my life when I know I'm doing the right thing. The first was going to teachers' training college and now, twenty-four years later, starting another degree course. I was so disappointed last time when I only got a pass; this time I hope I'm going to do much better. I've enrolled to study Theology and Religious Studies, part-time, which means it will be six years until I graduate, but that's fine; I'm retired, I've got plenty of time.

I'm at St Mary's at Strawberry Hill, Twickenham, near the River Thames. It used to be a Catholic teacher training college, but now it's part of London University. I was here for a course in Religious Education two years ago, so I'm already familiar with it. The old part of the college is housed in an eighteenth century country house, formerly owned by Horace Walpole. There are wooden panelled walls in the corridors and three wide shallow flights of stairs to get to the Waldegrave drawing room where we had to register. It's a huge room, decorated in red and gold, with high ceilings and big chandeliers.

That was eighteen years ago. That first day I met Andrea, much younger than me. She'd just done a full time access course. I'm still in touch with her, although our paths went different ways. She graduated in three years, went on to do a masters in Chaplaincy, and has since worked in the field of mental health. I also met Caroline, who like me had already done a degree some years previously. She switched to the masters course a year later and did very well, although dogged by ill health. We were in touch until recently.

We went on lots of visits that first year. The most memorable was a Sikh Gurdwara; after we'd visited the temple, we were given lunch in their *langar*, which supplies free meals daily. Eighty or ninety students sat cross-legged on the floor, eating *chappatis* and *dahl*. It was staffed by volunteers; everyone was very welcoming and hospitable. I was impressed and wished that more of our Christian churches would do something similar.

Another gorgeous place was the Swaminaryan Hindu Temple at Neasden, newly built by volunteers. This amazing edifice, which looks a bit like a wedding cake, stands in its own grounds, incongruous in industrial Neasden with its drab factories and bleak housing estates. Inside, shoes were left in a cloakroom, with ceiling to floor storage, before we entered the huge entrance hall, with carved wooden pillars and luxurious carpets, all scrupulously clean. Up a wide marble staircase to the place of worship, which had carved marble pillars, and where many deities, richly-clad and adorned, stood resplendent in glass cases. During the brief midday service, chanting monks carried brass trays with lit candles, wafting the smoke towards us as we sat cross-legged on the marble floor.

As well as visits, I enjoyed the lectures, remembering how windows had opened during my previous studies. I was learning more about the Bible, and about the major world religions. My library at home was expanding rapidly, and I was very happy using the extensive college library.

During the second semester I heard about a planned pilgrimage to the Holy Land in July, just after term ended. I'd always wanted to go there, so put my name down and paid the deposit. I told John about it.

"I wonder if I could go too... can you find out, darling?" So I said I'd enquire.

Clare and Gabby were very amused by this, as their father wasn't usually keen on going abroad.

"I bet Dad wonders what you'll get up to on your own, Mum..."

"Not a bit of it... I'd like to see the place myself," said John, and it was duly arranged.

We set off from home early, barely light, and at college, joined the rest of the party of about thirty students, with two lecturers: Father Michael, and Duncan. A coach took us to Gatwick Airport where we had quite a wait before our Dan Air flight took off. We arrived at Ben Gurion Airport in early evening, and as we set foot in Israel we stepped into the hot, exotic atmosphere which I recalled so vividly from Malta days, fifty years ago.

We were delayed at the airport waiting for John's penknife, confiscated at Gatwick and which had been transported in the hold; I'd been somewhat embarrassed seeing him being searched there.

It was exciting driving to Jerusalem, seeing palm trees and unfamiliar road signs. As we neared the city, Father Michael chanted Psalm 122.

I was glad when they said to me
  "Let us go to the house of the Lord"
Our feet are standing
  within your gates
O Jerusalem.

We soon arrived at a Syrian Christian hostel in the Arab quarter, where we were all staying. John and I had a double room, en suite, on the third floor. Downstairs we all sat round long tables for meals. The hostel was near the Damascus Gate into the Old City. After dinner, Duncan took several of us there. We walked through the narrow, paved streets, up shallow steps, under archways. Some houses had tiny balconies, precariously attached to the walls, and we saw lots of churches.

The next day, we had an early, delicious breakfast, before boarding the coach. We were going to visit St George's Monastery, in the Wadi Kelt, part of the Judean Desert near Jericho. The coach dropped some of us on a hill, so we could walk there, while the others would go by coach and we'd meet up later. It was very hot, but we all wore hats and carried water with us. We walked downhill, then along a narrow path with the hillside on our left, to the right a sheer drop of a few hundred feet to the *wadi*, or valley, below.

After a while, we became aware that we should have arrived at our destination.

"About twenty minutes, the walk," Duncan had said. I was fine, but John began to flag a bit. Eventually we walked down many steep steps until we reached the monastery, the extensive buildings jutting out of the towering cliffs. John immediately lay down on a low wall, in the oasis shade of palm trees, bourganvillea, and spiky cedar trees. I refilled our water bottles from an outside tap. We must have walked for about two hours. I stayed with John, but some of the students went inside the monastery, which was Greek Orthodox.

Duncan then said he'd go ahead to the rendezvous with the coach, taking most of the students, leaving Father Michael with us two, Andy, and Alec. John was struggling badly by then, so Alec and I went ahead, still within shouting distance; then I stopped and Alec went on. After a while Andy shouted to me,

"Judy, John can't go any further," and I relayed the news to Alec.

"I'll go and get help," yelled Alec.

I sat down in the shade of a tree, leaning against a rock. Although virtually alone in that huge, barren desert I wasn't afraid or worried. I thought it was a beautiful place; I loved the barren rocks, the occasional olive trees, the blue, blue sky.

A while later a young Bedouin trotted past me, with two students, and not long after that, I could see him coming towards me carrying John piggy-back, Andy close behind, with poor Father Michael limping along in the rear.

We must have walked another couple of miles, when Andy said, "Look! There's the coach... not much further now."

A cheer went up as we joined the other students; one of them burst into tears. Duncan gave the Bedouin, whose name was Ashram, a hundred American dollars, which he reluctantly accepted. John repaid Duncan later. Ashram told us that had we been in Israeli territory, rather than the Palestinian West Bank, John would have been rescued by helicopter.

Apparently the other students hadn't got back unscathed; a couple of them were sick, one had a panic attack, and most of them had blistered feet. It seems that the coach had dropped us at the wrong place that morning, but as we'd all got back to the coach in the end, it didn't seem to matter. It must have been a headache for Duncan and Michael though.

The next day I had very stiff legs, especially going downstairs, and I had an upset tummy, but John was none the worse for our adventure. It was our thirty-fifth wedding anniversary, so that evening we bought several bottles of wine, to celebrate and to thank everyone who had helped John and been so nice about waiting so long for us to get back to the coach. It had quite a bonding effect on the party; the young students were very nice to us after that, John in particular seemed to be quite a father figure, especially to the girls. Duncan and Father Michael were happy to have an older man with them, too; they and John had several convivial evenings sharing some duty-free whisky.

The rest of the pilgrimage passed without further drama. I found it fascinating that there were churches of all denominations commemorating events in the gospels: the Shepherd's Field, the Last Supper, the Garden of Gethsemane, the Wedding at Cana, and many more. We visited Bethlehem one day, and for a few days we stayed at a Christian hostel in Nazareth. One of the most spiritual experiences for me was a boat on the Sea of Galilee, and the ancient stone steps outside the church of St Pietro in Gallicantu, on the Mount of Olives. It marks the site where Jesus was imprisoned, St Peter denied knowing him, and the cock crowed. Each day, Father Michael and Duncan celebrated mass at one of the churches, including the crypt of the Church of the Nativity in Bethlehem, where we sang carols. At all our visits, too, one of us read the appropriate passage from the gospels.

One day we visited the Western Wall, sacred to Jewish people. The wall towers over the extensive plaza, which teemed with people. A rope divided the area into separate space for men and women; there were chairs for the elderly and disabled. Men with tall hats, long beards, and curling sidelocks were swaying as they said their prayers. People were writing prayers on scraps of paper and pushing them into cracks in the wall, and we were told that we could too, if we wanted to.

To the left of the Western Wall was the covered walkway leading to the Temple Mount itself, which is sacred to Muslims. A huge, paved space with trees and shrubs growing, at one end the Al Aqsa Mosque, at the other wide steps leading up to several arches, beyond which is the iconic building of the Golden Dome. We were lucky enough to go inside it, as since the second *intifada* it has been forbidden to tourists.

Richly embellished outside and within, it contains the huge rock where Abraham is said to have been willing to sacrifice his son Isaac and from where the Prophet Mohammed ascended on his horse Barak, on his journey to Mecca. It was an amazing experience visiting there, very beautiful, peaceful, and uplifting. I much preferred it to the vast church of the Holy Sepulchre, home to six Christian denominations, who all argue with each other, and the keys to the sole entry door have for centuries been in the safe keeping of a Muslim family. It was full of noisy tourists with flashing cameras.

Very emotional was visiting the tiny Holocaust Memorial: a room of plaques commemorating lost communities in Europe; display cases of shoes, spectacles, children's toys, almost unbearable to think of the pain and suffering.

One of my abiding memories of the trip is of walking down the Mount of Olives, looking towards the panorama of the Old City, spread out below, flowering trees and bushes everywhere. I took masses of photographs and kept a nightly diary to record all we were doing. It was a great trip, and we were sad when it ended.

"Darling, I've really enjoyed the trip. Do you think I'd be able to come to college with you next term?"

"I've no idea… I'll ask the office when term begins." This I did, and John duly enrolled as an audit student. This meant that we would just attend lectures together and John wouldn't be doing any coursework.

This year was different because I wasn't returning to the Theology Department. Everyone had to study a second subject, and being part-time I'd only done half of the first year courses. I'd always enjoyed history, so this was what I chose to do. John liked history too, luckily. I was looking forward to it, but was also slightly apprehensive as I hadn't studied history since O-level, and I'd be with youngsters fresh from doing their A-levels. At the end of the year I'd have to decide whether to continue studying only history, or to return to the theology department, or to do joint honours.

John and I soon got into the swing of it, getting to college in good time, a lovely drive there past Kew Gardens and over

Twickenham Bridge. We often had lunch in the excellent refectory, before or after lectures. Sometimes we met Andrea or Caroline, friends from my first year, for lunch, and we often bumped into the young students we'd met in Israel. After a while we made friends with other mature students and would often meet them in the refectory for breakfast before lectures. It was good fun John being there too, even though I sometimes had to nudge him when he fell asleep during lectures.

I particularly enjoyed the social history courses, the history of the family in pre-Industrial and Industrial England. Children were just mini-adults, regarded completely differently to how they are now. Of course, so many of them died before they were five years old, and a small coffin under the table was commonplace. The other thing that struck me was that divorce was practically unknown. Life span was much shorter, so that couples were seldom together even for twenty years. And there were John and myself going on for forty.

At the end of the year I decided to go back to the Theology Department, as there were lots of modules I wanted to do there. I didn't think I was a particularly good historian; my marks had been better in religious studies, and I wanted to do well. John didn't mind which subject I chose.

One module I was looking forward to was Judaism, having done lots of reading and an essay about it in my foundation year. Caroline, my colleague from St John's, was married to a Jewish doctor and had converted to Judaism so that their son could have his Bar Mitzvah, the coming of age rite of passage for boys of thirteen. Caroline converted to the Liberal tradition and had to learn Hebrew, but another teacher at St John's converted to the Orthodox tradition, which is much stricter. Margaret had to have an Orthodox Jewess living with her for six weeks to check that she was following the tradition correctly, using two sets of utensils as meat and milk cannot be cooked together. It sounded very daunting.

Anyway, John and I were invited to the ceremony; I loved the haunting, minor key of the music, the Psalms, the worship of the Old Testament God, so familiar from my Christian background. That I had recently been to Israel made me even keener to learn more.

One of the first books I read about Judaism was *On Being Jewish* by Julia, now Dame, Neuberger; I couldn't put it down. In Judaism, the mother has special importance, as Jews can only be born to a Jewish mother. She teaches her children about their heritage, beginning with the weekly family celebration of *Shabbat*, the Sabbath. This begins at sunset on Friday evening with *Kiddush*, when candles are lit and the family eat a special meal together, often joined by extended family members and friends. Sometimes they go to the synagogue for a service afterwards, but in any case they go to the synagogue service on Saturday morning. Everyone greets each other saying "Shabbat Shalom", and it is a joyful occasion.

I suppose our Christian Sunday used to be a day of rest, as no one hung out washing, much less went shopping. Sunday opening has changed all that. But Sundays in my childhood were never very joyful, just church, Sunday school, and more church. Having said that, I do think it is a pity that Sunday is little different to the rest of the week, not that I have any scruples about shopping then, but I do draw the line at shopping on Good Friday.

The essay topic I chose was 'Will We Have Jewish Grandchildren'. My extensive reading highlighted some of the overriding concerns of the Jewish community, particularly in England and America. Their population are aging and declining and there is a low Jewish birth rate. Many young Jews are choosing not to marry other Jews and have Jewish children, and there is a high divorce rate. A huge issue is the definition of 'who is a Jew?' Religious law recognises as Jewish children born to a Jewish mother, or to a convert to Orthodoxy, which accepts very few converts. Israel allows anyone with a Jewish parent or grandparent to live there, but they still cannot have a Jewish wedding, unless they go to Cyprus. However, some years ago American Reform recognised as Jewish children born to either Jewish parent, provided that they have been brought up in the faith. This caused considerable upset, in England too, and was resisted by many traditionalists who dislike change.

Some writers think that if Judaism were more welcoming to people wanting to join their ranks, such as a marriage partner, there might not be such a problem of Jews drifting away from their faith. Jews who 'marry out' are often shunned.

Judaism is so much more than a religion, it is a way of life, especially the observance of *Shabbat* and the numerous colourful festivals throughout the year. I think it is amazing that it has survived in the Diaspora, with all the persecution, and not least the Holocaust. It seems to me that it comes down to the family. As Julia Neuberger said, 'For many of us family and close community have given us our love of being Jewish.' There will be Jewish grandchildren as long as there are families who carry on the traditions.

I did a module on Islam too, the youngest of the three major monotheistic religions. Those who practice Judaism, Christianity, and Islam are known as 'People of the Book'; at times they lived in harmony with each other, sadly no longer the case, as can be seen in the Middle East generally and Israel in particular. Unlike the older two, Islam has no leader like the Pope or the chief rabbi. The faithful follow the traditions laid down by the Prophet Muhammed, and *Sharia* law, interpreted by scholars of four different schools of law. The worldwide community is known as the *Umma,* but there are wide differences in the culture of the twenty-two countries the majority of whose population is Muslim.

There are two traditions, dating from disputes as to who would lead the community after the death of Muhammed. The major tradition is *Sunni,* the minor tradition is *Shi'a,* chiefly practised in

Iran, and today it is often associated with terrorism. There are few doctrinal differences but often resentment and even violence between the traditions, as *Shi'a* are regarded as underdogs. Both traditions have further sects within them, and there is also mystical *Sufism,* known for the 'whirling *dervishes'* and some beautiful poetry.

One of the *Shi'a* sects is *Ismaili,* whose spiritual leader is the *Aga Khan.* There is a wonderful building near the Victoria and Albert Museum in London, the Ismaili Centre. I visited there from college; the interior is decorated entirely in geometrical pattern; the walls, the ceilings, the floors, with beautiful use of colour too. It's an incredible place to see. Representation of the human body is forbidden in Islam, hence the use of pattern. The centre holds many social, educational, and cultural events.

I was brought up on the Bible so studying it in depth was so interesting. It was sad that Fish had died before this time in my life, because I wish I could have discussed what I was doing with him; he loved the Bible and I can still remember his husky voice reading the lessons in church on Sundays. To do her credit, Mum read all my essays.

"Thank you, darling, that was fascinating," she'd say.

I couldn't do the module on the Psalms, my favourite part of the Old Testament, because it clashed with something else. But I did do a module entitled 'The Wicked and the Righteous', taught by an American lecturer. Lectures covered topics from the Old and New Testament, and I chose to do an essay on the sermon on the mount, from the Gospel of Matthew. Arguably one of the best known passages in the Bible, there was a wealth of literature on the subject, not least in a huge tome, the *New Jerome Biblical Commentary.*

I also discovered Thomas Cahill's lovely series, *The Hinges of History.* In the third volume, *The Desire of the Everlasting Hills,* Cahill writes about the world in the time of Jesus. There was so much to comment on that I had no trouble with the word count. My favourite part is the parables near the end of the sermon. '*Do not store up for yourselves treasures on earth, where moth and rust consume and thieves break in and steal...; consider the lilies of the field, how they grow... even Solomon in all his glory was not arrayed like one of these...; sufficient unto the day is the evil thereof...*' and the best of all, '*Do not judge, so that you may not be judged*'. The last one is the Golden Rule, contained in most religions: '*In everything do to others as you would have them do to you*'. So easy to say, but so hard to do.

Another enjoyable module, Israel Wisdom Literature, was taught by an immaculately dressed, well-organised lecturer from Malawi. We studied the Proverbs, the Book of Ecclesiastes, The Wisdom of Solomon, the Song of Solomon, and the Book of Job, on which I did my essay. What I gained from that was that it is quite all right to shout at God when bad things happen which are no fault of yours. Job did that, yet somehow did not lose his faith, and he overcame his tribulations in the end.

One of the best lecturers of all was Kathleen O'Gorman, a New Testament specialist. I did the Synoptic Gospels, Matthew, Mark, and Luke, with her, and separately the Gospel of John. We'd be given extracts from the gospels and asked to expand on them. I had my own biblical concordance which I used extensively with those extracts; there was a huge amount of information available, it brought the New Testament alive and was rewarding research.

Robin Gibbons was an ordained Orthodox Catholic priest. I did Religion and Art with him. He used take us on field trips; we visited the V+A, and the British Museums, and Southwark Cathedral. We were having lunch in the National Gallery one day.

"I used to come here when I was a student," he said. "My friends and I would watch other people, and after they'd gone, would quickly grab any leftover food for ourselves."

Another time he took us to some of the Wren churches in the city, and was always full of anecdotes and information. I did an essay on Caspar David Friedrich, one of my favourite artists whom I'd come across whilst at Thomas Huxley. The task set was to consider Friedrich's contribution to theology and art; I was very fortunate that there was an exhibition of his work at the National Gallery at the time. I found his paintings very spiritual; his poignant, imaginative landscapes, often with a lone onlooker, convey the glory of nature, which is where I too find the Almighty, and in times of personal sorrow I find comfort in his images of medieval cathedrals in the sky.

I had already done modules on Judaism and Islam and had been to Israel on pilgrimage, when to my joy there was a module on the Holy Land. The lecturer, Nur Masala, was a Palestinian, so he was well-versed in the subject, but also very even-handed.

Before the First World War, Arabs, Christians, and Jews lived in harmony with each other. The rise of Zionism in Paris in the early nineteenth century, and many Jews fleeing to Palestine from the pogroms in Russia, changed all that. We learned about the political promises made concerning the establishment of a future Jewish state, the growth of the *kibbutz*, the communal settlements, and the increasing Jewish population in Palestine. Finally, partition in 1947, which gave the Jews an official homeland, but led to many Arabs fleeing their homes, some never to return. What constituted victory for Jews was the *Nakba,* disaster for Arabs.

I told Nur how much I'd enjoyed the module.

"You should do a PhD on the Holy Land, Judy," he said.

"Hold on, Nur, I haven't got my BA yet..." But it did give me ideas for the future, if I wanted to continue studying.

Of all the modules I did, only the one on Christian Ethics was disappointing, which was such a pity because the topics were interesting. The lecturer, a nun, had no class control, and allowed one particular student to hold the floor during discussions. I was glad when the module finished, it was such a contrast after all the other well-organised ones.

As each academic year passed, the work became more challenging, and involved doing a class presentation in addition to an essay. I got very nervous and didn't enjoy that bit at all. But I did get very involved in another assignment. Being fascinated with Judaism, I'd been to a *Shabbat* service at the Orthodox Synagogue in Ealing, sitting in the upstairs gallery with the women, who were all very friendly. I was most amused at their chatting to each other throughout most of the service, and I loved the music. Ealing had a Liberal synagogue too, and it was there that I went for a *Shabbat* service, asking if I might speak to the rabbi afterwards.

"My name is Judy Corry, and I'm a student at St Mary's University in Twickenham. I've got to do a study of a worshipping community, and I wonder if you'd allow me to do it in your synagogue?"

"Certainly you may, that will be interesting for us too. Why don't you make an appointment to see me another time, and we'll talk about it."

I chose the Liberal synagogue because the rabbi was female. The Church of England had fairly recently ordained women as priests and I was interested in the role of women in religion. The rabbi was most helpful; the congregation spoke highly of her, and the atmosphere of the place and range of activities there reflected her leadership. There were clubs for badminton, bridge, books and lunch, a women's 'Nite Out', mother and toddler group, and a singing group. Adult education was provided, and the rabbi herself spent time in the *cheder*, the synagogue school, and had links with the local schools too, as there was no Jewish school in the area.

The synagogue had a membership roll of 220, and, unusually, an organisation called 'Friends of the Synagogue'. The members were those who had a Jewish husband, wife, or partner and wished to have a formal relationship with the community. There were 35 members who paid a considerably reduced membership fee, and it was of great benefit to people who had 'married out' and were sometimes ostracised, causing them to abandon Judaism. I had already read about this problem in research regarding my 'Jewish grandchildren' essay.

I met some lay people too, who were interested that an outsider wanted to study their community. I went to several services, on Friday evening and Saturday morning, including a Bar Mitzvah. I especially liked the part when the Torah, the Jewish Holy Book, was taken from the special cupboard where it is stored and carried in procession round the synagogue, followed by some of the congregation, including children. The address given by the rabbi was lively as people in the congregation sometimes asked questions during it, so different from staid Christian sermons.

I liked the *Yahrzeit,* the memorial board where the names of the deceased are inscribed. The congregation included elderly members who survived the Holocaust, and remembrance of the dead is important to them. I really enjoyed my study time there, and I got a good mark for my work too.

All too soon it was time for the final dissertation, the last big assignment of the degree course, quite a challenge and a period of anxiety, I must confess. John wasn't well and had dropped out of lectures, so I was on my own. I had thought I could compare the role of the female Jewish rabbi with the female Christian priest, but in the end decided that it was impractical, and chose instead to do my dissertation about Judith, my Biblical namesake, whose story is found in the Apocrypha or Deutero-Canonical Bible. I had a problem deciding the focus for my research, and was helped considerably by Lynne, the lecturer who had taught me about Judaism and Islam. She suggested that I look at the different interpretations of the book in traditional literature, feminist literature, and also in art.

Once started, I worked hard and was fortunate that there was a lot of literature available. I went to Heythrop College in Kensington, which had an extensive theological library, spending days there as I wasn't able to take books home. I walked through beautiful gardens tended by Maria Assumpta nuns whose convent was on the same site, and it was a good excuse to wander round Marks and Spencer on the way home.

Thought to be one of the first historical novels, its mythical heroine Judith challenges and contradicts many of the conventional values of society. Judith cut off the head of the Assyrian general who was besieging her home town, having first got him drunk. The army fled, and her town was saved. The book has been extensively studied and interpreted, and it was fascinating to read how differently feminist scholars viewed Judith, in contrast to the traditional male approach. She was variously regarded as a pious, saintly widow that saved her people, or as a sexual symbol who ensnared a man to his ruin. One of the books I read was entitled *Judith Sexual Warrior: Women and Power in Western Culture*.

The chapter in my dissertation which was the most fun was looking at how Judith was interpreted in Christian art; there are literally thousands of examples. She can be found in illustrated Bibles, statues, stained glass windows, walls, ceilings, and carved doors of medieval cathedrals. In the secular field too there are sculptures, woodcuts, ceramics, wax tablets, jugs, carved furniture, screens, jewellery, tapestries, and embroideries. Judith's story seems to have inspired a commercial response not unlike that of a modern royal wedding. I could equally have looked at Judith in literature; her story has been the inspiration for many novels, plays, and films.

I chose to discuss six very different paintings of Judith and the severed head of Holofernes. I was lucky that one of the loveliest paintings of her was on display at the Queen's Gallery at Buckingham Palace, by Cristoforo Allori; said to portray a local beauty with whom he had fallen in love. Holofernes' head is a self-portrait; Allori's jealousy and his fights with woman were well-known. The visit to see it is chiefly remembered for John having his penknife confiscated by security, and they wouldn't return it to him afterwards.

Giorgione's painting of Judith is demure and dreamlike, despite her standing on the head of Holofernes; Gustav Klimt portrays a decorative, sexual Judith; she has no sword and Holofernes' head is barely visible, although in birthday cards sold in Israel, his head can clearly be seen. The sole female artist I chose, Artemisia Gentileschi, shows a dark, violent painting, said to reflect her experience of rape. It bore out my point that women view Judith differently than men.

I duly finished my ten thousand words and submitted it, with some relief. The course ended not long after that. Gabby came with me to see the results posted on the college notice board. I had got a First. I was very elated, but then the excitement evaporated. The graduation ceremony was in Westminster Cathedral, an impressive setting, but I wasn't with any particular friends, so it was quite unlike my first time, curtseying to the Queen Mother. I should add though that I received a prize for my dissertation, about which I was more than delighted.

So what was I to do next? After some deliberation, I signed up to do a masters course in Religion and Conflict, also at St Mary's, starting in October. It was such a contrast after the BA, which had been great. This was in the evening, for three hours, and only a ten minute break, so no time to socialise with other students, of whom there were only six. There was a lot of reading too, some of it quite hard going. I did like some of the modules, especially one on the Crusades. We had an enthusiastic young lecturer who gave us stuff to prepare beforehand, so the evening was very stimulating. The module on Fundamentalism in Israel was interesting too. I studied the assassination of Yitzak Rabin, Prime Minister in Israel, by an extremist Jew; it triggered one of the many times when the peace process foundered.

Finally though, having completed two years study, I became eligible for a post graduate diploma, so decided to opt for that, and not finish the MA. I wanted to spend more time with John, not just bury myself in books. It was sad to be leaving St Mary's after spending so many years there, but I had learned such a lot, it had enriched my life so much, and I had such happy memories.

What I remember best about college was the anticipation of starting a new module. What would the lecturer be like, if I didn't already know them? What would the content be like? Who else was doing the same module? And then of course looking at the essay titles and seeing what appealed to me, I think that was usually easy. And the joy of going to the library and seeing what books there were; sometimes the library came before the final essay choice, when the perfect book would trigger my interest. I always went to both my local libraries too, and searched the Internet for material, but of course that was a while ago now and there was much less information to be found.

What I gained most, in retrospect, was learning about Judaism and the Holy Land. I often wondered if I'd been Jewish in a previous existence, but of course that is fanciful. During my extensive reading I'd come across Rabbi Shmuely Botteach. I can't of course remember his exact words, but the essence was that there was no need to convert to another religion, one's relationship with the Almighty was unchanged by the human practice of it. I think that was it, it made sense, and that is why I didn't go down the path of conversion myself. But Judaism has remained fascinating.

Through the Council of Christians and Jews, John and I went to Israel again, on several study tours, of which more in the next chapter.

Chapter 15

Study Tours

There had been an *intifada*, a Palestinian uprising against the Israeli occupation, since our pilgrimage to the Holy Land in 1999, and it was only recently that tourism there had resumed. In the summer of 2004 I saw an advertisement in *Common Ground*, the magazine of the Council of Christians and Jews, of which I was a member.

"Darling, look at this... there's a study tour to Israel in the Autumn... can we go? Please? I've been dying to go back since we went last time. I'm sure it's all right there now..."

"Well, we could find out more details about it," said John, ever cautious.

I phoned straight away. They still had places available, and it sounded wonderful. Entitled 'Pilgrimage and Spirituality', it was for eleven days, spent in Galilee and Jerusalem. We went up to CCJ Headquarters for a preliminary meeting, where we met Beryl, the course leader, and some of the other participants, and were given a large pack of information to read through.

Edward drove us to Heathrow on November 22nd 2004, where we joined the party of twenty or so, Christians and Jews. Whilst waiting to take off we talked to Barnabas and Stephen, Catholic priests who were celebrating the twenty-fifth anniversary of their ordination. I told them that John was a Catholic convert.

"Oh dear, we'd better behave ourselves," said Barnabas.

I later discovered that he knew one of my numerous cousins, Michael, and his wife Margaret; he was their parish priest. They were great fun, both of them, unlike the Church of England lot who were the opposite, rather 'cliquey'; they all sat together at meal times. Tedious, I thought.

After a flight of four hours we landed at Tel Aviv Airport and went by coach to Kibbutz Lavi near the Sea of Galilee. It was a lovely hotel; our room was comfortable, the food delicious, and the spacious grounds had an extensive, beautiful rose garden. A succession of Jewish scholars joined us during the tour and shared their knowledge of the sites we visited.

Especially memorable was a service at a Greek Catholic church in the Arab village of Rama, where the cantor sang an eight tone setting of the liturgy. It sounded wonderful.

One day we went to Kinneret, where there was the cemetery of one of the first of three *kibbutz* set up at the turn of the twentieth century. The first baby born there had died soon afterwards, largely because everyone on the *kibbutz* was so young; no one had any experience of childbirth and the baby wasn't taken to the hospital in time. I put a stone on his tiny grave, as is the Jewish custom. After that, children's houses were founded; they were controversial but the peer bond in them was strong, and most heroes of the War of Independence were raised in them. Lavi still had a children's house, but it had never been residential. Near the rose garden, it had delightful floor level windows so the little ones could look out.

An attractive place was the medieval city of Safed, on top of a hill, where the *Kabbalah*, mystical Judaism, developed. A quaint place with cobblestoned streets, we saw many young Orthodox families each with lots of small children. Lots of synagogues, too; we went to a short service in one of them. In Cana we saw the 'wedding church', and street stalls outside tried to sell us special 'wedding wine'. At a Franciscan school we met the head teacher, an Arab nun; the nursery children waved at us while at play, which brought back happy memories of my teaching days.

We left Galilee after four days and set off for Jerusalem, arriving at the wonderful Hotel Zion just before *Shabbat* began; originally a hospital, the building was set into the cliff and had spectacular views as well as sumptuous marble-floored reception rooms. We had to go down six floors in the lift to get to our room. We attended a service in the crowded synagogue, people swaying as they sang and the rabbi beating time with his hand on the prayer desk. Most uplifting.

After the service we were invited for *Shabbat* dinner by Rabbi Joel and his wife, Susannah, who played the violin in the Israeli chamber orchestra. I discovered that Joel had done his rabbinical training with Melinda Carr, the rabbi at the Ealing liberal synagogue where I'd done my study of a worshipping community. Small world. Joel said I should go to the Leo Baeck College Library to get information about biblical Judith, for my dissertation, which I subsequently did. We had a lovely evening with them, their family and friends, and delicious food.

The next morning we went on a *shul* crawl; for Jews it is perfectly acceptable to go into a synagogue for part of the service. We visited three or four, walking past many more, all very different, one just a house with the former owner living in one adjoining room. It was very cold, and one by one, people went back to the hotel. The thing I chiefly remember about that trip was the temperature; the forecast said it would be warm, but it was cold and I hadn't taken enough clothes with me. It was a relief later that day when I went to the market and bought a sweatshirt. I was a lot warmer after that.

With our group was Jill, working for International Jewish Christian Relations, living in Jerusalem with her husband and four children. She'd looked very tired the day before.

"How are you, Jill?" I asked her, during our visit to the church of the Holy Sepulchre.

"Two of my children are attending a funeral today," she said. "One of their friends threw herself off the roof and died three days later... We all live with the daily reality of sudden death... but it's different if it's someone you know..."

"That's so sad... having to experience bereavement at that age."

"Yes it is... adolescent problems get neglected in our tense society..."

Another day we visited the huge Dormition Abbey, built by the Kaiser after the First World War; a beautiful, spacious, and peaceful church, and with an excellent gift shop. Outside Zion Gate we walked past a seated camel.

"Isn't he lovely?" I said. Just as I spoke he growled loudly at us. How we laughed, once beyond the reach of his large yellow teeth.

Soon the tour came to an end, and we were at the airport again. We'd been in churches, synagogues, and mosques, visited lots of places, met five archbishops, and had talks from a wide range of people. I'd learned such a lot and it complemented what I'd been studying at university; I couldn't wait to go to Israel again.

Less than a year later, another study tour was advertised, this time entitled 'The Land', and we set off again in September, with me in particular full of excitement. We also had new purple-wheeled suitcases, easy to spot at luggage arrival. There were some familiar faces from our previous trip and some new: Beryl was accompanied by her husband Bill, a retired Anglican priest and a delightful addition to the group. Our Jewish guide this time was Ophir, a lovely man, full of knowledge and enthusiasm.

We found ourselves in Israel during the forty days of penitence leading up to *Rosh Hashanah*, Jewish New Year, and Ophir organised a *shul* crawl, in the middle of the night, starting off at 2am. I should explain here something about Judaism. After the fall of Jerusalem to the Romans in 70 AD, Jews fled from Palestine and migrated all over the world. This is known as the Jewish Diaspora, Jews settling in northern and Eastern Europe became *Ashkenazi;* they spoke *Yiddish.* Those around the Mediterranean were known as *Sephardi,* and they spoke *Latino.* For both groups their sacred language is *Hebrew.* Each group has their own synagogues and slightly different liturgy. I believe the *Sephardi* are known to be more informal, and joyful, as befits those living in sunnier climates.

Ophir told us that it is rather remarkable that in the relatively short time that the modern state of Israel has existed, the official spoken language is modern *Hebrew.* I've learned recently that an early immigrant to Israel from Russia, in the 1880's, decided that only Hebrew would be spoken in his house, regardless of the fact that his poor wife didn't speak or understand it. He was furious when he found her singing German songs to their young son.

"Father," said the upset child in Hebrew, having heard his father shout at his mother. After that they all spoke Hebrew, as did their friends and neighbours. In time there was a Language Institute that 'invented' words for the modern world.

Ophir took us to the Spanish *Sephardi* area, a world of tiny narrow streets and lots of synagogues. We went in one to hear the most famous cantors in Israel; they had fabulous voices. In another synagogue the men got offered cups of tea, but we women didn't. Just before dawn, we went to an open bakery for most welcome coffee and patisserie. Back to the hotel for a bit more sleep before the day's activities.

One day we left busy Jerusalem behind, and as we emerged from the tunnel, had a sudden glorious view of the open, rocky countryside, with sparse vegetation and occasional Bedouin encampments, flocks of goats searching for food amongst the sparse vegetation. We drove mainly downhill towards the Dead Sea, to Masada, the huge mountain fortress a thousand feet above it. It is possible to walk up a winding path of many steps, but we went up in a cable car, an adventure in itself. The top is large and fairly flat. Herod the Great built a palace there on three levels, carved into the rock; there was a sophisticated bath house with running hot water, a synagogue too, and extensive storage for grain to feed the large garrison stationed there.

During the Jewish revolt against the Roman occupation, which led to the fall of Jerusalem, about a thousand Jewish zealots camped there. Rather than be slaughtered by the besieging Roman Army, they apparently chose to commit suicide. There was an excellent museum on the site too.

We stayed at *Kibbutz Lavi* again, arriving in time for *Shabbat*, the hotel full of excited children, their parents, and grandparents, all dressed in their best. Ophir had brought his wife Sara, and baby Shamai, ten months old, so of course I was in my element.

We walked through the gorgeous gardens to the synagogue for the service. Then there was the festive dinner with over a hundred people seated round tables. It began with singing *Kiddush,* the blessing, and breaking *challah,* the special bread. During the meal, people were singing, clapping, and dancing, the atmosphere so joyful, I'd never experienced anything like it before. The food was delicious too. Having finished my meal, I took little Shamai out for a walk so that his parents had a chance to enjoy theirs.

The following evening, Ophir arranged another festive dinner, *Tu b'Shevat Seder,* a mystical celebration of nature. We sat round a large table on the veranda, taking it in turns to read aloud from the book of *rabbinic mitzvot* and *barakhot,* commands and blessings. We ate sacred foods mentioned in the Bible: barley, nuts, dates, grapes, and figs. Wine is sacred too, and we drank toasts during the meal. White wine symbolised winter; red added made it pink for spring, light red for summer and finally just red wine for autumn. At the end of the meal, Ophir and Sara sang the *Havdalah*, the prayer that concludes *Shabbat*.

There are seven High Holy Days throughout the year, each with their own ritual significance. It was soon to be *Rosh Hashanah*, New Year. It is traditional to greet people by saying, "Happy New Year, may you be inscribed in the Book of Life." As God has decreed the time of death of an individual, so he inscribes their name only if they have done well. Maybe this tradition ensures good behaviour. It's a lovely idea.

A few days later some of the residents at *Kibbutz Lavi* invited us to their homes. We visited Edith Gold, taking presents which we'd been advised to bring with us from the UK. Edith talked about life on the *kibbutz*; she and her late husband were founder members, and their two sons, daughters-in-law, and nine grandchildren all lived nearby. She was dismissive of the *Haredim,* the ultra-Orthodox Jews who have a lot of political influence. She said there was much good happening in Israel, and most people wanted to live at peace with their Arab neighbours.

"After all you can't tell the difference between Arabs and Jews if you see a bunch of teenagers," she said. "They all look alike... dress alike... play the same music. My husband had an Arab Christian carer. He was a wonderful man and became a great friend. He's looking after another old couple on the *kibbutz* now..."

Next we went to Tel Dan, a nature reserve, from which part of the River Dan flows into the Sea of Galilee. The surging flow of water, wide, deep, and very clear, was an incredible sight. We wandered through winding paths alongside the river, and Ophir quoted the beautiful Psalm 137; "By the waters of Babylon... at the willows there we hung up our harps." He told us that the ancient Israelites in exile had continued to worship their God, rather than the gods of captors, and this was what made Judaism unique, and why it survived. Time spent at Tel Dan was a highlight for me.

Our last visit in Galilee was to Dalmanutha, an ecumenical, open air chapel by the Sea of Galilee. It had a stone altar and log seats around it, fringed by flowering trees and bushes. I'd been there before and loved it, a beautiful, spiritual place. Bill took a service there. We sang several hymns, and said Psalm 27. Afterwards I paddled in the sea and collected some shells and stones.

Back in Jerusalem after peaceful Galilee, a different atmosphere with the armed guide outside the door of the Mount Zion. The next day we visited Yad Vashem, the Holocaust memorial. First we saw the Avenue of Righteous Gentiles, with carob trees planted in memory of those people who helped the Jews during the Second World War, twenty thousand to date. At the children's memorial we filed through darkness surrounded by tiny symbolic candles, while a voice read out the names of the million and a quarter children who died in the camps. The main underground museum had a zigzag layout; the excellent guide kept us moving through, looking at maps, facts, and figures, and hundreds of artefacts; very sad personal effects, but also beautiful paintings, poetry, and accounts of theatre groups and schools for children.

The final memorial hall had shelves of files containing the stories of identified victims, empty shelves bearing witness to the unknown lost whose stories will never be known. There were photographs too. We went out up a slope and came out to see a panoramic view of forests and Jerusalem, symbolising the world emerging from the darkness. It was such a relief to come out into the open air again, none of us could talk for quite a while.

Study tours always included talks from a variety of scholars; one we met was Dr Ilan Pappe, an Israeli 'revisionist' historian and writer, friend of Nur, my Palestinian lecturer at St Mary's. Dr Pappe told us that he is a controversial figure in Israel, his views unacceptable to many Israelis; among some he is even regarded as a traitor.

"At the moment I'm involved with a charity which runs kindergartens for Jewish and Palestinian children; we believe that peace in Israel will eventually occur through similar projects... especially among children and young people."

Asked about the wall, Dr Pappe said, "It is akin to apartheid". He was immediately challenged by several people.

"No surely not! What about Jewish safety? Israelis have to prevent suicide bombers coming in…"

"It is how it is routed, rather than the wall itself. It makes it difficult for people to work, to take their children to school… they have to get permits to get through it… to get to hospital appointments… or to visit friends…"

David, a Jewish judge, had already walked out of the room and others of our party clearly weren't happy with what Dr Pappe was saying either. We had seen the wall earlier, from the Palestinian side; covered in graffiti, the towering concrete structure literally cuts villages in half. We could see it from the hotel, too, snaking across the land. I thought the wall was horrible, but didn't feel confident enough to say so, in front of those in our group who clearly knew more about it than I did. In my opinion it was a good thing that Ophir had invited speakers who sympathised with the Palestinians, especially as Dr Pappe was Jewish. Incidentally, from the Israeli side, the wall is landscaped with trees and bushes and doesn't look so menacing.

During dinner that evening, David, who had Zionist views, had a heated discussion with Ophir about what Dr Pappe had told us. Zionists, the original founders of the land, believe that the Jews have a God-given right to live in Biblical Palestine, regardless of the indigenous population. Ophir clearly disagreed, although he didn't say so directly.

On our last evening, Ophir took us all to a concert of *Sephardi Latino* music in a newly built concert hall, with a buzzing, excited atmosphere. There were eleven very lively items; dancing and singing, with a full orchestra, and it included an especially good act by some Turkish children. John hadn't been to a concert for forty years, and really enjoyed it, and I loved the music.

Before going to the airport, we drove to the Ben Shemen Forest, part of which was being re-forested following the felling of diseased trees. We were each given a seedling tree to plant there. Holes had already been dug, and we could choose from a cypress, a pine, or a 'crown of thorns' tree. What a lovely idea; they must have grown quite tall now, ten years later.

We didn't have long to wait for the next study tour; we set off again at the end of April 2006, our third visit in eighteen months. Ophir met us at the airport, with Uri, the driver we had had the year before. This time the theme was 'Memory'. We stayed again at the gorgeous Mount Zion Hotel; it was exciting to be back in familiar surroundings and with some friends from previous tours.

The next day we went to *Har Zikkaron,* Memory Mountain, to see part of the rehearsal for Independence Day. A verse from Genesis, in Hebrew, was displayed about the grave of Theodore Hertzl, whose Zionist vision led to the founding of modern Israel.

'May he give to you the blessing of Abraham, to you and your offspring with you, so that you may take possession of the land, where you now live as an alien, land that God gave to Abraham.' [Genesis 28:4]

We sat in tiered seating overlooking a large parade and watched the young men and women soldiers of the Israeli Defence Force, marching with a military band, parading their colours and forming complex patterns. It was quite uplifting seeing them, all clearly enjoying the occasion. That evening we sat on steps overlooking the Western Wall, watching the brief, solemn ceremony marking the beginning of Memorial Day, commemorating the fallen. It was very crowded, full of young people, with the army and security police much in evidence. We walked back through the Jewish Quarter of the Old City; the stone alleyways and arches looked beautiful at night.

The next day, *Yom Ha Zikkaron,* Memorial Day, we went to the military cemetery on Mount Hertzl. It was very busy. Stalls were piled high with bunches of flowers and bottles of water, given away free. All the graves are standardized; engraved on the headstone (known as the 'pillow') are details of the deceased, including their name, age, and date of death. The grave is surrounded by a low wall enclosing a rectangular bed planted with rosemary and lots of flowering plants: roses, lilies, etc. Flowers were placed on the 'pillow'; some had many bouquets already. Ophir told us that at the end of the day, soldiers would place flowers on graves which had none. Using flowers is recent in Israel; the original custom was to place a small stone on the grave as a mark of respect.

As we sat on a low wall, a siren went off, and an eerie hush fell. We could hear, but not see, the ceremony; a rabbi led prayers, a cantor chanted a psalm. People walked past, but quietly; Ophir explained that however secular they were personally, most Jews showed respect for religious values. As the civil speeches began, the mood lightened. We spent the rest of the morning looking at various memorials – amongst them one to Jewish soldiers who fought with the Allies in the Second World War – and the long, high Memorial Wall for the Jews with no known graves.

That afternoon a talk by Father Kamal Farrah, a Palestinian Christian priest, originally from Bir'am, a village on the borders of Israel and the Lebanon. During 1948 it was evacuated for security reasons, ostensibly for two weeks; in fact the villagers were never able to return there. As an Israeli citizen, Father Farrah respects what Jews have been through and their longing to return to Jerusalem, but Palestinians have rights too, to have their own state. The role of Christians in the Middle East is reconciliation, starting with the recognition and acceptance of others; people should be talking to each other of the future, not the past.

Father Farrah considered that the West bears some responsibility for the extremism of Islam; ironically, as I write this some nine years later, the situation has escalated, worldwide. He said that Arabs see the injustice of the West dealing differently with Israelis and Palestinians. They also think that the West is ignorant about Islam.

That evening, the Independence Day celebration began; first we went to the Great Synagogue, where we stayed just a few minutes to absorb the atmosphere and beautiful haunting music, which Ophir says he can't stand. I love it. We had dinner in a bookshop cum café cum restaurant; someone found a book saying that women are psychologically ill and a menace to society and themselves. We thought it hilarious but it was obviously a serious treatise, published in 1947. Afterwards we walked along crowded streets, full of families, young people dancing to street musicians, people bonking each other on the head with squeaky hammers (on sale at stalls) or spraying each other with shaving foam. It was a very exuberant, happy evening and with no drunkenness or litter to be seen.

The next day we set off for Galilee, stopping in Tel Aviv en route. Israel is such a small country, journeys are never very long. There we saw the superb Independence Museum, which tells the story of the Jewish Diaspora, ending with the foundation of the State of Israel. The best part was the architectural models of synagogues from all over the world.

After dinner at Kibbutz Lavi we met Sheila, who came to Israel in 1951, with a group of thirty-five members of the Zionist Youth Movement. Some had arrived in England in 1937 as *Kindertransport* children, much affected by the Holocaust. Wanting to build a place of safety they were assigned a hilltop near the Sea of Galilee. They lived in tents, clearing the land with no equipment. Water was delivered in tankers and had to be boiled as it was polluted. By 1955 they had some houses, piped water, and crops growing. They built a synagogue and created a religious *kibbutz*. Today they are a community of four generations, some seven hundred people. They have a thriving hotel, a synagogue furniture factory, as well as a running farm with a dairy herd, growing fruit and vegetables.

We visited Bir'am the next day, which we'd recently heard about from Father Farrah. We were taken round the ruined, overgrown village by a former resident; it had wonderful views looking towards the mountains of Lebanon, and was still a beautiful place despite its sad history. There had been about a thousand people living there, who for two weeks sheltered in the olive groves at night. Bitterly cold, seven children died. Everyone then scattered; families were split and some never saw each other again. There are now about four thousand Bir'am descendants, some of whom still own the keys to their former homes. The church there was later restored and is still in use, as is the cemetery.

Another day we met two young women talking about their work with volunteer pupils from Jewish and Palestinian schools. Initially, meetings are separate, so the young people can learn about who is the 'other' for them. After a while they meet together, to discuss things even if they disagree. Sometimes friendships are formed between Jewish and Palestinian youngsters, which can only be positive for the future. Another positive initiative is the unique Christian Kibbutz, *Nes Amin,* founded in the fifties by Dutch and Swiss Christians, an important part of the interfaith community. They have a hotel and run educational programmes, but have recently had to close their rose-growing hothouses due to the decline in tourism. We had an excellent dinner there.

Back in Jerusalem again, some of us went shopping in the Arab market in the Old City. We saw a distressed young man, handcuffed between two policemen, being marched along the street; minutes later an Arab man swore at Scottish Barbara, "F*ing Jew", which wasn't nice, but luckily she didn't mind. We saw again the gorgeous view of the city from the Mount of Olives, rays of sunlight glinting from the Golden Dome; nearby a camel drinking from a bottle of water. I love camels.

It was Sunday. Visiting the Church of the Holy Sepulchre, or the Church of the Resurrection as it is known by Eastern traditions, we heard chanting and saw a procession of Franciscan monks. Our guide had explained the complexities of the church so lucidly, that hearing the monks, it wasn't just an ugly confusing building full of tourists with flashing cameras; instead it was several worshipping communities collected under one huge roof. I found it a moving experience.

On to the Garden Tomb, popular with Americans and Europeans as an alternative site of Jesus' crucifixion and burial; a rocky cliff overlooking the bus station was reputed to be Golgotha, and nearby was a tiny tomb, in the hollowed rock. General Gordon of the Battle of Khartoum particularly favoured this site. John told us all that General Gordon was a sapper, generally regarded in the Army as 'mad, married, or Methodist' and not to be taken too seriously. This caused some hilarity. It's an attractive, peaceful place, full of flowering trees and bushes, but the weight of tradition is behind the Holy Sepulchre as the most likely site of the crucifixion.

The next stop was Mount Hertzl, and the Valley of Lost Communities, a man-made quarry fashioned out of huge, cyclopean blocks of stone, in areas of different levels, linked by narrow alleyways. Each area geographically represents a European country: Germany, Poland, Russia, Romania, France, Czechoslovakia, etc., with the names of communities carved into the stone. It conveyed the sheer enormity of the numbers of people lost in the Holocaust, but understated, which made it all the more poignant. It had the silence of death, but was also peaceful, with trees, grass, and flowers above the towering cliffs. Visiting it was an incredible experience, one of the abiding memories of the trip. On entering it, I thought, *This couldn't possibly have happened*, whilst knowing all too well that it had.

Ophir was unable to come with us to visit Bethlehem; as an Israeli citizen he is not allowed by law to go into an Arab town on the West Bank, it is potentially too dangerous. We went through the security centre, a horrid place like an aircraft hanger where we had to show our passports, then go through endless revolving gates. We were met by Elias, our guide, and taken to the ecumenical international centre, run by the Lutheran church for the Palestinian community. They have centres for media, craft, and sport, and run courses for children on Friday and weekends. An impressive place, and it had a super gift shop.

The highlight of the visit was to Dehaishe Palestinian Refugee Camp, established in 1950; initially the people lived in tents. There are 10,000 people there now, three thousand families, Christian and Muslim. It is one of the largest refugee camps. There are sixteen refugee camps altogether, ten in Gaza, the rest in Jordan, Syria, and Lebanon. Dehaishe has hospitals, schools, a computer centre, and a library donated by Norma Major. During the *intifada,* Japan donated a physiotherapy unit and Italy a maternity hospital. Some of their people are highly qualified scientists, lawyers, and doctors, but work permits are needed and hard to obtain, there is very little work available. Most families have someone injured or in prison. When questioned, our host admitted that neighbouring Arab countries had not helped to any great extent.

They were so hospitable, the family we visited. Sitting on sofas and chairs in a large, L-shaped room, we were given tiny cups of coffee and then glasses of mint tea, served from a tiny adjoining kitchen by our host's wife. Her daughter and three small children were visiting and sat with their grandmother, all very friendly and happy to entertain us. I felt very emotional when we said goodbye, it was a privilege to have been there.

We said goodbye to Jerusalem and set off for Be'er Sheva, in the Negev, en route picking up a lovely Palestinian scholar, Fatmeh, about to complete her PhD about Arab women's memories of the 1948 War. She told us that 80,000 Bedouin are living here in forty-five unrecognised villages. Since 1948, their semi-nomadic way of life has been affected by modernity; many have been expelled, their land confiscated and movement restricted.

We arrived in Abu-Kaf, which had no signpost. As we got off the minibus, a small boy came up and held out his hand to shake mine – what a touching welcome. We were taken to a nearby house and sat on cushions against the wall. Again, like Dehaishe, there were most welcoming, hospitable people plying us with refreshment as we listened to our host. All the time small children were wandering quietly in and out, and the little boy who shook my hand was listening to everything, chin on hand.

Five hundred people were living at Abu-Kaf, with no sewage system, rubbish disposal, or electricity provided – they have their own generators. Initially they were well-disposed towards Israel, and they did military service. Then their land was confiscated and their appeal for its return was rejected by the Supreme Court. Now they feel that the world does not distinguish between Muslims in general and Muslim fanatics, and the press is not sympathetic either. After the talk we were shown round their farm, containing camels, sheep, and goats.

We went next to a recognised Bedouin town, Laq'ia, and to see a Centre for Women's Advancement and Improvement. There we met a dynamic woman who runs a desert embroidery project, keeping alive traditional skills and employing over a hundred women who supply their shop. The needlework is done with cross stitch on fine, woven fabric, using bright colours often on a black background; they do traditional geometrical patterns. They produce most attractive table mats and runners, purses, bookmarks, shawls, and garments. There is also a young leadership camp for 15 to 18-year–olds, and a mobile library and special needs centre for children under six. Bedouin society is changing rapidly and this project is helping women to adjust.

A talk by two professors at the Ben Gurion University of the Negev informed us of the positive education intervention programme amongst Bedouin youth, to help them use their talent and potential. This year their graduates include a young woman gynaecologist, the first Bedouin woman to qualify as a doctor. She will be able to undertake vital work in their community amongst women who often refuse to see a male doctor. It was inspiring hearing these very enthusiastic speakers. Even John stayed awake.

Also at Be'er Sheva, John was delighted to see the Allenby Memorial, a plaque which commemorates the successful charge of the Australian Light Horse in 1917, which captured the town's vital water supplies from the German-led Turkish Army.

Our final day was great because we were taken to see the Negev Desert. In the Avedat National Park we walked by a river along a valley, towering cliffs each side, a beautiful, awe-inspiring place. It was very hot. Later, in jeeps, we were taken for a drive through the heart of the Negev Desert. It was so exciting, not least because the jeep was bumping and lurching about and I couldn't stop laughing. The views were spectacular, with hills, valleys, a pool below a waterfall, where some boys were swimming. It was wonderful. I loved every minute.

We'd left the hotel that morning, already packed. After a long drive, we arrived at the Carmel Winery, at Rishon Le Zion, a Jewish town. It was a huge place with several hundred other people in celebratory mode. The food was delicious. There was live music, with a singer and keyboard; people were singing along, clapping, dancing – even getting onto tables and benches. It was the most exuberant, uninhibited, infectious atmosphere I'd ever experienced.

John got up; I thought he was going to the loo, but no, he grabbed me and started dancing. It was so exciting, we hadn't danced together for thirty years or more. Ophir took a photo of us with my camera; he was most amused, as were our fellow travellers, some of whom were dancing too.

It was sad when midnight came and we had to leave. We went straight to the airport for a night flight, but I was too excited to sleep on the plane. It had been the absolute best of our study tours in Israel.

Chapter 16

My Mother

I'm in Nottingham for the weekend, and I'm thinking about my mother. On July 24th it will be six years since she died, just before her ninety-fourth birthday, and next month on August 18th it will be a hundred years since she was born. It's quite hard to believe that actually. Until fairly shortly before she died she never seemed old, and now here I am officially old myself, although I don't feel it.

In the course of writing my life story, my relationship with my mother has figured quite a bit, mostly the difficult times, and there were many years of that after I got married. But after Fish had his first stroke, just before Christmas 1992, I went to stay at Park Hall to help Mum, and Fish had to go into hospital. After that, Mum and I talked and talked; we caught up on events of the last thirty years. We laughed a lot and began to get on well again, as we had when I was first grown up. David came over too, and we had a lovely time together in spite of worry about Fish. I want now to write about Mum's life and to record some family history too.

My mother's father was Arthur Llewellyn Meyricke, from an ancient family that originated in Wales. He had wanted to marry Winifred Mary Richardson, my mother's mother, when he first met her, but couldn't afford to until seven years later, as he was a curate at St John's church, Whitby, and earning very little.

Winifred, or Winnie as she was generally known, was the eldest daughter of the Reverend John Horsfall Richardson. He'd been a vicar in Hedon, Yorkshire, until 1902, when he inherited Park Hall from a cousin, who had bought the house in 1856. He promptly retired and lived at Park Hall with his family until he died in 1941, on my first birthday. His other children were Mabel, known as Mamie, Jack, who was wounded in the First World War and died just before his father, and Clifford. Winnie was the only one who married.

The Richardsons were a close family; after he inherited Park Hall, my great grandfather John had his siblings to stay during the summer. They all used the tiny two up, two down cottage behind Park Hall. He had a studio built in the garden, above the tennis court, for his younger brother Frederic, an artist who became well known; he was a contemporary of Dame Laura Knight, and for a while part of the Newlyn School of painters in Cornwall. Frederic married Elsie, who was thirty years younger, in his late sixties, and they had two sons, John and Patrick, who were contemporaries of Mum and her sisters.

John's half sisters, Evie and Ethel, ran a girls school in Rickmansworth. Janet was the matron and Arthur the headmaster of St Peter's Court, Broadstairs, a boys prep school in which my brother David was subsequently educated. I like to think that my teaching career arose from Richardson roots.

Arthur and Winifred were married in September 1911, and the reception was held in the garden at Park Hall, the Richardson family home. I have a lovely photograph of them taken in front of the house; a hundred years later, Emma, David's daughter, and Hugh Griffiths had their wedding reception there too, in teepees erected on the old tennis court.

My mother was born in Whitby on August 18th, 1915, the eldest of three daughters, and soon afterwards the family moved to the newly built vicarage in Aislaby. Mum's father was appointed the vicar of St Margaret's church there, where he ministered for the next thirty-seven years. Catherine (Kate) was born on April 29th 1920, and Joan on 16th September 1922.

Arthur Meyricke had an older brother, Robert, who was killed in the First World War, in France. He also had three Meyricke cousins. Robert was killed during the Boer War in 1902, Edward died in steeple chasing in 1905, and Rupert died in the First World War. This meant that Arthur was the only male survivor of that branch of the Meyricke family, and as he had no sons, when he died on April 22nd 1950, the line ended with him.

From her father, Mum inherited Dinham Lodge, the erstwhile Meyricke family mansion, in Ludlow, Shropshire. It was originally owned by her great grandfather, Robert Meyricke, who was reader of Ludlow; it was his three grandsons who predeceased their cousin Arthur. For some years it had been rented to the council, who were using it for offices. They said she couldn't take possession; instead they issued a compulsory purchase order. At the time Mum was upset about it, she told me,

"After all, we didn't have a home of our own, we were still living at the vicarage."

Recently, I saw Dinham Lodge when John and I were staying nearby. Quite big, an imposing red brick, three-storied Georgian house with a high-walled garden. I felt emotional seeing it; I stood outside for ages and was almost tempted to knock on the front door. Equally moving was finding memorials to Uncle Robert and other Meyricke ancestors in the nearby parish church of St Lawrence.

My mother's grandmother, Kate, had a younger brother, Charles Clarke, who had been an Army officer, but as was the custom, resigned his commission when he married Emmy, who was Irish. Family legend has it that when Uncle Charlie died suddenly while on holiday in Italy, and his wife didn't want him to be interred there, his nephew, Mum's father, went to the rescue and smuggled Charlie's body back to England hidden in a grand piano. His wife, Aunt Emmy, continued to live in their large mansion, Frensham Grove, near Farnham in Surrey. Still young, childless, and wealthy, Emmy wanted to train as a nurse. She travelled up to a London hospital daily in a chauffeur-driven car, did her training, and nursed there for a number of years.

Mum used to visit Aunt Emmy when she could, as had my grandfather; quite a character, and very deaf, her visitors communicated with her via an ear trumpet.

One day she said to my mother, "Eve, if I leave you this house when I die, will you live in it?"

Mum was astonished, of course, but thrilled. "Thank you, Aunt Emmy, that's terribly kind of you… of course we'll live here. It will be wonderful to have our own house…"

I hadn't long been away at the naval school when I heard from Mum that Aunt Emmy had died. It was lovely for me that the house was only ten miles from school, so I'd be able to go back there for days out and half-terms. David wasn't so lucky, as his school was in Kent.

I couldn't believe the size of Frensham Grove. We drove up a tree-lined drive and parked in front of a large, three-storied red brick house. Behind it was a pine wood; to one side a lawn surrounded on three sides by flower beds. On the other side of the house, a fair-sized vegetable garden. In front, there were extensive lawns and, beyond, more woods. At the edge of one lawn was a giant sequoia or redwood tree, very tall and with fascinating spongy bark. As we explored the path through the woods below we came across a lake, with a rickety bridge across it.

The estate included a fair-sized house at the bottom of the drive; at the other end, a bungalow where Mrs Hine lived. She helped Mum in the house, and also made us marmalade custard puddings;

delicious at first, I'm afraid they appeared so regularly that we ungratefully got heartily sick of them.

Inside the house a wide staircase with a shallow tread, which led to an open landing edged with a balustrade, with several bedrooms opening off it. Through a swing door was a bathroom and loo, and another staircase led upstairs to ten attic bedrooms. It really was a superb place for children to explore and play in, inside and out. In one attic room was a table tennis table, and billiards in another; we enjoyed both games and made full use of them. It was particularly good fun when we had friends to stay.

To the left of the bathroom door were a couple of steps leading to a half landing; there were my parents' bedroom and bathroom, and another staircase leading down to the kitchen area, and upstairs to the attic rooms. There was a huge kitchen, a separate larder for food, a pantry where the china and glass were kept, and beyond the kitchen a scullery for washing up. Outside the back door was a vegetable garden where Fish grew potatoes, Jerusalem artichokes, and lettuces.

Downstairs were several reception rooms, a huge, forty foot drawing room, an equally large dining room with a conservatory beyond, and another, much smaller sitting room which my parents used most of the time. They had a television in there too. Our school fees were expensive, so Mum had to stop smoking, she told us. They couldn't afford to run the central heating either; in winter the house was icy upstairs, it taught us to get dressed very quickly.

The house was full of beautiful antique furniture and paintings, but a bit dark; the woodwork was all brown. However, my parents, nothing daunted, set to work with paint brushes and soon transformed it. They kept the large garden going too, cutting acres of grass. Rather to our dismay, David and I were press-ganged into helping in the garden too, during our holidays. But we did have time for family games of cricket, which Fish always loved. There was a set of croquet hoops and mallets too, which Fish set up on the lawn by the sequoia tree, and in the evenings, we all played mahjong. It was the only game Mum joined in with.

"The tiles are pretty," she'd say. "I don't like playing cards…"

Mum and Fish were hospitable and often entertained. They gave a seventieth birthday party for Gar, Fish's mother. Six of his seven siblings came, plus their other halves, and Fish employed stewards from the royal yacht to wait at table. I remember part of Fish's speech:

"We were so lucky as a family to come through the Second World War without losing anyone… unlike the First. Mummy lost her two brothers, and Daddy lost two brothers, a stepbrother, and a brother-in-law… it must have been an awful time…" It was my first 'grown up' occasion, and I was the youngest there.

In October 1955, we heard that Uncle Clifford, Ducky's brother, had died. It was expected that he would leave Park Hall to John Richardson, his nephew, the elder son of John Richardson's artist brother Frederic, but instead Uncle Clifford broke Richardson entail and left it to Mum instead, so that she would have a home near Ducky. I loved my room overlooking the valley. Years later my son Edward and daughter Clare were born there, and Mum added an adjoining 'nursery', a room with a shower, built over the garage.

David and I knew the house well already; we'd spent a lot of time with Aunt Mamie, who was an indulgent great-aunt. Uncle Clifford we knew less well; he was a music teacher at Aysgarth, a boy's prep school near York, and was only there during the holidays.

Mum and her cousin, John Richardson, a doctor with a busy practice in Devon, had always been good friends. John visited Yorkshire every summer for many years and never minded that Mum inherited Park Hall instead of him. Recently I met one of his daughters, the third of his eight children. Diana is three years younger than me. Thanks to her I have photos of our shared great-grandparents and other relatives. It was quite an event to acquire a 'new' cousin, and we get on very well.

Park Hall is built on a hill, facing south; outside it a flight of stone steps, steep grass banks on either side, leads from the terrace to the sloping lawn below. Beyond is a sunk fence and steps to another lawn on the left, a tennis court on the right. Fields below drop down to the valley, the River Esk, and the North York Railway; above them is the large, sprawling village of Sleights, and beyond, a distant view of a very steep hill and the road which leads to the moors.

The old studio (built for Great Uncle Frederic) overlooked the tennis court; David and I were allowed to play in there. It had an old iron stove; we used to light it, boil a kettle, and make powdered tomato soup. Beyond the studio was an upward sloping stretch of garden full of old gooseberry bushes, then a wood of huge beech trees, hollies, and rhododendrons, which led up to a high stone wall. Set in between tall stone pillars, two side gates and two large central wooden gates opened on to the gravelled drive, leading down to the front door at the side of the house. The wall extended from the gates, sweeping round behind the old cottage and the kitchen garden. A back drive led from the garage, past two cottages on the left, and Park Lodge (my grandmother's house), behind its own high walls. I can picture it clearly even if I haven't conveyed the size and layout of the property.

The front door opened onto a tiled hall; to the left was the morning room, beyond it the 'Home Guard Room', so named during the war; a door to a large greenhouse was on one side and on another a door leading to the garage. Off the hall on the right a large drawing room and dining room, with French windows and a panoramic view. There were lots of family portraits on the walls, some very large and imposing.

The kitchen had an adjoining larder and pantry; on the wall was an array of bells, with connections leading to the main rooms. They still worked, with a loud, echoing clang, and we always enjoyed trying them out. There was a large, dark, creepy cellar below, full of dusty wine bottles. Beyond the kitchen was a separate, self-contained wing, initially occupied by Mrs Cowburn, the housekeeper. After Ducky died, nine years later, Hilda, John, and small daughter Gillian moved there from Park Lodge.

We had lived at Frensham for about four years when Fish heard that he was being posted to Malta. It was impractical and expensive to keep both

houses, so my parents sold Frensham and moved all the antique furniture from there to Park Hall, on March 8th 1958. They lived there full-time after Fish retired in October 1973.

Mum was tall and slim with light brown hair which went blonde in summer. I always thought she 'helped' it but she assured me she didn't when I asked her. It eventually went a silvery grey. She always had it permanently waved in the same style. She loved clothes and was always very elegant, even in her gardening clothes. She was reserved and very self-contained. She kept a diary daily all her life, which must have reinforced that reserve; she rarely showed emotion, she had the 'stiff upper lip' approach typical of her generation. She had a great sense of humour though. Mum got on particularly well with men, for whom she 'sparkled'.

She especially enjoyed parties and entertaining, and was in her element supporting Fish in his naval career; several of his confidential reports commented on that. She was devoted to Fish and he to her. I went with Fish in the ambulance when he was admitted to Whitby Hospital. Later that evening I took Mum to see him. As soon as he spotted her, Fish held his arms wide, saying,

"My beautiful darling." That's what I call romantic.

Mum and Fish taught themselves to paint, he with oils, Mum with watercolours. Mum did some landscape, but mainly flowers. Fish did landscape and still life, and he did lovely pen and ink sketches too. We have many of their paintings in our house, as well as our daughter Clare's heraldry and calligraphy; she inherited their talent.

Mum was known as 'Mummy Eve'. This came about when her sister Kate's children were small. Mum occasionally looked after them, and as their voices were similar, they called her Mummy too; as Kate had married fifteen years after Mum, my Edward was only seven months younger than Kate's Robbie. In time our children called Kate 'Mummy Kate', and their grandmother 'Mummy Eve' too. The title suited her well. I had the impression that Mum never really wanted to be a grandmother, not that she ever said as much, but she did like her grandchildren when they were older.

When Mum was seventy, Fish wrote to tell me that Mum was going to have an operation for breast cancer; she'd ignored the symptoms for about three years. I was very shocked, having had a feeling that all wasn't well with her some weeks earlier. She denied anything being wrong, of course. Apparently the surgeon didn't rate highly her chances of recovery, but Mum was indomitable; despite radiation burns and being hospitalised the following year with a bad attack of the psoriasis which had plagued her since her teens, she did completely get over it, and lived for more than twenty years afterwards.

Mum and Fish were very involved with village life. Mum was chairman of the parish council and organised the church flower rota. She and Fish mowed the village green outside Park Hall and the churchyard. Mum got many prizes for flower arranging in local competitions as well.

When Fish had his series of strokes, Mum looked after him faithfully, although not a natural carer, being impatient of illness herself, and hating hospitals. Fish often had accidents.

"Don't tell Mum," he'd say, downing another half pint of bitter at lunch time in the pub opposite Park Hall.

After his final stroke, she couldn't have him at home again; he went into a nursing home in a converted country house, about a mile down the valley. Mum visited him daily, often walking there. The only time she didn't was when she had a cataract operation. Fish died eighteen months later; Mum was devastated, but very stoical.

"I'm not going to cry at the funeral," she said, firmly. I'm afraid that a stiff upper lip isn't a quality I inherited.

Mum survived Fish by fourteen years and stayed at Park Hall, although she didn't like living alone. She loved her garden, working in it every minute she could. I visited her regularly, and she was always very welcoming when any of our children were in Yorkshire; she entertained them and their friends.

"Mummy Eve was a lovely grandmother," Edward told me recently. "I was very fond of her and very sad when she died."

I gave her a large toy polar bear for her eightieth birthday; she was delighted with it. When it got grubby, some years later, we were crying with laughter trying to wash it in the bath. I still have Bear lying on my bed.

I offered to take Mum to New Zealand to see an old friend of hers, but she wouldn't go.

"I don't want to leave Park Hall... I'm not leaving until I'm carried out..."

When Mum was nearly ninety, David had to stop her driving, much to her annoyance.

"I can drive perfectly well, David... I've driven all my life..."

She became very forgetful and unkempt, with stained clothes and a fridge full of food which needed throwing away. David organised daily carers, which Mum hated, and once when David had booked overnight care she locked the front door so they couldn't get in. Eventually she was diagnosed with vascular dementia.

John Marshall, Hilda's husband, still living in the wing at Park Hall, was very kind to Mum after her car was sold; he took her shopping every week. Mum used to wake in the night and go looking for him, and John took her back to her bedroom. In the evening she often went through to John's kitchen saying, "I'm hungry," and he would cook something for her, as she had forgotten that she'd already eaten. "I used to read to Mrs Dalglish," John told me recently. "She liked that. We watched television together too." It was an unlikely but touching friendship.

Then one day David phoned me. "Judy, I've just been talking to John Marshall. He's very sorry, but he can no longer cope with Mum... I've booked an appointment to see the home I told you about. Can you come up to Park Hall and bring Mum over?"

David's sister-in-law Maralyn worked in a care home in Harrogate and spoke highly of it. It wasn't far from where he lived, so he and Lynda would be able to visit Mum there.

"Of course I will, David..." I went to Yorkshire soon afterwards and we took Mum to see it. They had an elderly infirm unit, for just six people. "What do you think of it, Eve?" Maralyn asked her.

"Very nice," said Mum, looking rather grim. "Can we go home now?"

It seemed a happy, comfortable home and I liked Maralyn very much, but I was so sad that Mum would have to leave Park Hall; I had a big lump in my throat at the thought of it. I had a dream about Fish, too.

"Look after Mum," he'd said. It was fleeting but so vivid.

A month later a place became available. It fell to me to take Mum there. It was awful being unable to prepare her for it, because she would have flatly refused to go.

"We're going to have lunch with David and Lynda," I told her that morning, and we set off in my car, sixty miles over the moor. After lunch, David said to me,

"Let's go. Mum, we're going for a drive." They set off in David's car.

"Why is Judy following us?" she demanded. "Why is she in her car, not with us?"

Mum realised where we were as soon as we got there. She let out a terrible wail.

"How COULD you do this to me?" and she started sobbing. Maralyn took us to her room, spacious and bright, with a photo of Fish on the chest of drawers. I tried to explain.

"Mum, it's only for a short while. John isn't very well, he needs a rest. You'll be looked after here."

"I don't need looking after... this is the worst day of my life..."

"Mum, you do. Your body is fine, but your mind isn't... you forget things... You aren't safe on your own anymore." I was so upset I couldn't stay much longer. "Mum, I've got to go back to London... I'll come and see you soon."

I could hardly see to drive through my tears, but David rang before I got to the A1.

"Mum's ok now, she's calmed down. Don't worry, she'll be fine. She'll soon forget all this." Mum's short-term memory was ten minutes at the most, by then, and David said she soon stopped asking to return to Park Hall.

A few weeks later, Maralyn reported a conversation she'd had with Mum.

"Eve, do you know where you are?"

"Yes... I'm in an old people's home."

"What do you think about it?"

"I'm happy... I never thought I would be... but I am."

Another conversation was overheard; "I don't know what I'm doing here," said a fellow resident.

"Neither do I," said my mother. "You just have to sit back and be looked after."

Maralyn looked after Mum beautifully, always made sure she had matching tops and trousers, and socks too, nice beads round her neck, her hair washed and set. It was such a nice home. I went up there regularly, initially staying nearby, then just for the day, which was long enough for Mum. David saw her often and always let me know if anything happened.

"Judy, Mum cut her knee badly this morning, and I had to take her to hospital to have it stitched… You should have heard her with the doctor… 'You bloody man, what are you doing to me? Ooooooooh… you effing bastard… you're hurting me'."

David and Lynda took Mum to a pub for lunch one day. A child was crying.

"Slap it!" said Mum, in a loud voice.

And another time, brandishing her stick she shouted at someone in front of her, "Get out of my way, you fat pig."

We were in Portugal when David phoned.

"Judy, Mum's lost the use of her legs… she can't stand up… we're going to have to move her to a nursing home." Then she couldn't swallow. About six weeks later, she died peacefully, during the night. She did still recognise David and Lynda right to the end, and Robbie too, who went to see her just before she died. I didn't see her as I couldn't leave John. Mum would have understood; she always put Fish first. I was really sad when she died; in spite of our often strained relationship, I did love her.

At times, Mum and I were good friends. We weren't a bit alike, but I did appreciate her qualities. She was always positive, rarely complained; she was well-organised, and made the best of her life, wherever she was.

"I'm so lucky," she'd say.

The last time I saw Mum I was sitting beside her when she said, "I do like your hair, darling."

"It's just like yours," I said, holding up a mirror so she could see.

"So it is," she said, laughing. "You've made my day!"

Mum's funeral was on a sunny August afternoon. As we had done with Fish, the hearse came to Park Hall and we all followed it through the village on foot, her nephews, Kate's children, amongst the pall bearers, the church pretty full. David gave an excellent tribute, and we raised the roof with the hymn *Thine be the Glory.* Mum was laid to rest with Fish; nearby were the graves of her parents, great grandparents, uncles, aunts, sisters, and tiny nephew, David's son William, who died at three months old. It was a fitting final resting place, especially as her father had been the first vicar of the church.

It's ironic really. Fish's step grandfather tried to stop their engagement.

"Jim, you can't possibly marry an impecunious vicar's daughter." My father took no notice, and neither of them had any notion that my mother would inherit three houses.

Now Park Hall has been sold, and it's the end of an era.

Chapter 17

Further Travels

I thought we'd had our last trip to Israel, as lack of interest had led CCJ Study Tours to become unviable. Fortunately though, Lynne Scholefield, a lecturer whom I'd got to know quite well during my BA, was teaching one of the MA modules too.

"Judy, I'm hoping to organise a study tour to Israel just before Easter. I wonder if you and John would like to come with us."

"We'd absolutely love to, Lynne," I said. "I don't even have to ask John, he'll be delighted. When would you like a deposit?"

We were given handouts and the itinerary well in advance; twenty-two students were coming, and in addition to Lynne, who was the leader, Kathleen, a lovely Irish lecturer, a New Testament specialist whose lectures I'd so enjoyed in my undergraduate years. We set off on the 9th of March, 2008.

It was the first time we'd been to Luton Airport; I drove there, managed to miss the turning, and had to go on to the next roundabout to approach it from the other direction. I had pre-booked a car park, but it wasn't clear where to go and, being so early in the morning, there was no-one to ask. In spite of all that we were the first to arrive.

The flight was four hours or so; from the airport we were taken by coach to Tantur, an ecumenical institute outside Bethlehem.

The rooms were comfortable and the food, Palestinian cuisine, was delicious, lots of my favourite salads, humus, and falafel.

This time, the tour was different as we were with a young party; after supper we'd often gather in the large sitting room, a student called Gemma played the piano, and we'd have a sing song, and sometimes people would start dancing too. We'd chat about the places we'd been that day, too, but mostly we'd just listen and watch the youngsters enjoying themselves.

Some evenings speakers came to talk about their life in Israel. We met a Jewish professor, a Palestinian Christian, and lastly Dr Mohammed Hirani, an Israeli Arab.

"I live in Israel, not the West Bank," he told us. "I was born near the Lebanese border. More than half of we Israeli Arabs live in the Upper Galilee, northern Israel; some live in a small area near Tel Aviv, and the rest in the Negev, in the south."

He went on to talk about the 'present absentees' in Syria, Jordan, and Lebanon. The 'Right to Return' is always a point of conflict in peace negotiations; there is resentment that the military chief of the Arab Army is a Jew, and there is only one Israeli Arab member of parliament. Education is an issue too; children are taught the Jewish narrative, about Independence Day rather than the Arab *Nakba,* or disaster.

"This has led to our youngsters receiving religious education in the mosques, and to the rise of Fatah and Hamas... they are both radical and very anti-Israeli."

Dr Hirani told us about positive aspects too. Israeli Arabs living in Israel have a higher standard of living, resented by those in the West Bank and Gaza. Israel is the only country in the Middle East which has no leprosy. There is a hundred percent literacy, whereas in Syria it is only twenty-five percent, and there are a hundred million illiterate Arabs worldwide. There is no Arab university in Israel and only one teacher's training college, but Arabs can attend the Hebrew

University, as he did. Perhaps most importantly, women are much better treated in Israel; thousands are highly educated as well as having freedom of speech and movement.

Dr Hirani said that during partition many villages were destroyed, and seven hundred thousand Arabs became refugees, but many villages were all right, there was no ethnic cleansing. People were given the choice of whether to leave or to stay in Israel. A hundred and fifty thousand remained, now still twenty percent of the population despite all the Jewish immigrants from Russia, Ethiopia, and the Sudan.

Dr Hirani concluded his talk by saying, "I have a good life in Israel and all my children are professionally qualified. I think that very few Israeli Arabs would choose to live in an independent Palestinian state." We all applauded him; such an interesting speaker, and so good to hear an Israeli Arab view, to balance the dominant Israeli political debates about the country.

It was lovely seeing familiar places in Israel and good to visit new ones too. We hadn't been to the Fair Trade Centre near Bethlehem before; a huge emporium full of local crafts, including carved olive wooden objects and jewellery. I bought several presents to take home, and John gave me a silver and opal Jerusalem cross.

"Ooooh, Judy, that's gorgeous," said some of the girls. "How sweet, John giving it to you…"

One afternoon some of us went on the Rampart Walk, something I'd wanted to do for ages. We climbed up steep steps to the top of the broad stone walls round the Old City, starting at Jaffa Gate. The views were fabulous: dwellings, playgrounds, roof tops, backyards, lots of cats. There was a football match in progress, as well as familiar landmarks of churches, which Lynne pointed out from the map. Most dominant was the Dome of the Rock, which glinted in the occasional shafts of sunshine. The walk took us up and down; it took over an hour and was quite strenuous, as well as chilly, and by the time we got to Lion Gate, where it ended, spotting with rain. It was a great thing to have done. It gave me a quite different perspective of the Old City as not just a place of churches, museums, and markets, but a place where people lived and worked.

Our visits included Yad Vashem. Having been there several times, we didn't want to see the Holocaust Museum again, but instead explored the site, including the lovely bookshop, the synagogue, the café, and the hall which commemorates the concentration camps; I think I counted twenty-one, many I'd never heard of.

After lunch back at Tantur we gathered in one of the lounges.

"We've all had an emotional morning," Lynne said, "but I think it's important that we don't dwell on it, or let it spoil the trip... I want to discuss the issues it raised. Most of those who died in the Holocaust were Jews," she went on. "The rhetoric against them took away their humanity... they were regarded as non-people, parasites... less than animals. The Germans were gullible and easily influenced. Hating Jews became a bandwagon, so what chance was there to challenge Hitler? And after all, we Christians had been guilty of anti-Semitism."

We talked about survivor guilt, of the people who'd had to live with what they did to each other through desperation. We talked about heroism, that although people could barely stand for hunger, culture in the ghetto continued with education, music, and drama. Above all they had hope, and despite everything, kept their faith alive.

Someone had read the story of a pregnant survivor, who after the war wanted an abortion because she thought the sound of a crying baby would remind her of the suffering. I mentioned that I'd heard that for those who'd reached Israel after the war, getting married and having children as soon as possible had been important to Jewish survivors.

Lynne thought that European guilt about the Holocaust meant that the terms of partition of Palestine in 1948 were not fully considered, leading to repercussions ever since. Also recalled was a speaker earlier this week who'd said that Jews "play the Holocaust card". After today, no-one found this surprising; we'd had a real reminder of the immense complexity of Israel. It was a really good discussion, enjoyed despite the harrowing subjects talked about.

Our last afternoon at Tantur, Kathleen took us on a walk to Bethlehem, a lovely thing to do. We'd travelled on local buses too, rather than going by coach. Good fun. When I got back later, I went to find John, who hadn't been on the walk.

"Did you have a nice time?" he said. "Darling, I'm afraid my mouth is bleeding, where I had those teeth out last week…"

"I did tell you to delay the extraction…" I said, with more than a little irritation. "We'd better tell someone about it." I was worried as we were leaving Tantur the next day, to go to Galilee.

We went to see the vice rector, Sister Bridget, an Irish nun, who'd been most friendly and helpful.

"You could see a dentist in Jerusalem tomorrow," said Bridget, "or you could go to Galilee with everyone else and see a dentist there. I can ring the hotel and ask them to make arrangements."

"That's very kind of you, Bridget… I think we'd better stay with the group, don't you, darling? You're not in pain, are you?" So that is what we decided.

When we woke the following morning, John's pillow was soaked with blood, and we arrived in Tiberias too late to see the dentist that day. We stayed at the Ron Beach Hotel, which bordered the Sea of Galilee, a gorgeous place with a swimming pool in the grounds. John's tooth sockets bled all over the pillow again that night. After breakfast we went by taxi to a hospital with a dental department. All the signs were in Hebrew, but luckily most of the staff spoke excellent English and were most kind and helpful. John had several tests; after a long wait the blood clot was removed from the tooth socket, and the bleeding stopped, which was a relief.

We had a late lunch in Tiberias.

"I want to look round the shops," I told John. "We're too late to join the others."

"You go, darling, I'll stay here. Why don't you get some earrings to match your Jerusalem cross? I'll pay for them… I think you deserve it after the business with my teeth."

"Thanks, darling… the hospital was quite an experience, but I was disappointed to miss today's visits." I did find some lovely earrings.

It was now the end of the trip; we'd been in Israel for nine days, and we'd so enjoyed it. It was great fun being with the students. Amusing too to hear their plans for exploring the night life and how hungover some of them were the next day. We'd got very fond them all.

"Thanks so much for letting us join the tour," I said to Lynne at the airport. "It's been great… I've learnt so much."

"It was great having you both. Judy, I think you know more about Israel than I do!" Lynne replied.

I soon got itchy feet again. "Where shall we go next, darling?" I asked John. "Turkey? Syria? I've always wanted to go to Damascus… or what about a cruise down the Nile?"

"No, not there…" said John, to most of my suggestions, but we did eventually decide to go on a Saga trip to 'The Imperial Cities of Morocco' for eight days in November.

I had a window seat in the aircraft; as the sun set there was a bright, broad glowing ribbon of yellow and orange on the horizon, silhouetting the wing of the plane.

It was dark when we arrived at the Mansour Eddabhi Hotel in Marrakech. It had four hundred rooms, marble floors and pillars, squashy sofas, chandeliers, expensive boutiques, painted ceilings. I'd never seen anywhere like it before.

I looked out of the window in the morning to see that all the buildings were pink, and there were palm trees everywhere. We went first to the huge Khoutiba Mosque, which could be seen for miles;

unique to Morocco is the live, atmospheric, haunting call to prayer by a *muezzin.*

Next we saw the Bahia Palace, built in the *riad* style, plain outside but WOW, inside it was stunningly beautiful, with a huge open courtyard, while in the centre was a fountain, trees, and shrubs. Through archways were a series of rooms; every inch of the floors, walls, ceilings, archways, windows, and doors were richly, colourfully decorated with geometric patterns. I particularly liked the Qu'ran school, with a niche for the teacher, and in the entrance a large water container for the children to wash their slates. The palace was enormous, but our guide told us we'd seen less than half of it.

The *souk* or market was huge too, much bigger than the one in Jerusalem. We saw a man operating machinery with his foot, making kebab sticks; we saw metal workers with sparks flying and leather workers in tiny little alcoves, sitting amongst piles of hides. There were hundreds of shops with leather goods, ceramics, clothes in dazzling colours.

The next day we spent a few hours at Casablanca. Lunch at a café overlooking the sea, and we explored the newly built, enormous Hassan II Mosque which accommodates twenty thousand worshippers inside and a further eighty thousand in the vast paved courtyard outside. It is hard to visualise such numbers of people.

The interior of our hotel in Rabat was like a ship, the central lounge and dining area surrounded by balconies with rooms opening off them. I was downstairs when I heard John shouting from the fifth floor,

"Darling, I forgot the room key… will you bring it up, please?"

We had a super room with a rooftop view of the city. We visited the *Challah,* the ancient burial place of the fourteenth century royal dynasty. A broad pathway with shallow steps led through trees and large bushes covered in orange flowers. At the shrine was a wishing well, dozens of roaming cats, and on the tops of walls, masses of storks' nests. Rabat is a most attractive town, with wide spacious boulevards, and none of the yellow lines and white arrows that grace our streets at home. There is evidence of the Moroccan French heritage in the many Art Deco buildings, cream-coloured, as are the fleets of taxis.

The next city was Fez, and we stayed at another elegant, spacious hotel with a panoramic view. The *Medina,* the medieval part of the city, has many different areas, each one containing a fountain, a *hammam* (bath house), a bakery, a mosque, and a kindergarten. There are over three hundred mosques and thousands of streets, but no house numbers so the postman has to ask directions at the bakery. There were laden donkeys with men yelling *"Bellak… bellak"* – "Get out of the way." From the balcony of a shop selling leather goods, we held bunches of mint to counteract the smell, as we saw rows of huge vats and people in bare feet trading hides through various stages of curing and dyeing.

We looked through an open door and through the beautiful white, curved arches of Kerrouaine University, said to be the oldest in the world. I felt a sense of awe that we'd been able to glimpse this ancient institution.

The Roman ruins at Volubilis were stunning, as were the King's Stables at Meknes. Built in the seventeenth century in the same pink stone as Marrakech, the arched interiors were vast and apparently accommodated twelve thousand horses. I loved the extensive, paved spacious square in Meknes too, like that of all Moroccan towns; it comes alive at night with musicians, entertainers, and many food stalls.

Leaving Fez, we were driven through the Atlas Mountains. It was pouring with rain, forested, and is known as the 'Moroccan Geneva'. The houses have red-tiled, pitched roofs typical of Swiss chalets. Wealthy Moroccans have second homes here, to ski in winter and escape the heat in summer. It looked very European. In the open countryside I was struck by the soil in the fields, ranging in colour from burgundy to palest ochre. I enjoyed the drive, seeing such varied scenery. Some of our party were complaining about the leaky bus though; they found wet clothes in their suitcases. Wet pyjamas didn't bother me, I was having such a good time and was happy to be back at the Mansour Eddahbi Hotel too.

On our last day we went to the coast. We saw goats perched in the *argan* trees; they looked comical but they actually pick the nuts, otherwise used for cosmetics, amongst other things. After three hours we reached Essaouira, with a stunning view of the Atlantic Ocean beyond. All the houses were painted white, with bright blue doors and shutters. We walked through bustling streets and alleyways of the *souk;* there were pyramids of colourful spices, many varieties of fruits and vegetables. There were pens of chickens, a rabbit in a hutch, lots of cats, and the air was warm and spicy.

By the sea were rows of cannon pointing through embrasures in the stone wall, the Atlantic waves crashing against the rocks below, spray rising high in the air. Many gulls swooped overhead, and there was a prevailing smell of fish. There was a busy working harbour nearby with lots of trawlers, and rows of small, bright blue rowing boats drawn up on the beach. The town is a haven for artists, being so attractive; we passed many galleries and paintings propped against stone walls too.

I loved the day we spent at Essaouira; I think it was the best one of all, but then I enjoyed everywhere we went. Funnily enough I have no recollection of the other people in the party, apart from a couple of moaning minnies who found fault with everything. The tour manager, Anyes, was lovely, as was Madani, the guide.

Soon after our Moroccan trip, I went to college for the graduation ceremony. I was the very last student to go up on the stage to receive my post graduate diploma, which I felt was quite an achievement. Nur came up to me afterwards.

"Hullo, Judy," he said. "What a pity you didn't finish your masters."

Then I saw Lynne in her academic robes.

"Congratulations, Judy," she said. "By the way, I've been meaning to get in touch with you. I'm organising a pilgrimage to Rome just before Easter. Would you and John like to come along too?"

"Thank you so much, Lynne, we'd love to… are you sure that's all right now I'm no longer a student?"

"That's no problem. You'll already know some of the students from our visit to Israel, they're a nice bunch. We'll be there for five days."

This was just what I needed, as I was feeling a bit 'flat' now my student days were over. I went to the bookshop to buy an Eye Witness Guide. I'd been to Rome with my parents as a teenager and had thrown a few coins into the Trevi Fountain, said to be a way to guarantee a return visit there. Little did I expect to find myself there as a rather mature ex-student.

We stayed in a guest house in the centre of Rome, run by some Belgian nuns. It was quite spartan but very adequate, and we were lucky enough to have an en suite bathroom, unlike everyone else.

One of our first visits was to St Peter's. The piazza is imposing, with all the rooftop statues, but I was absolutely bowled over when we went inside; the interior had a huge impact on me, by its sheer size, the sumptuousness of its marble floor, the paintings, the statues, the painting ceiling, and the light. There was so much to look at, to marvel at. Unbelievably enormous; we walked on and on. There were lots of people there but it did not seem unduly crowded. The equivalent of one and a half football pitches, it holds sixty thousand people and a further million in the piazza outside. I'd been impressed by the huge mosques in Morocco, but somehow St Peter's had an extra impact.

We walked for miles in Rome and travelled on local buses too; we saw many churches, ate delicious food in the cafés, explored architectural excavations, and heard speakers. One day in the Piazza

Navone I glanced behind me to see where John was, and I couldn't see him anywhere.

"Has anyone seen John… I've lost him…" I said anxiously. I tried his mobile as we searched; eventually I spotted him strolling across the piazza.

"Where WERE you?" I said… "I thought I'd lost you… we've all been looking for you."

"I wasn't lost… I knew where I was," he said, quite unconcerned.

The highlight of the visit for me, although I'm not a Catholic, was going to the general papal audience at the piazza outside St Peter's, for which we had tickets. There were rows and rows of seats, and there were crowds of excited people of all ages, from many countries, lots of school and college groups waving flags and banners. Digital cameras were flashing constantly. There were two huge screens on either side, so we could see what was happening. A row of cardinals in brilliant red robes were waiting too. At ten, thirty people started cheering as the Popemobile entered. Many of us stood on chairs (including me); the atmosphere was electric. The Pope was slowly driven round behind us, up the side, and across the front to the steps leading up to his throne; we could see him quite clearly. It was quite wonderful. I felt like an excited child.

The Pope addressed us first in French, then Italian, English, German, Spanish, and Polish, talking about his recent trip to Africa. After each speech a cleric announced the names of visiting groups from that country, everyone cheering loudly as they heard their names. The ceremony ended with the Pope chanting the Lord's Prayer in Latin; the words were on our tickets so we could join in. For John this was the most moving moment.

It had been unbelievably exciting, we all thought. As it ended, the rain started; the piazza was empty within minutes, and no litter was left behind. We had a wet walk back to the guest house, a slight anti-climax.

On our last day we had the morning to ourselves. We duly threw coins into the Trevi Fountain and I marvelled at the Italian shop windows, with such intricate displays and wonderful variety of goods. Back home again, we much enjoyed talking about what fun it was being with the students and what a lot of interesting things we'd seen.

We were looking forward to our next Saga trip, to Portugal, when one morning I heard a loud crash and John groaning; I rushed into the hall and found him draped across the bottom of the banisters, having fallen downstairs.

"Whatever happened?" I said, as I helped him up.

"I tripped…" John said. "My side hurts…" I called the doctor, who came to examine John.

"You've broken a rib," he said. "Here's a prescription for some painkillers… Just rest, they'll take a while to heal."

A few weeks later I phoned the doctor, who said John should be all right to go to Portugal.

So on June 6th 2009 we set off again. There was quite a delay in the flight, we seemed to sit at Heathrow for ages, so it was very late in the evening when we had a late meal at our hotel in Oporto, Northern Portugal. The next day we toured the very ornate cathedral, with lots of gilded statues. I was surprised to find that the votive candles were lit by electricity, rather than matches, and the statues of Our Lady were dressed in real robes. Unusual too was the mural of blue and white tiles at the station. We had coffee at a very upmarket McDonalds, which amused me, as did the fact that we had to ask for the loos to be unlocked for our use.

The next day we set off for a cruise up the River Douro, taking us part of the way to Lamego, where we were going to stay. It was a perfect few hours, the scenery just gorgeous, with lots of trees, churches, and houses interspersed amongst them, a loch or two, and later fields of vines clothing the steep hills on either side of the river.

The hotel was lovely too, with its own swimming pool and grounds full of flowering bushes. At dinner we met a couple with a similar age gap to ours, except the man was younger by sixteen years. When they had got married she was a widow, he still single at sixty. We had such a nice time talking to them and others of the party.

Amarante was the destination the following day, fifty miles away by coach. A beautiful medieval town built either side of a river, it had a busy market and an ornate cathedral, with a paved courtyard outside. We had lunch at a café there. Afterwards, John had gone inside to the loo and I was outside taking photographs, when a strange man came up to me.

"Excuse me, I think your husband has had an accident…"

I rushed inside to find John, white-faced, sitting on a chair. "I've hurt my back… I fell down… that kind lady helped me up," he said. "Please thank her for me…"

I asked the proprietor to call a taxi. Two men carried John on a chair to the taxi, and I said to the driver,

"Please take us to the bus station."

I told the tour driver what had happened to John, and he told the taxi to take us on to the hospital. When we arrived there, John was taken away in a wheelchair and I saw him disappear behind closed doors.

I couldn't speak Portuguese…

My mobile phone needed charging…

Where had they taken John?

What was I going to do?

Chapter 18

What Happened Next

What a good thing I had our EEC Health Cards with me, I thought, as I sat in the dingy waiting room. I hadn't a book to read, but at least I had my diary and a pencil so I started to write; *I expect John has a broken pelvis.*

At that minute, Carol, the tour manager, arrived. Almost never was I so glad to see someone I knew. She went to find out what was going on and soon returned to say that John had just been x-rayed. They found that his femur was broken near the hip joint, he would need an operation, and we were going to be taken to another hospital with an orthopaedic department. Carol informed the insurance company about the accident and then she returned to the group, who were visiting a nearby winery.

It seemed ages, but can't have been long before John was rolled onto a stretcher and wheeled into an ambulance, a red one because in Portugal the ambulance and fire service are combined.

We were looked after by a handsome young *bombeiros* or paramedic called David, who bore a striking resemblance to our erstwhile son-in-law, Robert; David frequently patted John and said,

"Are you all right, sir? Are you in pain?" He told me that he'd learned English at school. "I like to practice speaking, otherwise I'll forget it," he said, and we chatted about the Queen, Buckingham Palace, football, and Portuguese history, amongst other things. "I hope I can visit England some day," were his parting words as we said goodbye and thanked him for looking after us.

Then I had to say goodbye to John too. The pouring rain echoed my feelings. It was a desolate moment.

I re-joined the rest of the group, who were very kind and supportive people, and returned with them to our hotel in Lamego, forty or fifty miles away. I phoned the insurance company, and Carol came to see me.

"Judy, I think you should stay here for the rest of the week... when the rest of us go back to the UK, the local Saga agent, Antonio, will take you to a hotel in Penafiel near the hospital."

"Thank you, Carol, that sounds a good idea," I said.

The next day, Carol put me in a taxi to go to the station in Regua, with a timetable for trains to Penafiel. Luckily, the taxi driver spoke good English and helped me get a ticket. I got a taxi to the hospital too, but when I left, the taxi driver didn't understand the word 'station'. Being a Bank Holiday, the ticket office was closed, and when I asked a passing couple where to catch a train to Regua, I was met with a torrent of Portuguese.

"Sorry, I'm English..." I said, which amused them, but they were very helpful. The same thing happened when I asked for the bus to Lamego. Finally, a dozen blank faces later, someone pointed across the road, so I did get back to the hotel. Phew. Later, Gabby told me,

"You don't know what you are capable of until landed in a foreign country, not speaking the language..."

The next day, Carol suggested that I go on the train to Pocino with everyone else, and go back to Penafiel from there. This sounded ok and the trip was spectacular, but it was another Bank Holiday and there were NO RETURN TRAINS. I was very upset not to be able to see John. Near to tears, I joined the group who were having lunch. Afterwards, we visited Pendormo Castle, and I climbed up to the top, quite hazardous, few safety rails; John would have been horrified, but the view was well worth it.

On Saturday, the holiday ended and I went with the group to Porto Airport. There I met Antonio, the holiday company agent, a cheerful, kindly, rotund man. It was a great relief to have someone local who could find out what was going on. Antonio took me to check in at The Pena Hotel, actually just a B&B, and then to the hospital. John and I were expecting to be flown home by air ambulance the next day, but when I got to the ward I was told that John wasn't fit to travel due to suspected internal bleeding. Suddenly, the UK seemed far away and the present rather uncertain. I phoned Edward and Gabby, telling them, rather tearfully, that we wouldn't be coming home after all.

Edward flew out to Portugal on the Monday. Antonio kindly met him at the airport and they joined me at the hospital. When John saw us he said,

"Where's the car? Get me out of here," and was very cross when we said we couldn't.

"Dad looks so thin, doesn't he?" said Edward.

A doctor came to see us to say that he would operate on John's hip the next day, and I signed the consent forms. At last something positive was happening.

Edward had an adjoining room at the hotel, and we found a nice restaurant to have dinner that evening. The next day we walked for miles, exploring Penafiel, stopping at intervals for a drink and something to eat, and kept looking at our watches. Such a relief when Antonio rang to tell us that the operation had gone well and we could now visit John. We went straight away, but he was still rather sleepy so we didn't stay for long. Dinner that evening was celebratory; Ed had an enormous steak, and I had some local fish.

The day ended with a nightcap sitting on the balcony outside my room, enjoying the warm night air.

Edward had to return to England on Thursday, so we had one last day together. A travel agent in the town was very helpful finding a flight; Ed bought some presents to take home, and I was happy seeing a school group of small children, in immaculate uniforms. We visited John, taking refuge in the nearby air-conditioned McDonald's while he rested, and we found another different place to have dinner. We were very sad saying goodbye the next day, but had made the most of the few days together, despite the worry about John.

Edward had bought me a Portuguese phrase book at the airport, and I learnt how to say good morning, please, thank you... And "Excuse me, I'm English." However, it didn't have the word for 'bedpan'.

I soon got into a routine after Edward left. I usually walked to the hospital, which was downhill, looking at the shops on the way. Whilst with John I read a book, or did a puzzle or two in my codeword book. I often stayed to try and get him to eat some supper. The buses didn't run after five, so if it was very hot I took a taxi back to the hotel, otherwise I walked back, admiring the colourful gardens and flowering bushes. I found a swimming pool my last day there and wished I'd found it earlier. At night I occasionally had dinner out, but usually I just stayed in my room and had biscuits and cheese, yogurt, and lots of fruit.

'Mr John' was the only English patient in the hospital, and everyone was very kind and helpful. John wasn't an easy patient; he kept trying to get out of bed and hated the food. Luckily he slept a lot. There was an elderly man with dementia in the bed opposite John. His daughter was very friendly, and we managed a conversation of sorts. I was so touched when she gave me a carrier bag containing useful things like tissues, drinking straws, and a pretty artificial flower which I still have.

There were numerous calls from the insurance company about flying us home; it was impossible to get a clear answer, as they wanted John's haemoglobin reading, then access to his medical records. Finally, Gabby intervened and phoned the insurance company.

"Get my parents back to England, please!" Gabby had been a great support the whole time I was there; no day had begun or ended without a text or phone call. I don't know how I would have managed without her and Edward.

On Sunday 29th June, over three weeks since we arrived in Portugal, departure day finally arrived. Antonio collected me and our luggage and took me to the hospital. An escort nurse arrived to take charge; John, very confused, was taken to the ambulance. I said goodbye to Antonio, who had been wonderful, and after going through endless security checks at Porto Airport, John and I were flown home in a tiny Cessna plane; the nurse was rather bad-tempered, although it was me, sitting beside John, who had to stop him undoing the belt across his stretcher.

After a four hour flight we landed at Northolt Airport. An ambulance took us to Charing Cross Hospital, where Edward and Gabby met us. I was thankful to see them. In the Accident and Emergency Department we were received by a delightful young doctor who examined John.

"I'm afraid your husband will be here for a few weeks," he told me, but by then I'd already realised that John was quite seriously ill. He was tossing and turning, and he pulled out a canula soon after it was inserted. It was midnight before John was taken to a ward, and Edward took me home.

The next day I was waiting by the row of four lifts in Charing Cross Hospital. I got in one, just, as it was so crowded and it stopped on every floor. I rang the bell by the door of Ward 5 West. No one answered for several minutes, and I was back to that feeling of acute anxiety when John was whisked away from me in Portugal.

"Good afternoon, I've come to see my husband John Corry, he was admitted here yesterday."

"Oh, he's just been transferred to the Orthopaedic Ward downstairs," said the nurse.

So off I went again to find him. It was like this for several days; he was put in several different wards as the doctors decided what to do with him. One day I was sitting with John, who was fast asleep, when a doctor came in.

"Mrs Corry, I'm Mr Lewis, an orthopaedic consultant. I just want to bring you up to date with your husband's treatment. I'm afraid John's hip has become infected, and I shall have to operate to remove the prosthesis. Then he will need to have antibiotics intravenously for about six weeks, to get rid of the infection. After that I hope to be able to replace it."

"Thank you so much, Mr Lewis. Will John be able to walk all right in the end?"

"If all goes well he should be all right... I'll keep you informed. By the way, John certainly keeps us amused... yesterday he asked us, 'When am I going to have this baby?'"

On the day of the operation, I went blackberry picking with a friend. My mother had died a few days earlier. I was very sad, but too worried about John to be upset for long. The operation went well, and I think it was about eight weeks or so later, a very up and down time, that John had another operation to replace his hip joint. Of course, with yet more anaesthetic he was very confused afterwards. There was some talk of time in a rehab ward, then one afternoon the ward manager came to see me as I was visiting.

"Mrs Corry, John is going to be discharged next week. He'll have a home support package for six weeks... we'll let you know when it's all been arranged."

I was shocked, I must admit; it wasn't that long since John's third operation. He was very confused, and he had hardly even walked across the ward. He'd been in hospital nearly five months. I dreaded him coming home and wondered how on earth I was going to manage. I had spent the last few weeks reorganising the house. We already had a room downstairs with an en-suite loo and shower, so I got a new carpet fitted and bought an electric bed and armchair.

Late afternoon on November 4th 2009, John was sent home in a taxi. The supervisor from the care agency showed me how to empty his catheter bag, and I sorted out a carrier bag of medication. Poor John didn't really seem to know where he was; he kept looking round and saying,

"I don't remember this…"

For six weeks, John had a twice daily carer helping him wash and get dressed. A physiotherapist gave him exercises, an occupational therapist arranged for grab handles and a shower seat, also a commode. She warned me that John would continue to need help. A social worker assessed my state of mind, which was about as confused as John's with all I had to learn about being a carer. After the discharge package ended, John continued to have a carer in the morning, for which we paid. He had been awarded attendance allowance, which was a great help.

I bought a wheelchair and applied for a blue badge, and I was told about a day centre at St David's Nursing Home for ex-service people, which was a blessing as it gave me a few hours free time. Occasionally John stayed there for a week's respite care. I found those early days very hard and cried more than I had when Clare died; at times I detested John too, but I did know that I was very fortunate in having support from Edward, Gabby, and friends, having good health myself, and not least being able to pay for help.

For weeks, John woke up several times a night, often calling, "Auntie," as if he were a child again, or telling me that the sergeant wanted something, as if he were still in the Army. He had frequent urinary tract infections, which mimic the confusion of dementia, which I thought John had; a specialist in elderly medicine assessed John but said it was too early to tell.

I had a scare after John had been at home for about four months. I'd been out in the garden for a short while, and when I came in I heard John calling from upstairs. Somehow he'd gone up, with his zimmerframe, looking for me. I was horrified, and called the surgery for advice.

The doctor said, "Call an ambulance, to be on the safe side."

The paramedics could find nothing wrong. John just said,

"My wife seems to think I'm confused... I can't think why she called you."

The ambulance was still outside when John suddenly started talking absolute gibberish, so I rushed out to tell them. The kind paramedics took us to A&E at Charing Cross Hospital.

I can't look after him if he can't understand me... I was thinking.

"It's a urinary tract infection," said the doctor. They kept him in for a week, so I had a few days' respite.

A few months later, John was again so confused that I couldn't keep him in bed at night... he was waking up so often that I slept on the sofa downstairs to be near him. I'd taken urine samples to the surgery and he'd had two lots of antibiotics which seemed to have had no effect. Finally, one night I lay on the floor in his room, trying to sleep.

"The colonel was asleep on my floor last night," John told me when I took him a mug of tea. "I can't think what he was doing there."

"That wasn't the colonel, it was ME," I said... but he clearly didn't agree, so I took him to the doctor.

"I think he needs to be in hospital," he said, so off to A&E we went.

I was so agitated that I forgot to display the Blue Badge, so got a parking ticket, but it was cancelled when I appealed.

I was visiting one afternoon, and took John for a walk down the corridor.

Suddenly he turned to me and said,

"Who are you?"

"I'm Judy...I'm your WIFE," I said... but he just said, again,

"Who are you?" So I stopped a passing nurse.

"Excuse me... my husband doesn't know who I am... I don't know what to do," I said, near to tears.

So she took him back to the ward and told a doctor. "We'll get him assessed," they said.

The verdict was vascular dementia... and haloperidol prescribed. He was sent home again not long after, awake most of the night, as before; very sleepy, very confused in the day. One morning I found him about to swallow his hearing aid. I emailed Mr Walton, the kind specialist at Charing Cross. He phoned me.

"Take him off the haloperidol straight away, Mrs Corry," he said. "Come and see me next week." At the appointment he said to me, "You had probably better start thinking about the future." At this stage I was sleeping in a folding bed in the hall, so I was near him when John woke in the night.

John was taking zopiclone sleeping pills, which might as well have been smarties as they certainly didn't send him to sleep.

Then a friend said, "Have you tried temazepam?"

The GP agreed to prescribe it, and miraculously John began to sleep at night. Within a month or two, he was almost back to his old self. The confusion gradually went, and he was more mobile, helped by the physiotherapist at St David's. His confusion had all been caused by the urinary tract infection.

Now John was better, we spent many happy afternoons sitting by the pond at Gunnersbury Park. We became members of Kew Gardens, which is beautiful at all times of year, and has lovely flat paths on which to push the wheelchair. We went to films at our local arts centre, often first having a curry lunch at the restaurant. I was getting used to 'living in the moment' and finding pleasure in it too. The folding bed was banished upstairs and life seemed pretty normal again.

Of course nothing stays the same for long, but I think we did have about two peaceful years. However, during the summer of 2013, John started to have a skin disease, first on his hands, then his body. He was soon covered in a very itchy rash, the soles of his feet and palms of his hands seemed as if covered by cardboard. We had several emergency dermatology appointments at Charing Cross Hospital. No ointment or cream seemed to help. Finally it was diagnosed as something rare, needing medication. John only took the tablets for six days; his hands and feet started to swell, then his body.

I took John to see a doctor.

"He must be allergic… stop the medication."

"I already have," I said.

The swelling got worse, and after three abortive GP appointments and one A&E visit, I phoned the Out of Hours Service.

A visiting doctor examined him and said, "Take him to hospital straight away".

After a lengthy time in A&E, John was admitted to a ward. The swelling subsided but he contracted pneumonia. He was discharged two weeks later. My friend Ann came to help me take him home; it was snowing and I was almost running down the street pushing the wheelchair, to get John out of the cold. That evening the carer found a canula still in his arm and an unexplained dressing on his heel. He was very confused, too.

The next day, John refused to get up to have a shower, so I had to send the carer away. I phoned the hospital, who told me to call an ambulance. I tried to get John up but couldn't manage by myself, so I had to ask Ann to come and help. John was shouting and flailing his arms.

"No, no, stop it... NOT that shirt..." Finally we got him dressed, and the ambulance arrived. "Where are we going for lunch?" John asked the paramedics. It was another long day in the hospital, but finally John was taken to a different ward. "Why have you done this to me?" he said. "I'm very disappointed in you." His behaviour was so uncharacteristic, I was somewhat upset when I left him.

The next day, Edward and Annette picked me up and we all went to visit John.

"Mum. I've been writing a eulogy for Dad," says Edward.

"SHUT UP, Ted," says Annette.

"Don't worry, Annette, we'll need it sometime..." I said, one of many occasions when laughter has saved the day... but not for long.

When we got to the ward, John was very agitated, shouting "Get me out of here," and trying to get out of bed.

Two days later, he was delirious, tossing, turning, and moaning with pain. He was put into a side ward, and a nasal feeding tube inserted. For the next three long weeks I visited him daily. Edward and Gabby often came as well, but John was usually asleep, and when awake, didn't seem to know us. As well as pneumonia, the doctor said he had an infection in his brain. I had to cancel a mini-cruise to see the tulips in Amsterdam. I was disappointed but couldn't have left John in that state.

I'd started writing a bit of poetry a year or two earlier; the following words were my thoughts about our life together.

John

I was twenty-three when we first met
he was going on thirty-nine.
"what a good looking man"
I thought.

married the year following
three children in quick succession

bought a big house
did it up
I was plumbers mate

John did silversmithing
at weekends
we had
happy times in Yorkshire

children grew up
moved away
moved back
two of them
married twice

then
one of them died

after forty years
just us again
time for travel
Israel our favourite place

John now in hospital
he may not recover

God grant me the serenity to accept
what happens
and gratitude

for
the better, the worse
of forty-nine years
so quickly lived
together.

John was full of surprises as ever, and he did gradually get over his illness. He was very confused at first and still slept a lot. He was transferred to Ealing Hospital for two weeks, and then came home again, almost three months after it had all started. We were told that he'd had meningo encephalitis; I looked it up on the internet. It is usually fatal.

Soon after John came out of hospital the first time, after his broken hip, I had some alterations done in the house. The following chapter is an account of this. Like our holiday in Portugal, it had unexpected consequences…

Chapter 19

The Attic & The Lai's

After my mother died, I decided to use part of my inheritance to have a shower and loo put in the attic, rather than have a new kitchen, as I didn't like cooking enough to do that. I got in touch with Mick Gleeson, a builder whose four sons I had taught years ago. He came over with his plumber, Mr Sharma. They measured up and discussed it at some length, before saying,

"This is a job for Gordon."

So one snowy evening along came Gordon, who agreed that it was just up his street, as he really enjoys attic conversions. He started about three weeks later. It was really exciting going up every day and seeing his progress. He worked very hard, rarely leaving before eight at night.

Gordon extended the wall on the left of the alcove and built the frame of the bathroom in the attic space. He did all the plumbing, electrics, and tiling himself, with colleagues doing the plastering and decorating. He put in a large dormer window, letting in daylight. He installed a semi-circular shower, a loo, and a basin set in a work top. The finished bathroom looked very spacious and was a really great job, worth every penny, although it cost more than the original estimate.

I went to the local Japanese estate agent to say that I had an attic flat to let, and would they be interested? They were. A friendly, chatty man called Toba asked me,

"Mrs Corry, do you have a car? Can I come and see the flat straight away?" So off we went, just round the corner, and he liked it very much.

"I have a young man looking for a place; he's not Japanese, but he has a wife and baby in Japan, who will be joining him soon... can I bring him here this afternoon?"

"That will be fine... three o'clock... I'll look forward to meeting him," I said.

I was a bit taken aback... but then I thought if the tenant thinks they can fit in one room, why not? And I've always loved Oriental babies.

Toba introduced his client.

"This is Pal Yin Lai," he said.

We shook hands, and I felt an immediate rapport, because he had such a friendly, smiling face. *He'll do*, I thought to myself. Shortly after they left, Toba phoned to say that his client wanted to rent it, if I could put in a washing machine. I agreed to this. As the attic kitchen alcove was rather small, Gordon suggested putting it in the small back bedroom on the first floor, where I hung my own washing. So I bought two more racks and said they could use the washing line in the garden too.

On May 7th 2010, my new tenant moved in. Stockily built, with a round face, brown eyes, shaven head, and a beaming smile, he was very easy to talk to.

"Call me Andix," he said. "We Chinese people always have an English name too... I come from Hong Kong, but I've been working in Japan for the last ten years... I work in the media, doing computer graphics... I specialise in hair and beards."

"Would I see your name in the credits?" I asked him.

"Yes, you would." He showed me photos of Kayo and Sola, their baby son. "Kayo is Japanese… but she speaks good English… my family were very surprised that I got married… I was a bachelor for a long time."

Six weeks later, on June 12th, I took Andix to Heathrow to meet his wife Kayo and son Sola, aged twenty-one months. We chatted all the way there.

"Kayo is very thin," he said, and told me all about their traditional Japanese wedding.

I waited in the car while Andix went to the arrivals lounge. I was feeling quite nervous, but as soon as I met Kayo I felt at ease, and Sola was the most gorgeous little boy. I fell in love with him straight away. Somehow we managed to fit them and their luggage into our car, pushchair and all, and set off for Oakley Avenue. John was waiting for us, and his expression, normally serious, was a picture of happiness when he met Sola.

Quite soon it seemed as if the Lai's had always lived upstairs; it made such a difference to our lives to have a young family up there. We saw them often, as they always brought Sola down to say goodnight. Until he arranged broadband services, Andix used my WiFi and he brought his laptop downstairs at weekends. Sometimes he brought Sola down too, if Kayo was resting. I took them shopping to Morrison's; our car could take all five of us with a wheelchair and buggy in the boot. They came with us to Gunnersbury Park on the morning of our 46th wedding anniversary, and frequently after that too. Sola played on the swings, and they joined us for a cup of tea, sitting by the pond.

I heard Sola crying one night, and the next day Kayo apologised. "Please don't worry, Kayo, I don't mind a bit… I don't have to see to him… and anyway, you might hear Mr Corry calling for me…"

Soon afterwards John did call me, loudly, several times. When I saw Kayo In the morning I said,

"I hope Mr Corry didn't disturb you in the night... he was shouting for me..."

"Andix and me fight... I sleep on bathroom floor... I hear Mr Corry..." she said.

"What happened?" I asked her. "Are you all right?"

"Yes... I angry with Andix, he go out too much with friends after work..."

"Men can be a bit selfish..." I said. "I think you should talk to him, tell him it's all right to see his friends, but sometimes he must take you out too..."

It reminded me of when I was teaching, and I used to give advice to young mothers... and Kayo was a long way from home. After that she sometimes asked me what to do when Sola was naughty.

I took Kayo to see a nearby nursery; she and Andix wanted Sola to mix with other children, not just Japanese ones. He went there for two mornings a week, and Kayo started English classes on the same days.

Kayo and I were often hanging out the washing at the same time, and we began to get to know each other.

"Where did you learn to speak English?" I asked her. "You speak it so well."

"I go to Australia when I was twenty-one... I not speak English before." she told me. "I was there three months."

"How very brave of you..." I said.

Kayo was very thin, quite tall, and pretty, with a heart-shaped face, large brown eyes, and thick, shiny black hair, beautifully cut. She loved clothes, and looked stylish and colourful. Sola's face looked like his mother's, and he had his father's build. They were both very involved in his upbringing and Andix often took Sola out at weekends, to lunch at Chinatown, or to various museums. Kayo didn't like crowds so usually stayed here.

On the eve of my seventieth birthday they brought me some gorgeous flowers and a card. It was Sola's second birthday two weeks later; I made a cake which sank in the middle. Andix took lots of photos and I said,

"Don't show your family, they'll think English people can't make cakes!"

Kayo's thirtieth birthday was in November. John and I took them to Kew Gardens, which they explored on their own and we met up later.

Andix was eight years older than Kayo. For his birthday we went to the Wetlands in Barnes.

Kayo said, "We are family now," and that's what we were.

Especially helpful for me was that Andix sorted out any problems I had with the television or computer.

Their first year here they joined us for lunch on Christmas Day, along with Edward, Annette, her mother Jackie, and dog Tara. I did a Christmas stocking for Sola (having asked Kayo if that was all right; "It's an English custom," I told her). Sola said, "Oooh," looking closely at everything he was given. They all enjoyed the food, Andix especially liked sprouts. Later in the afternoon, Edward and John were both sound asleep, Kayo was playing with Tara, Jackie and Annette were sitting on the floor playing with Sola and his new toys, I was ensconced on my new purple bean bag, watching them. Then Sola came and stood beside me, so I lifted him onto my knee; he talked and talked, just babble, hands waving. His eyes closed for a few seconds, then he was talking again. Eventually he did go to sleep, and it was one of the most lovely, touching, and abiding memories of the day.

I often looked after Sola when Kayo was unwell or had an appointment. I got a couple of jigsaws in charity shops and kept them downstairs, with some felt-tipped pens and paper, and a set of wooden bricks. I collected books too; Sola liked me reading to him, the Hairy McLairy books were particular favourites. He was a quiet little boy, very polite and well-behaved. He didn't talk much unless I asked him questions, and I only had one altercation with him, when he wouldn't have his seat belt on after a trip to Gunnersbury Park.

Kayo and Sola went back to Japan to see her mother and sister at the end of February 2011; I took them all to Heathrow. Two weeks later, Andix came down, on his way to work.

"Mrs Corry... there's been a huge earthquake in Japan... it's caused a tsunami..." I switched the television on immediately and we saw it all happening... it was an appalling sight...

"That's terrible, Andix... please let me know as soon as you hear anything." Later on we heard that they were all right, which was a huge relief.

We were glued to the television all day. Ships, cars, and broken buildings tossed about on the heaving seas. The tsunami didn't quite reach Tokyo, where Kayo's family lived, but the earthquake did. The nuclear power plant at Fukoshima, 150 miles away, was badly damaged and the escaping radiation caused immediate problems in Tokyo. We heard that much of the coastline of Northern Japan was devastated and over twenty thousand people died, many of whose bodies were never recovered. There were constant aftershocks, rationed electricity, and food shortages, but being Japan, the northern motorway was repaired in a fortnight.

Every day we asked Andix how Kayo was and what was happening.

"The drinking water is contaminated... it's dangerous for Sola... I'm going to try and get them an earlier flight home..."

A week later he succeeded and they returned. We were so happy to see them again. I hugged Kayo.

"Are you all right? It must have been awful... we were so worried about you."

"We had to go outside, lie on the ground... it was shaking for about five minutes. My dad fell down, broke his leg..."

"I'm so sorry you had to come back early, leave your family..."

"I'm just glad we are safe now..."

Sola started going to the montessori school at St Martin's Church Hall soon after they got back, three days a week, 8.50 to 2.50. He settled in happily. It did seem a long day for a two-and-a-half year old, but I supposed that was the modern way, and he was an only child living in one room. I collected him a time or two, and Kayo asked us to accompany them to the Christmas play; Sola was a shepherd and carried the toy lamb I had bought at Nazareth some years earlier. It reminded me of my teaching days.

Kayo made several friends but some of them returned to Japan as their husbands only had short contracts here, which was sad for her. She told me that her friends envied her living with us. One friend, Junko, wanted to meet me, so we had her and another friend to tea just after Christmas. They couldn't stay long as they had children to collect from school, so we arranged another date. Junko, Akiko, and Yuko came, chattering non-stop and looking at all our photos, asking lots of questions about my family. Junko made some origami, now hanging in the hall.

Kayo loved animals.

"We had three dogs in Japan," she told me.

After our old cat Mo died I adopted Tilly, a pretty black and white cat from the RSPCA in Southall. Sola loved Tilly and was very gentle stroking her. She was good with him too, she never scratched him. He always went to look for her when he came home from school, especially if any of his friends came to play.

For Sola's third birthday we went on the miniature train at Ruislip Lido, which was great fun, and had lunch in a funny little café afterwards. For Andix's birthday we went to the Horniman Museum in Forest Hill. Kayo navigated. It was pouring with rain and the journey took ages. We found a small, compact museum full of artefacts, including a wonderful gallery of musical instruments. The restaurant was crowded with families; we only just found a table. John had fish and chips, Andix a sandwich, cake for Kayo, chips for Sola, coffee for me.

"Chinese people love peas, but Japanese people don't," Andix told us, as he and Sola finished off John's peas.

Sola had two years at montessori nursery, and time passed quickly. The pushchair in the hall was replaced by a scooter, then a two wheeler bike, soon without stabilisers. Sola grew up so fast. Just before his fifth birthday he started at West Acton School, where he got on very well; his first reports from the reception class and year one were both excellent. There was less time to do things together by now but we did still have birthday outings, to the RAF Museum, as well as the Steam and Musical Museums. He still occasionally came down to say goodnight too. Sola blew John a goodnight kiss, while I still got a proper one.

Sola had just started year two in September this year when Andix came home one evening.

"Mrs Corry, I've just heard that I may be made redundant… I'll be informed in two weeks…"

"That's terrible, Andix… does Kayo know about it?"

"Not yet, I don't want to spoil Sola's birthday."

I was devastated… and very worried. It was totally unexpected.

The next day, Sola was seven, and had a party in the garden. There were eleven Japanese children ranging from three to eight or nine years old. What a delightful occasion, not a cross word between them, they all played happily… John and I watched them for ages.

Andix told me that he and Kayo agreed that he would apply to be transferred to Canada, as his firm had jobs available there. Two weeks later, Andix emailed Kayo one lunch time, and she came down to tell me.

"Mrs Corry, we are going to Vancouver in January."

I hugged her. "I'm so sorry, Kayo… I hate the thought of you going… but I've heard that Vancouver is one of the best cities in the world to live in… beautiful countryside… much more space than in London."

I could hardly bear to contemplate what life would be like without them, but felt I must put on a good face, especially as I know they wanted to stay in London and have Sola educated here. I felt near to tears whenever I talked about them leaving, there was going to be such a big gap in our lives.

As honorary grandparents, we have watched Sola grow from a toddler to a schoolboy. John always has the same fond expression when he sees him. Kayo has been so good looking after John, and I don't know how I'll manage computer problems without Andix. We've been very blessed. One day I hope I'll be able to visit them in Canada, and in the mean time there is Skype; if I can learn how to use it, that is.

Chapter 20

Reflections

Today I'm staying in my favourite place, Sandsend in North Yorkshire. The sun is shining on the sea just across the road, and there are 'white horses' rushing towards the shore, as there is a strong wind. I'm thinking about my life and wondering where this chapter will lead. I was born in Aislaby, three miles inland from here, at the vicarage, built for my grandfather as vicar but long now in private ownership. I spent the first thirteen years of my life in the village until I was sent away to school, and even now I identify with this part of the world and miss it if there's too long a gap since my last visit.

I've been thinking about the various different periods of my life. When grown up I had about four years as a naval daughter; almost three living on my own in a bed sit in London – I loved that time. Then getting married, giving birth to three children in four years, moving to Ealing, getting involved in playgroup. The excitement of being accepted for teachers training college, and finding out how much I enjoyed studying. There followed almost eighteen years teaching, most of that in the same classroom.

After retiring I went back to being a student again, another good time, during which I discovered the joy of travelling. John and I had several memorable times abroad, with built in study of the country. Having finally finished academic study and missing writing, I started doing autobiographical writing courses: Birkbeck first, then the City Literary Institute and now I attend a writing workshop.

What I'm realising is how quickly time has passed... especially the last few years. It seems no time since I was seventy, and now I'm seventy-five. I used to joke about saving for my zimmerframe when I was teaching; hopefully it will be a few more years until I need one, and in the meantime I am doing my best to make the most of my life.

Today I walked barefoot along the beach to Whitby, not that comfortable as it's very stony. I walked close to the water's edge; the tide was going out but one wave came rushing up and swished round my knees. Luckily, I kept upright, just, despite being almost helpless with laughter.

Near Whitby there was a wide concrete promenade above an outcrop of rocks. I don't remembering it being there before but perhaps because the tide was further out then and I could stay on the beach. Anyway, I dried my feet with my socks and walked shod for the rest of the way. To my surprise too I found a Costa Coffee in Baxtergate. It used to be a shoe shop.

I bought some sunflowers in the Co-op, caught the bus to Aislaby, and put flowers on Kate's grave, as well as my parents', grandparents', and Hilda's. Hearing the organ, I crept into church to find Evensong in full swing. So I stayed and enjoyed the lovely old prayers and singing familiar hymns. After the service I had a brief chat with a few people I knew.

I walked back through the village and down the drive to Park Hall, thinking I'd have a last look round before the house is sold. I noticed how huge some of the trees and shrubs are now, and remembered my parents wanting me to photograph them, newly planted, while they were in the Far East. I recalled us playing cricket with Fish on the tennis court, the paddling pool on the lawn when our children were small, and Fish mowing the lawn on his tractor. I felt emotional too, tears lurking, but they were happy memories.

I was thinking about Fish, my father, too. He learnt to use a computer in his seventies, and wrote his autobiography, *The Life Story of a Fish,* published in 1992. We were all very excited about it. Six years ago I thought I would follow his example and I began to write mine too. My story begins when I met my father for the first time, aged one year, which is why I have called it *Fish's Daughter.* This is the concluding chapter.

I left Park Hall to walk down Featherbed Lane, another abiding memory as it was one of the ways David and I used to go to school. Very overgrown now, I couldn't at first find the way. I went down it very cautiously, as it was slippery in places, and I didn't see a soul. In Sleights I waited in the sunshine by the bus stop, and was so lucky; an empty bus picked me up about ten minutes later.

I then had a most delicious early dinner at the Magpie, reading my Kindle and enjoying being on my own.

A passing waitress said, "Is everything all right, little lady?"

"Yes, thank you," I said, smiling as I've never been called little before.

Having paid the bill, I walked along the harbour front, looking at the boats, and up at the abbey and parish church at the top of the cliff opposite. At the bus station I caught the last bus back to Sandsend, beautiful in the evening light, and with the tide coming in again.

It was such a lovely weekend. The weather was perfect, and I did all my favourite things: hearing the swish of the sea at night, walking on the beach, visiting familiar places. It was so good to have time to take stock of my life. It was six years since John broke his hip in Portugal, which changed our lives so suddenly; mine because I had to take responsibility for the house and learn to be a carer, and John who had to cope with illness and disability. The Lai's moved in soon after that, making such a difference to our lives. It was two years since John's second period of acute illness, when he spent another three months in hospital.

I thought about what it was like first learning to be a carer: medication, wheelchairs, commodes. It was a huge learning curve, endless, exhausting, and unremitting; I'd not taken to it easily and have to admit to great impatience and a lot of bad language. My father swore a lot, I was brought up hearing it. My mother used to remonstrate with him, so I laughed when David told me that Mum had called the doctor an "f*ing bastard". Now it was my turn.

"What the f*ing hell do you want now?" I'd shout at John... the f word escaping my lips in spite of myself. I usually apologise and feel slightly ashamed about my impatience.

After a year or two, when John was a lot better, he asked if I could make some tea.

"I want to talk to you," he said. So I duly made a couple of mugs, and sat down on the sofa.

"What do you want to talk about?" I enquired.

"Your swearing..."

"F*&k OFF!" I said. "I'm not a child. I'll swear if I want to... don't you DARE tell me off!"

He said no more, and my language hasn't improved. Not that he always hears... his deafness does have some advantages.

The thing I am probably most proud of, and thankful for, was being taught how to insert a catheter. Hardly dinner party conversation but such a blessing not to have to rely on hard-pressed district nurses, especially as in the last couple of years it has blocked frequently, needing to be changed. A catheter should be replaced every twelve weeks. John's sometimes last less than two.

After John came home again he resumed going to the day centre once a week and occasionally stayed in a care home for a week's respite care. However, he had always hated this and he finally rebelled.

"I won't go, I'm too old to be told what to do," he said. It was no good arguing.

I had never found being a carer easy, I don't suppose anyone does, come to that, but I'd found time off essential. So I asked Kayo if she would be prepared to give John his lunch and/or tea sometimes, and I would pay her. She was happy to do it, although protesting about being paid. I insisted, however; it wouldn't have been fair otherwise.

I then had another brainwave. I'd had girls cleaning the house for some years, my current one was Kamala who comes from Sri Lanka. She needed more work.

"Have you ever done any caring?" I asked her.

"Yes, I looked after an old lady of ninety-nine; I gave her a shower and her meals."

"Would you be prepared to look after John for a weekend sometimes, and stay the night on Saturday?"

"If John doesn't mind, I'd be happy to," she said.

John didn't mind, luckily, as it meant he could remain at home. So that is what happens. Once a month I go away, sometimes for two nights, and come back on Sunday evening. It has worked out well. Kamala likes the work, I like the freedom, and I've explored some lovely towns: Ely, Eastbourne, Nottingham, Deal, Solihull, St Albans. I like Windsor best and have been there several times.

So life was calm and settled for the next year, and I never minded returning home, which I used to when first caring for John. Not long after my weekend at Sandsend came the sad news about the Lai's going to live in Canada. The next three months leading up to Christmas weren't the happiest time. Kayo usually asked me if I'd like to go to Sola's Christmas concert; I'd gone most years so this last one was especially poignant. I talked to several of Kayo's friends, all very sad about her leaving, especially as Kayo had been an active member of the school parents' association.

Sola and Kayo decorated the Christmas tree, which they had done every year with us, so the house looked very festive. On December 17th 2015 we celebrated John's ninety-first birthday. Edward and Annette came from Enfield, plus Tara their chocolate Labrador, Gabby and Hugo from near the New Forest, with Stessy, their Border Collie. The dogs get on very well. It was a happy day. Beforehand I had made Christmas cake in two silicone cake moulds, a nine and a one, rather fiddly to do but they looked good. Unwisely, I left the cake on the sideboard, and I caught Stessy taking a large mouthful out of the nine; we all had a good laugh about it, especially Sola. He and Kayo helped John blow out the candles after everyone else had gone home.

The last time I looked after Sola we played pairs, and snap, and looked at one of his books together.

"What would you like to do now?" I asked him. "Shall I get you some paper for drawing?"

"Yes please," he said, and settled down on the floor with pens and paper. Sola never talked very much, it was usually me asking him questions.

"What are you going to draw? Cars... trains... buses... Mr Corry?"

Sola grinned at me and began work, drawing John sitting in his arm chair, glasses on his nose, a book on his lap, fleece hat on his head. He wrote *Mr Corry sleeping,* with an arrow pointing towards him, and *Sola Lai 23.12.15.* Andix and Kayo were so pleased when they got back. So were we. Later I got a frame and hung it beside the grandfather clock.

On Christmas Eve I gave Sola one of my long knee socks on Sola's bed.

"This is for Father Christmas," I said. "Ask Mummy to pin it on the end of your bed... in the morning you'll have a surprise".

After Sola was asleep Kayo substituted the other one, which I had filled with small toys, pens, fruit, a book, a chocolate Father

Christmas and some crisps, and left in a black bag in the spare room. Next morning, Sola came downstairs.

"Mrs Corry… can I show you what Santa brought me?" Later, Kayo gave me the card Sola had left out, *to Santa from Sola*.

Dear Santa Merry Christmas. Thank you for giving me presents. You must be busy. From Sola Lai. Please have a rest tomorrow. On the other page he had drawn two faces, and written *me/Sola Santa/you*. That is kept in my 'Treasure Box' along with the note he gave us, with some drawings of Tilly, in a homemade envelope decorated with flowers. He must have spent ages doing it…

Dear Mr and Mrs Corry

Thank you for letting us live in your house. I hope London is always great.

From Sola, bye bye. Friday 1st January 2016

They all came downstairs and we had Christmas lunch together, but it was rather a subdued occasion…

A week after Christmas the hall was full of suitcases, an excited Sola standing guard over them. A few of Kayo's friends came to see them off, all of them in tears, and taking photos too, so I had to compose myself… Andix seemed particularly moved, saying goodbye to John, giving him a big hug. Then a large taxi took them all to Heathrow, and that was that. The following day we heard that they had arrived safely.

The house seemed very empty and quiet after that, not that the Lai's were ever noisy, once Sola grew out of having tantrums. It was like losing part of our family, them going so far away. We felt very bereft, even Tilly was wandering round the house, looking lost.

We sometimes talk to them on Skype and regularly exchange emails and photographs. They have rented a house near the school, where Sola is doing very well. Andix already knew several colleagues and has an old friend living in Vancouver too. This summer, Kayo sent us a card:

How's the weather in London this year? I guess you are enjoying flowers and sunshine. Oh how I miss you and parks in London (always remember that like yesterday)

She also told me that there are an elderly couple next door "just like you two." The move must have been the hardest for Kayo, who is on her own all day, but recently her mother came to stay from Japan, which was lovely for her and Sola. Japan is nearer Canada than England, and flights are cheaper.

I got the attic flat decorated, which was not entirely straightforward, and I had a few problems with the new tenant, a single Japanese girl, who moved at the beginning of April. The shower had to be replaced, the kitchen tap leaked, the smoke alarm shrieked as the battery needed replacing. I got it all put right, and we hardly see her as she is at work all day.

So now there are just the two of us again. We have been married for fifty-two years, which I think is quite an achievement. Inevitably there were less good periods, starting when our three were teenagers; there were times when our age gap seemed wider than others; learning to be a carer was a 'for worse' time. Once organised though, it was satisfying trying to make a good job of it. Now I feel the wheel has come full circle, and we have found closeness and contentment.

John is pretty amazing for his age, apart from his hearing, which isn't good, and makes communication hard at times. He doesn't want to go out much now, unless it's an extra nice day, when we go to Kew Gardens. He's happy in his armchair with his newspaper, the television, and the odd book to read, even happier if it's a sunny day. He recently bought an air pistol and can still hit the centre of the target, firing it into the garden through the dining room doors. Recently we have much enjoyed watching the Olympics on television, which is so funny as neither of us was the least bit sporting in our youth. The best thing is that John is completely *compos mentis* – I couldn't have coped if he'd had dementia, which at first seemed likely.

I always appreciated how John encouraged me to go to teachers training college, and for a while came too when I was at uni after I retired; he himself was enthusiastic about many diverse topics, with shelves of books to prove it. Our children never lacked reference books, or the example to 'look it up'. He always backed me when our children were small. If one of them asked him if they could do something, he'd always say,

"What does Mummy say?"

"Mummy said no…"

"Well I'm saying no too…"

We were never in debt, didn't live beyond our means. He was very good at 'do-it-yourself' and I was happy being his plumbers mate. He made beautiful silver things, too. I could only have wished for a bit of help in the garden; it's always been me mowing the lawn.

I am more than thankful that I didn't marry a naval officer as my parents would have wished me to. John has always 'been there' in his own quiet way, for me and our children. And not least he seems to enjoy my writing. So now it seems as good a time as any for me to finish writing this account of my life, while we are still together. We have many happy memories to look back on, many blessings to count, and hopefully we will have some time to enjoy the here and now, with family and friends nearby.

Judy Corry
September 2016.

Acknowledgements

Grateful thanks to Caroline Natzler and the members of her Writing Workshop, Karine Hetherington, Kate Jefford, and Anne Nicholson. I learned so much from them whilst writing my memoirs.

My Poetry

Contents

Writing Class

Oh good it's Thursday
Writing Class day
the train transports me away from my life
briefly
into the life of others.
I go to different times, places, events
to other countries
I laugh, I cry,
I marvel at the written words read aloud.

Long pieces, short pieces
happy pieces
sad pieces
finished too soon…
so much more I want to know
about wartime
and homelessness

The class has taken me
back to my own carefree
childhood.
memories returning as I write
discussion so helpful
what to include, what to omit.

Oh good, it's Thursday again
I wouldn't miss it for anything

—November 15th 2012

JOHN

I was twenty-three when we first met
he was going on thirty-nine.
"what a good looking man"
I thought.

married the year following
three children in quick succession

bought a big house
did it up
I was plumbers mate

John did silversmithing
at weekends
we had
happy times in Yorkshire

children grew up
moved away
moved back
two of them
married twice

then
one of them died

after forty years
just us again
time for travel
Israel our favourite place

John now in hospital
he may not recover

God grant me the serenity to accept
what happens
and gratitude
for
the better, the worse
of forty-nine years
so quickly lived
together.

—April 8ᵗʰ 2013.

Life

"Darling
it's our wedding anniversary,"
he said

I hadn't forgotten......

forty-nine years ago
"for better, for worse"
"I will," I said

children,
family
friends
blessings counted
but oh,
how fleeting the years
how quickly "the worse"
is here....

—July 31ˢᵗ 2013

Golden wedding

in a long white dress
I made myself
on my father's arm
feel like a princess

in a big strange church
I promise to obey
a lovely man
I hardly know

that day remembered
with happiness
and now,

I'm glad
that I said
"I will"

—July 4th 2014

Today

balloons float
pile of cards
and presents
await

smell of curry, cooking

family arrive
dog and puppy play

John sits in his chair,
smiling

it's time to be together
to give thanks
to celebrate

John is ninety
today

—*17th December 2014*

Rage

Rage came from nowhere

exploding like a firework

angry words scattering in all directions

fizzing and sparking.

he is bewildered

then angry himself

"Totally unjustified

don't do this to me"

More hurting words escape from my mouth

mingled with tears.

not sure I understand it either.

I'll go out now

say sorry later.

—September 28ᵗʰ 2012

Pain
(First Version)

Ten years ago
my daughter Clare
sat on the stairs
and died

miles away
I knew
something awful was happening

John phoned
to tell me
"I'll come home now," I said

journey endless
thoughts confused
"I can't plant potatoes
Clare won't be there
to dig them up…."

Gabby saw Clare
icy cold
lying on the floor
sat beside her a while
saw her
zipped into a body bag
taken away
to the mortuary

we, now four
saw her in her coffin

our lives fell apart
from each other
and within

alcohol the wrecking ball

a long, painful lonely journey
through grief and loss

Clare was thirty six
somehow I always knew
she would never be old

—January 2013

Pain
(second version)

ten years ago
my daughter Clare
sat on the stairs
and died

far away
John phoned
to tell me.
"I'll come home now," I said

journey endless
thoughts confused
"I can't plant potatoes
Clare won't be there
to dig them up…"

beautiful Clare
thirty six
zipped into a body bag
taken away

our lives fell apart
from each other
and within

alcohol the wrecking ball

the journey now
through pain

—*February 2013*

Memories

Clare and Gabby
at the kitchen counter
making roll ups
talking non stop

possessions strewn
everywhere

I hear her voice
on the phone
"Mummy, it's Clare…..

eleven years
since Clare died
but I still remember
them
chatting….

—March 11th 2014

Gabby's Graduation

gowns, hoods, mortar boards

thronging people

excitement

photos

band plays
Queen of Sheba

solemn procession

graduates announced
one by one

families, friends
watch
with pride
applause echoes

memories
remain

—December 2013

Sandsend

sandcastles
cricket
paddling
laughter....
white capped waves

storm tossed boulders
sadness of
scattered ashes......

sunrise
across the sea

—February 1ˢᵗ 2014

Sandsend Again

high tide
surging sea
crashing waves

memories
of childhood
long past

welcome
solitude

—April 30th 2014

Sandsend at Midnight

a crescent moon hung
in the sky
reflecting
a shining path
across the restless waves
of the receding tide

swishing sea the only sound
in the night

—September 7th 2015

From the Train

frequent church spires
and towers
in the distance

the dome of
a solitary mosque

overflowing rivers

two swans
in a field

poplar trees
like paintbrushes
against grey sky

villages
towns
blocks of flats
and warehouses
flash past

Kings Cross Station
my journey ends
and life resumes…..

—*February 5th 2014*

Kew Gardens

autumn smells
vibrant colours
falling leaves

a pond
fringed by rushes
a breeze ruffling
the still water.

Canada geese
glide overhead
their harsh honking
sounds
like arguing

a lone heron
on the
dilapidated bridge.

distant aircraft discordant

a tall pine tree
where a falling branch
killed
a woman
a few days ago

bunches of flowers
still lie there
in her memory

—*September 30ᵗʰ 2012*

Windsor Castle

armed police
observe

as we quietly
file
into
St George's Chapel

the organ thunders
clergy and choir
process
(no girls though)

a tiny boy, bespectacled
solemn
his voice glorious
mesmerising

Evensong

uplifting
unforgettable

—October 11th 2015

Park Hall

the house
home to my family
a century
and more
is to be sold

it stands on a hill
the distant moors
beyond

portraits look down
with timeless gaze

babies were born there
lives lived
lives ended
but not forgotten

not yet

—August 2015

Remembrance

in the Great War
not long begun
one mother
lost two sons
a son-in-law
a stepson
their names recorded
on a Memorial Wall

a hundred years later
five descendants
stood there
reflecting

the sun shone weakly
a girl trumpeter
sounded the Last Post

beyond
traffic thundered past
unknowing

Judy Corry
(nee Dalglish)
a great granddaughter

—November 14th 2014

Depression

I try to smile to hide the pain
but it won't go away
where has it come from
I ask myself
life is just the same

I try to keep active
and read and write

the pain is there
just the same

in time it goes
it fades away....

but
always
comes
back

again

—January 17th 2014

More Pain

The pain is here
just like last time

no warning

life is good
but I can't feel
its blessings

just the pain
of depression

—April 8th 2015

Here Again

tears
tiredness
time dragging

unbearable
unremitting

but not
unending.....

(thankfully)

—June 9ᵗʰ 2016

20089225R00169

Printed in Great Britain
by Amazon